b24

The dynamics of
the one-party state
in Zambia

The dynamics of
the one-party state
in Zambia

Cherry Gertzel   *editor*
Carolyn Baylies, Morris Szeftel

Manchester University Press

First published by
Manchester University Press
Oxford Road, Manchester M13 9PL, U.K.
and 51 Washington Street, Dover, N.H. 03820, U.S.A.

British Library cataloguing in publication data

Gertzel, Cherry
    The dynamics of the one-party state in Zambia.
    I. Zambia — Politics and government
    I. Title   II. Baylies, Carolyn
    III. Szeftel, Morris
    968.94'04   DT963.8

    ISBN 0–7190–1069–1

Library of Congress cataloging in publication data

Gertzel, Cherry J.
    The dynamics of the one-party state in Zambia.
    Bibliography: p.247
    Includes index.
    1. Zambia—Politics and government—1964–
2. Zambia—Economic conditions—1964–   .
3. Zambia—Social conditions—1964–   .
I. Baylies, Carolyn L. (Caroline Louise),
1947–   . II. Szeftel,
Morris.
III. Title.
JQ2811.G47   1984   968.94'04   83–25535
ISBN 0–7190–1069–1

Printed in Great Britain by
Butler & Tanner Ltd, Frome and London

Contents

List of tables

List of maps

Preface

This study is concerned with the origins and working of the one-party state in Zambia, with the interaction of political forces that resulted in the introduction of the one-party state in 1972, and in turn with the impact of social and economic change upon the political process. The central concern is with the nature of social relations in the post-colonial state and their influence upon institutional change. We do not always approach this question from a common perspective. We are, however, agreed on the overall argument: that the creation of the one-party state in Zambia in 1972 is best understood in relation to the search for a viable formula for the management of political conflict, and that the nature of that political conflict requires, in turn, consideration of societal change at both local and national levels, and in the context of local/central relations. The study therefore seeks also to identify the basis of local/central relations in a country whose dominant characteristic, two decades after independence, remained a stark rural/urban gap. Ethnic diversity and uneven economic development have produced a regionalism that has had serious consequences for political as well as economic change. We have therefore sought to identify the consequences of rural under-development and urban dominance for integration, and for relations between centre and locality.

The study is divided into two parts. Part I looks at the origins and working of the one-party state from the national perspective and in relation to Zambia as a whole. It is concerned primarily with the nature of popular participation and the control of political conflict during and after the transition to the one-party state. This leads us to consider at some length the Zambian experience of elections in the one-party state. These issues also raise questions concerning factionalism and the nature of patronage in the Zambian party system, as well as the rise of presidentialism and the centralisation of power. They also lead us to consider a major development in Zambia in the 'seventies: the emergence of a new entrepreneurial class.

Part II is concerned primarily with the manner in which local/central relations in Zambia have been both influenced and changed with the transition from colonial to post-colonial state and from multi-party to single-party system. This section consists of three regional studies: of the Copperbelt and Western and Luapula Provinces. We have focused first upon the Copperbelt because of the dominant role of that urban region in Zambian politics. The centrality of the urban population in Zambian politics must not, however, obscure the fact that the fundamental issue which faced Zambia at the time of the introduction of the one-party state was the failure of rural development and the growing rural/urban gap. The two rural case studies highlight the critical problems of economic and political integration arising from that failure. We have sought to identify and analyse these issues as they appeared at the time of the first general election held in the one-party state in 1973, and to compare the outcome with that of the second election which followed in 1978. Those elections also presented an occasion when it was possible to identify the interaction of political forces at the grass-roots level, on which the success or failure of the one-party state as a democratic experiment would largely depend. Hence we have sought, in these regional studies, to focus on the dynamics of the one-party state in that context, and to consider their impact upon party and Parliament in the one-party state.

The research on which these studies are based began when all three authors were teaching at the University of Zambia. Over the years we have incurred many debts to the many people who have helped us in our work. We are especially mindful of those former colleagues and students in the Politics Department, University of Zambia, with whom we participated in a study of the first general election on the one-party state in 1973. We regret very much that unexpected difficulties finally prevented the publication of any part of that study. Our own regional case studies presented in this volume grew out of our individual contributions to that project. They have been expanded and deepened since then by subsequent research on the working of the one-party system itself, but we acknowledge, gratefully, the opportunities provided by that period of co-operative research, and also the university's generous support. We are greatly indebted to the many people in both party and government who have assisted our research both then and on other occasions. While it is not possible to name them all, we must make especial mention of the Chairman of the United National Independence Party's Elections Committee, and of the Director of Elections, whose generous assistance on all occasions made our field work possible. We alone of course remain responsible for the interpretation of the material presented in this book. We are also mindful of the number of people who have helped us keep up to date with Zambian politics, and who have read parts or all of the manuscript. We would like particularly to thank Ralph Young and Professor William Tordoff of the University of Manchester, Ian Scott now of the University of Hong Kong, and Robert Molteno. Bornwell Chikulo and Gervaise Maipose generously allowed us to use their material collected on the second general election in 1978. Again, we remain responsible for the use made of that material.

As editor and co-author, I would like to thank the Australian Research Grants Committee for research support which made possible two lengthy return visits to Zambia in 1976 and 1980. I am also grateful to Mrs. R. B. McKenna for assistance with the Bibliography. Finally, I must thank the secretaries who have typed successive drafts of the manuscript and especially Anne Gabb, Rae Tyler and Marie Baker of the Politics Discipline of the Flinders University of South Australia and Joan Marshall, who typed the final manuscript with great efficiency and cheerfulness.

Cherry Gertzel
Flinders University of South Australia, 1983

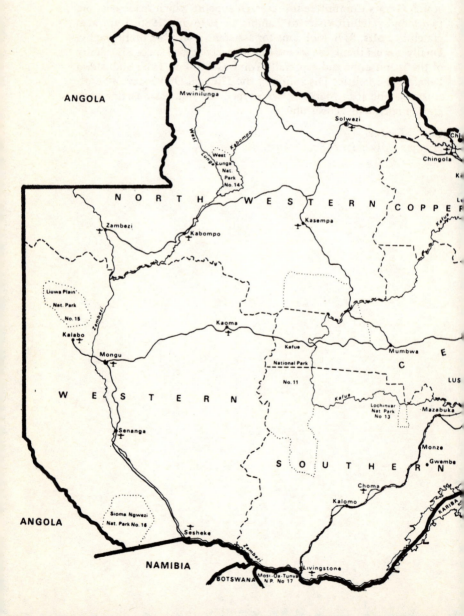

Miles 10 0 10 20 30 40 50 60 70 80 90 100 Miles

Provincial Boundaries . . . .
Provincial Headquarters . . . . ●
Towns . . . . ●
Roads . . . .
Railways . . . . +++
Aerodromes . . . . ✈

ZAIRE

ANGOLA

Mwinilunga

Solwezi

Chingola

West Lunga Nat. Park No. 14

NORTH   WESTERN   COPPER

Zambezi

Kabompo

Kasempa

Liuwa Plain Nat. Park No. 15

Kaoma

Kalabo

Mongu

Kafue

Mumbwa

LUS

Kafue National Park No. 11

C

Lochinvar Nat Park No 13

Mazabuka

WESTERN

Senanga

SOUTHERN

Monze

Gwembe

Choma

Kalomo

KARIBA

ANGOLA

Sioma Ngwezi Nat. Park No 16

Sesheke

Livingstone

NAMIBIA

BOTSWANA

Mosi-Oa-Tunya N.P. No 17

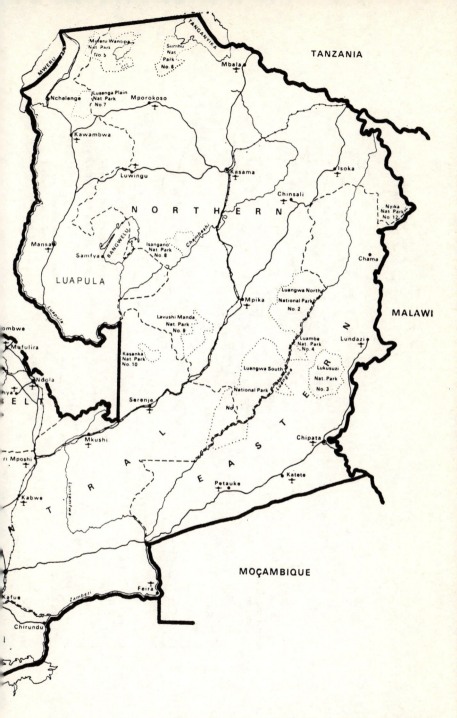

The Republic of Zambia (*by courtesy of the Ministry of Development Planning and National Guidance, Lusaka*)

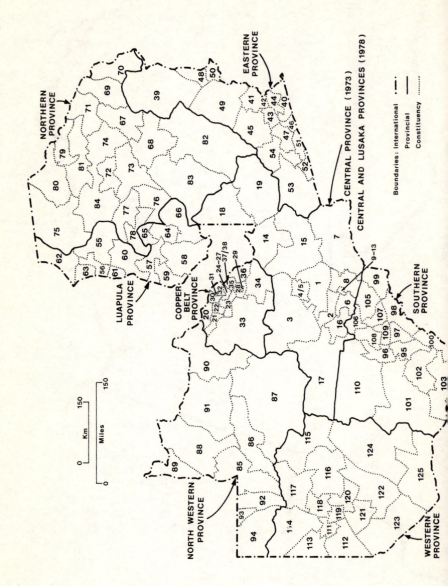

NORTHERN PROVINCE

EASTERN PROVINCE

CENTRAL PROVINCE (1973)

CENTRAL AND LUSAKA PROVINCES (1978)

LUAPULA PROVINCE

COPPER BELT PROVINCE

SOUTHERN PROVINCE

NORTH WESTERN PROVINCE

WESTERN PROVINCE

Boundaries: International ·–··–··
Provincial ——————
Constituency ············

Km 0 150

Miles 0 150

Parliamentary constituencies, 1973 and 1978. *Central Province* (in 1978 Central and Lusaka Provinces): 1. Chisamba, 2. Katuba, 3. Lukanga, 4. Bwacha, 5. Kabwe, 6. Chilanga, 7. Feira, 8. Kafue, 9. Kabwata, 10. Kanyama, 11. Matero, 12. Mandevu, 13. Munali, 14. Mkushi Boma, 15. Old Mkushi, 16. Keembe, 17. Mumbwa, 18. Chitambo, 19. Serenje. *Copperbelt Province*: 20. Chililabombwe, 21. Chingola, 22. Nchanga, 23. Kalulushi, 24. Chimwemwe, 25. Kwacha, 26. Nkana, 27. Wusakile, 28. Luanshya, 29. Roan, 30. Kankoyo, 31. Kantanshi, 32. Mufulira, 33. Luswishi, 34. Masaiti, 35. Chifubu, 36. Chiwala, 37. Masala, 38. Ndola. *Eastern Province*: 39. Chama, 40. Chadiza, 41. Chipangali, 42. Chipata, 43. Kazimuli, 44. Luangeni, 45. Malambo, 46. Katete, 47. Vulamkoko, 48. Chasefu, 49. Lumezi, 50. Lundazi, 51. Kapoche, 52. Minga, 53. Nyimba, 54. Petauke. *Luapula Province*: 55. Kawambwa, 56. Mwansabombwe, 57. Bahati, 58. Chembe, 59. Mansa, 60. Chipili, 61. Mwense, 62. Chiengi, 63. Nchelenge. 64. Samfya Central, 65. Samfya North, 66. Samfya South. *Northern Province*: 67. Chinsali, 68. Shiwa Ng'andu, 69. Isoka, 70. Muyombe, 71. Nakonde, 72. Kasama, 73. Lukashya, 74. Malole, 75. Kaputa, 76. Chilubi, 77. Luwingu East, 78. Luwingu West, 79. Mbala, 80. Mpulunga, 81. Senga Hill, 82. Mpika East, 83. Mpika West, 84. Mporokoso. *North Western Province*: 85. Kabompo, 86. Kalengwa, 87. Kasempa, 88. Mwinilunga East, 89. Mwinilunga West, 90. Solwezi East, 91. Solwezi West, 92. Zambezi East, 93. Zambezi North, 94. Zambezi West. *Southern Province*: 95. Choma, 96. Mbabala, 97. Pemba, 98. Gwembe, 99. Siavonga, 100. Sinazongwe, 101. Dundumwense, 102. Kalomo, 103. Katombora, 104. Livingstone, 105. Chikankata, 106. Mazabuka, 107. Magoye, 108. Bwengwa, 109. Monze, 110. Namwala. *Western Province*: 111. Kalabo, 112. Sihole, 113. Sikongo, 114. Liuwa, 115. Kaoma, 116. Luampa, 117. Lukulu, 118. Luena, 119. Mongu, 120. Nalikwanda, 121. Nalola, 122. Senanga, 123. Sinjembela, 124. Mulobezi.   *Source. Zambia Daily Mail* (Lusaka), 7 December 1973, from Elections Office.

Part one

The origins and politics
of the one-party state

Introduction
The making of the one-party state

Introduction

This book is a study of the political process in the one-party state in Zambia. In this essay we look at the background to the inauguration of the Second Republic in 1973, as a basis for the more detailed study of the working of the new system that follows. We do not attempt a full survey of Zambian politics since independence, which has been done with great skill elsewhere.[1] We focus instead on those features most salient to an understanding of the origins and working of the one-party state.

   The introduction of the one-party state in December 1972 constituted a watershed in Zambia's political history, since it brought to an end an intensely competitive multi-party system whose origins lay in the colonial state. Zambia thus followed, although a good deal later, the one-party trend which has characterised the politics of independent African states since the early 'sixties, and to which the ruling United National Independence Party (U.N.I.P.) had been committed since 1964.[2] The political environment had, however, changed a great deal in the intervening years, so it is important to bear in mind the extent to which our understanding of one-party systems has also changed over the same period. Early analysis emphasised the influence of the colonial legacy of bureaucratic authoritarianism, the political attitudes and beliefs of the élite, popular participation, and the role of ideology upon the movement of the newly independent states to one-partyism.[3] Writers stressed the differences between élite and mass organisations, revolutionary and evolutionary parties, and ideological and pragmatic strategies, and were generally sympathetic towards the one-party system as an agency of national integration and development. In 1966, however, the underlying assumptions of the existence of a broad national unity were called into question with a seminal study of West African party states, from which the single-party system emerged as a response to the dangers of fragmentation and loss of control.[4] The party was shown to have a limited capacity for mobilisation and the centre an often tenuous control over the periphery. Moreover, the shift of focus in the study of African politics in the early 'seventies to the local level and to rural change, provided further evidence of the difficulties of national control.[5]

Two particular developments are useful here. On the one hand, the notion of the political machine was explored, with its emphasis on party concern for material rewards rather than principles. It was suggested that:

African ruling single parties share many characteristics of decentralised political machines in that the organisation is held together in good part by the perquisites of and desire for office, and internal cleavages within the parties are often not over policy issues . . .[6]

The single dominant party was revealed as a coalition of interests rather than a monolithic, hierarchical body. On the other hand, the relevance of factionalism to African political conflict emerged more clearly. Factions, or conflict groups within the political party, arise in the struggle for power in the incompletely centralised state. They are typically informal, impermanent and illegitimate. They are inherently unstable, so that a factional system carries with it the potential for fragmentation and secession if the factions evolve sufficiently to break away from the permanent group and adopt an independent existence.[7] Political leaders build up networks of supporters, bound to them as individuals by mutual self-interest and perhaps by moral ties such as friendship, kinship or ideological commitment. To increase his prestige and political resources, the political leader at the centre seeks to advance his own followers. Patronage and personal following thus provide a critical element in local/central relations, ensuring those linkages that institutional arrangements have not yet been able to sustain. They carry with them, however, especially in a situation of scarcity, the potential for conflict between leaders at the centre and the exacerbation of cleavages in society.

We are forced, therefore, to look more closely at the nature of social cleavage, at a time when increasing economic inequality in African society has also focused greater attention upon the material basis of politics in the independent state. The evolution of the one-party state was seen from this perspective as part of the process whereby an acquisitive élite entrenched itself in power.[8] In due course, however, the debate focused upon class and class formation as a basis of politics, rather than 'ethnicity' and 'primordial ties'.[9] The dependency debate of the early 'seventies had a considerable impact on this shift of focus, while Marxist and non-Marxist scholars alike have had to identify more sharply the relationship between factionalism, ethnicity and class. On the one hand, it has been argued that both ethnicity and factionalism have vitiated class consciousness because they link individuals across social strata.[10] On the other hand, the empirical evidence of increasing stratification has grown, and radical analysis has sharpened the focus on those common social forces at work in the independent African states which follow a broadly capitalist set of economic and social policies — and indeed in populist-socialist regimes as well.[11] It is no longer possible, therefore, to ignore the potential influence of class formation upon the pattern of party politics where the party has survived. In those states where one-party civilian regimes remain in power, any analysis of the role of party must take into account the broader social process.[12]

While radicals have been generally critical of the existing one-party systems, the Tanzanian experiment led to some interesting analysis of the one-party state as an institutional arrangement to achieve a balance between control and participation.[13] Although the concern was primarily with the Tanzanian electoral process and the process of socialist transformation, the model none the less had a wider application to the broader issues of integration and disintegration, and to the problems of inadequate centralisation that the independent states generally encountered in the immediate post-colonial phase. In this context, the one-party state was interpreted as a conscious attempt to strike a balance between popular participation and central control, both essential ingredients of development.

The notion of the one-party state as an attempt to achieve an institutional balance between participation and control is a useful one with which to approach recent political change in Zambia.[14] Immediately after independence, the Zambian leadership had emphasised the importance of participation both as a prerequisite for, and a consequence of, development.[15] Increased participation, however, at a time of tremendous popular impatience for social and economic advance,[16] intensified political competition and exacerbated a factional conflict in the ruling party that had its roots in the colonial years.[17] The decision to introduce the one-party state was announced at the height of a bitter and prolonged political conflict, which had demonstrated the difficulties the leadership faced in asserting control.[18] It was subsequently justified as a necessary step to bring political violence to a halt.[19] We approach it, therefore, in this light: as a strategy employed by the regime to control social and political conflict. If we are to understand the nature of that conflict, however, we must look beyond the party to the broader processes of social change after independence to which we now briefly turn.

The background: post-colonial social and economic change

At independence Zambia demonstrated the classic characteristics of underdevelopment, with an economy dependent upon the copper-mining industry and a gross rural/urban imbalance. Historically its economic ties were with the south. Its land-locked position made it acutely dependent upon its neighbours to transport its copper out of and its imports into the country, while its position, as a front-line state on the borders of southern Africa and the white minority regimes, constituted a security problem that became steadily worse after Rhodesia's unilateral declaration of independence in 1965.[20] Nevertheless, in 1964 a sense of great optimism and abundance pervaded society, and Zambians at all levels had great expectations of independence.[21] After a colonialism characterised by intense racial discrimination, development was defined not only in terms of societal change for the community, but also of increased opportunities for the individual. The ordinary Zambian expected that life for him and his family must become better, while those who had fought in the nationalist struggle expected that their political role would be rewarded.

The first five years after independence appeared to justify those expectations. Zambia in 1964 was relatively wealthy, certainly by comparison with the majority of other newly independent African states. Copper produced a significant surplus, sufficient to allow the new government to embark upon an ambitious development programme. Over the period 1963-68, high copper prices enabled it also to increase wages, to provide material benefits and to achieve a significant programme of social development. The real purchasing power of the average Zambian employee increased by two-thirds. Zambia's urban working class became more entrenched.[22] Rewards were also liberally granted to those who had actively contributed to the independence struggle. Access to loans, licenses, employment opportunities and the early emphasis on agricultural co-operatives favoured local U.N.I.P. officials and strong U.N.I.P. regions.[23] Major economic reforms between 1968 and 1970 also opened up many areas of the retail and service sectors of the economy to Zambian citizens. Increased individual economic participation was thus enhanced following the acquisition of political power by Zambians determined to orient policy to the Zambianisation of the economy. The reforms, combined with credit facilities for small-scale business and the pressure of the state upon commercial banks to extend credit for larger Zambian enterprises, encouraged the emergence of an entrepreneurial group which had been actively discouraged for much of the colonial period.[24] One result was that after 1968 the growth of emergent bourgeois and petty bourgeois groups became the most significant feature of social change.[25]

The localisation of the private sector was less important, however, in terms of the overall economy than the extension of direct state participation through nationalisation, the general acquisition of property rights in some sectors, and the sponsoring of new enterprises fully or partially owned by the state. The result of these changes was a dramatic expansion in State participation in the economy.[26] The growth of State participation, moreover, had a profound effect upon bureaucratic, as opposed to political, control over economic policy and therefore upon political participation. The enlargement of the role of the State in the economy contributed to the growth of the parastatal sector, and of a parastatal management that assumed an increasingly central role in economic decision-making. It increased the need for technocrats and contributed to the extension of the power of the bureaucracy, rather than the party, which had neither economic expertise nor experience in that area. As a result, key decision-making responsibilities became far more concentrated in the hands of senior bureaucrats.[27]

The expansion that accompanied independence began to falter in the late 'sixties. Economic growth disguised but did not overcome Zambia's dependence upon copper and thus, when copper prices began to fluctuate in 1969, the country's basic underdevelopment became apparent. The government's first restrictive budget, introduced by Mr. Kapwepwe, as Minister of Finance, in 1969, made little impact on the public understanding of the constraints of underdevelopment. By the early 'seventies, however, increasing economic difficulties began to have direct repercussions upon urban society. Whereas the First National Development Plan had set a target of 100,000 new jobs between June 1966 and December 1970, employment rose only by 77,000 jobs or 24 per cent. Moreover the employment figures by themselves obscured the full social impact of the failure of employment to expand. Those seeking work had not only to contend with the difficulties of finding employment, but also with the fact that each year the jobs available were at progressively lower levels of status and remuneration.[28]

The most serious failure of the development programme in the early 'seventies related to the rural sector. Expansive access to credit and an ambitious co-operative programme had provided important patronage but had not resulted in agricultural development. On the one hand, African traditional agriculture had not been transformed, and on the other, the commercial farming sector had become a good deal less stable, with harmful consequences for the country's food supplies. While the gap between the earnings of Zambian workers and expatriate employees had been greatly reduced, the gap between the standard of living of urban Zambian workers and Zambian villagers had greatly increased. Whereas at the end of 1968, the average annual earnings of Zambian workers was K789, the typical village family's income was worth about K120.[29] Moreover, the economic reforms of 1968 and 1969 seriously disadvantaged the rural areas. First, increased State participation diverted resources to the industrial sector. Second, the rural areas lacked the capital necessary to take advantage of the Zambianisation of the private sector. In many cases rural retail stores closed down, contributing to the further rural/urban imbalance in economic participation and income distribution.[30] There was indeed no doubt at the beginning of the 'seventies that the benefits of independence had gone to the urban rather than the rural population; so much so that Kaunda himself could warn of the danger of 'two nations within one'.[31] What had not changed, however, were popular expectations, particularly in the urban areas, and the popular emphasis upon government responsibility in the allocation of resources. It is with this in mind that we must consider the pattern of political conflict over these years.

Uneven development and the regional basis of political competition

Zambia at independence was a multi-party state in which the ruling party faced a small but persistent opposition in the African National Congress. The most important level of political conflict, however, was not between U.N.I.P. and the A.N.C. but within U.N.I.P. itself. The successive stages of what became an increasingly bitter struggle for power within its leadership ranks are well known. The first was the expulsion in 1966, for alleged improper ministerial conduct, of Nalumino Mundia, one of the party's foremost Lozi nationalists, and of another Lozi minister; and Mundia's assumption in 1967 of the leadership of a new opposition United Party (U.P.). That party was banned in 1968 after an outbreak of violence on the Copperbelt. The second was the crisis which began in 1967 when a Bemba-Tonga alliance at the party's national conference defeated incumbent Lozi and Nyanja leaders in the election for U.N.I.P.'s Central Committee and made Mr. Kapwepwe, the senior Bemba politician, Vice-President. The third followed on from that election, ending with Kapwepwe's resignation to form the United Progressive Party (U.P.P.) in August 1971.[32]

At each stage the power struggle was frequently articulated by the protagonists in ethnic terms. Nevertheless, any simplistic attempts at explanation based on 'tribalism' need to be regarded with caution.[33] A more useful approach has termed the basis of the conflict as 'sectionalism', meaning a competition for scarce resources between interests which reflected the regional or provincial cleavages which at that time dominated Zambian society.[34] Sectionalism, in this sense, draws attention to the diversity of interests in Zambia beyond those relating simply to the ethnic group, and especially to regionalism.

While such a plurality of interests is common to all societies, they have been given particular salience in Zambia by the nature of that country's 'uneven and combined development' during this century.[35] The unevenness of colonial penetration across the country produced a variety of patterns of integration into the colonial economy, of migration to urban jobs, and of local integration into the capitalist market, as well as differing capacities for survival on the part of pre-colonial political and economic forms. Thus, in Northern Province, colonialism involved the destruction of traditional political forms as well as the trade and tribute on which they were based.[36] The province became a major source of migrant mine-labour, its agricultural economy declined and consequently it became in the 'fifties and 'sixties one of the main centres of militant anti-colonial nationalism. Its neighbour, Luapula Province, while also experiencing an outward drain of labour and decline in agricultural production, had benefitted from the fishing industry, stimulated first by the mining industry in Katanga and later by that on the Copperbelt. When the fortunes of the fishing industry declined in the late 'fifties, the frustrations of the residents of Luapula were expressed in a nationalist fervour whose militance approximated that in Northern Province.[37] In Southern Province, the alienation of vast tracts of land for commercial, settler farming created a rural proletariat and, unremarkably, many of the earlier leaders of nationalist politics.[38] Again, in Western Province, where Indirect Rule involved a measure of survival for the traditional ruling aristocracy and where the isolation of the province ensured only the most rudimentary development of commerce, pre-colonial political arrangements remained strong, nationalist politics tended to have shallow roots, migrant labour was integrated into the South African gold-mining economy rather than the Zambian copper mines, and political militants tended to be those socialised in the urban rather than in the rural areas.[39]

Uneven development gave Zambia a pattern of political competition which reflects varied responses to varied experiences.[40] It has also, however, ensured that in competing for the scarce rewards available only at the centre, Zambians have characteristically operated through factional networks which aggregate support roughly along regional lines.[41] Put differently, 'imperfect integration' at the national level made political alliances based on the locality and region a logical, even necessary, point of departure for the nationalist politician.[42]

Given such patterns of local patronage and regional alliances, political divisions, once formalised along party lines, became in the 'sixties relatively easy to maintain; the local base, rather than financial and other resources, became of primary importance to the political aspirant. U.N.I.P. itself had ultimately grown out of the 1958 schism within the A.N.C.[43] After independence, the A.N.C. became increasingly confined in its support to the Southern Province, thus constituting a formal regionally-based opposition.[44] Within U.N.I.P. itself, however, the coalition of various groups and factions proved more difficult to contain. The formation of the United Party in 1966, with support drawn primarily from Western Province (although it attracted some urban dwellers also), reflected the inability of the governing party to satisfy the needs of all sectional interests, and therefore its vulnerability to threats of secession from disgruntled factions dissatisfied over their allegedly inadequate share of the spoils.[45] The proscription of the U.P. resulted in many of its leadership joining the A.N.C. and the loss by U.N.I.P. in the 1968 general elections of nearly all the Lozi seats it held in Western Province. Thus, in the context of regional politics, events showed that secession from U.N.I.P. could clearly be maintained indefinitely and at little political cost to individual leaders.

Other, less dramatic, forces also contributed to the gradual erosion of U.N.I.P.'s effectiveness and popularity after 1964, and indeed can be seen to underlie the failure to control regional competition. We shall here briefly review three of particular relevance to the political process: first, the inability of the ideology of Humanism to take root among U.N.I.P. followers in such a way as to become a force for unity among political activists and to provide guidelines for national policy; second, the change in the function and status of the party after independence and its resultant failure to create for itself a satisfactory new role; and third, the change in the economic and social status of the U.N.I.P. leadership after the achievement of power. These factors, set against the failure of early development plans to realise mass aspirations, help to explain the failure of the party to overcome its own internal divisions.

The failure of ideology

Humanism was launched by Kaunda in 1967 after a request to him by the party Central Committee to formulate an official ideology for party and nation.[46] As such, it has been correctly identified as his contribution to the definition of national goals. He presented Humanism as a set of philosophical guidelines rooted in the Zambian cultural heritage, intended to unite the country in the common task of economic, social and political development. Its primary function (highlighted by its original presentation at the 1967 Mulungushi Conference) was to dispel conflict, since personal and regional competition were identified as contrary to the national good.

The ability of Humanism to provide an ideological basis for action and a cohesive and coherent direction for development was, however, inhibited by its own weaknesses. The first was its ambiguity. Despite subsequent attempts to elaborate and clarify its content, Humanism remained a set of ambiguous statements, many mutually contradictory, and depending on voluntaristic and volitional rather than structural solutions to social problems. Furthermore, it lacked any clear definition of the objectives of economic development, on which it was, in certain respects, inconsistent. While the ideology was described as an alternative to communism and capitalism, the relationship between Humanism and socialism was not spelled out. Although socialism was designated as a stage in the development of a Humanist society, capitalism was also accepted as a part of that development process.[47] While exploitation of man by man was condemned as inimical to Humanist precept and practice, there was no definition of what constituted exploitation.[48] Moreover the prescriptions for development were based upon a utopian notion of Zambian traditional society that now scarcely applied in the countryside, let alone to the realities of urban life. The consequence was that Humanism lacked conviction as a guide for development. Its prescriptions could be used to justify conflicting actions and to legitimise conflicting positions on both economic and social policy. Not surprisingly, while most politicians publicly accepted Humanism, as the party philosophy, it failed to take root or to constrain internal disagreement; it also failed to address itself to the problems of patronage and factionalism. It was widely accepted because President Kaunda espoused it, but was seen by leaders and followers alike as involving little more than volitional goodwill towards one's fellows.[49]

Decline of the party

Humanism, moreover, provided no specific role for U.N.I.P. New institutional structures, defended as a means for decentralizing power and enhancing mass participation, were not based on the party; they therefore did not revitalise the organisation or provide it with new purpose. In the event, the new organs of administration strengthened central control rather than the party or participation. Thus U.N.I.P.'s weakness was itself a mechanism for furthering control at the expense of participation, allowing the new managerial and bureaucratic groups to strengthen their influence over decision-making, and, at the same time, ensuring that the control of factional conflict was made more difficult. A lack of mass participation tended to leave few measures available against intra-party conflict other than coercion.

The inability of ideology to provide cohesive and coherent direction for the development process was paralleled and in part promoted by the gradual decline of the party after 1964 as a mobilising vanguard. During the struggle for independence, the party had served as the body which organized, educated and motivated people to act in concert; after independence, however, it gradually ceased to occupy a position of real national leadership. In part this failure stemmed from the very success achieved — party leaders were progressively lost to government service after independence so that the quality of party leadership declined.[50] In part it reflected the inability of the party to transform its objectives and functions once its primary goal of independence had been achieved and to identify a developmental role. Only in elections did the party appear to have a clearly defined function. Otherwise the internecine factional struggles pushed it to become an arena for confrontation rather than an agency for generating policy. The party was left as a vehicle for individual and group mobility rather than a national force for development, useful primarily to its leaders as a stepping stone to power and privilege, so that the potential for competition for leadership was exaggerated. Hence, cleavages often deepened at the local level as factions among party officials — or within constituency committees — attempted to ensure 'their' candidates were elected in the hope that patronage mechanisms might benefit them politically or in their businesses.[51]

Changes in U.N.I.P. leadership

The party's problems were, in turn, a reflection of the country's changing social structure. As noted, the attempts by government to redistribute wealth and gain local control of the economy promoted the emergence of a local bourgeoisie. The party, being embedded in the structure of political power, in the process became a means of access to economic power and thus one avenue of recruitment to that emergent bourgeoisie. Many of the most successful no longer held party office and their links with the party were often weak and sporadic. Among the growing petty bourgeoisie, however, many still retained political office or moved into the local levels of the party after having acquired their small businesses. Party patronage, moreover, had meant that a great deal of aid for petty trading and small enterprise had been made available for party officials. Thus its leadership ranks, once occupied by teachers, workers and marketeers, now manifested many shopkeepers, bar owners and aspirant entrepreneurs — some of them ex-teachers, ex-workers and ex-marketeers.[52]

In the rural provinces, where fewer opportunities for economic mobility existed because of the lower level of market development, a different pattern emerged. Branch and constituency officials, like other party members, frequently had neither paid employment nor business interests. Even in the rural areas, however, lower party officials were none the less oriented towards individual mobility and perceived the party more in terms of its capacity to grant individual rewards rather than to promote community ends. Thus, rather than providing a means of unifying the population, the party began to mirror the growing social divisions in the country. Its local leadership, frequently involved full time in business and only 'after five' in the party, had also come to identify — in aspiration as well as composition — with the more privileged strata of society.

The political system had thus become to a significant extent a spoils system, in which support was based on the ability to deliver benefits and power emanated from an ability to promote local demands. In this way, the potential for political secession, for regional groupings to leave (or threaten to leave) the party as a result of their frustration in the competition for rewards, had become built-in. To be unsuccessful as a patron and to remain an unprotesting party loyalist invited rejection by the local base, as was demonstrated in the defeat of a number of Lozi ministers by A.N.C. (former U.P.) candidates in the elections of 1968. Thus pressures from below and from the leadership for a regional articulation of interests were intrinsic to the multi-party system.

Intra-party conflict and the extension of control

In the multi-party state, the judicious use of patronage emerged as a necessary and accepted strategy against the sectionalism that threatened U.N.I.P.[53] Patronage alone, however, proved a costly and fundamentally inadequate safeguard against disagreement within the party ranks, so a series of other devices were also employed in an attempt to control intra-party conflict. Thus in 1966, following the formation of the U.P., the government amended the constitution to require any M.P. resigning from the party that had supported his election to resign also from Parliament and (if he so wished) to contest his seat again.[54] That amendment no doubt inhibited other U.N.I.P. M.P.s who might otherwise have resigned, both in 1966 and again in 1971. It did not, however, dissolve internal party disagreement.

Kaunda himself on successive occasions attempted to use both his personal legitimacy and his presidential authority to curb intra-party disagreement. On one occasion, in 1968, he threatened to resign in an effort to prevent open schism;[55] on others, in 1968 and 1971, he introduced a 'stringent set of regulations' designed to enforce collective responsibility in an attempt to prevent public ministerial disagreement.[56] In the face of the divisions within both Cabinet and Central Committee, he also, however, increasingly asserted his own independent authority as party leader and chief executive. The result was, in the period 1964 to 1971, a steady concentration of power in the presidency.

The independence constitution had placed executive power firmly with the President, and from the first Kaunda had used his position to initiate policy. Clearly he saw his role as that of innovator, as shown by the successive expansion of functions assumed by the Office of the President and the enlargement of an advisory staff in State House. Thus the key economic reforms of 1968 and 1969 emanated from State House, apparently without Cabinet involvement. The tendency on the part of State House to act independently of that body was, however, increased by the factional crisis of 1969 – 71.[57] Moreover, in the face of factionalism and the resulting divisions within the Cabinet, Kaunda also extended his control within the party as well, as for example in August 1969, when he appointed three ministers of state in the president's office with responsibilities at Freedom House, U.N.I.P.'s headquarters.[58]

Two presidential initiatives were most important in the context of control. First, Kaunda's administrative reforms of January 1969 may be interpreted not only as a response to bureaucratic weakness, but also as an attempt to exert greater control over sectional conflict by structural change. They created a new administrative structure by merging, at all levels, officers of the provincial and district government division of the president's office and the Ministry of Local Government. A Cabinet Minister and Permanent Secretary were posted to each province to head the restyled provincial and local government. The district level of administration was politicised by the creation of the post of District Governor as political head of the district. Appointed personally by the President, a governor was responsible to the Provincial Minister as the 'chief government co-ordinating officer in [his] district with reference to the task of political and economic development'.[59] The justification of those changes was the desire to involve the grass roots more closely in government by taking decision-making nearer to the locality, thus widening the base of participation. It was also hoped to expand the local planning function by adding development committees at village, ward and district levels to the local administration structure introduced in 1965. At the same time, the office of District Governor provided the President with his most important channel of direct presidential control over party organs and officials.

Second, Kaunda's single most important assertion of presidential power was his suspension in August 1969 of U.N.I.P.'s Central Committee, his assumption of authority as Secretary General of the party and his initiation of a movement for party reform out of which emerged a new party constitution. That constitution, finally agreed upon by the party in November 1970, represented a further attempt to control intra-party conflict by structural change. The nub of the problem was provincial representation in the general conference, the party's highest authority, which also elected the Central Committee, in which representation had been based hitherto on the party's administrative structure. The uneven growth of party regions across the country had produced an imbalance in provincial representation, and the dominance of the Copperbelt as the province with the largest number of branches. Copperbelt dominance was, however, seen by other provinces as the source of Bemba dominance, and thus of the Bemba success in the 1967 elections. The 1970 constitution attempted to overcome that imbalance by providing equal provincial representation at the general conference, going a long way to meet the complaints of those provinces that had seen themselves as underrepresented in the past. It was undoubtedly a major factor in U.N.I.P.'s ability to withstand the subsequent U.P.P. challenge, but it also undoubtedly disappointed many on the Copperbelt and in Northern Province. In the event, it contributed directly to the formation of the U.P.P.[60]

The U.P.P.: appeal to the dissatisfied

The United Progressive Party in 1971 epitomised the tendency for intra-party competition, in the guise of regional conflict, to culminate in secession from U.N.I.P. Its formation led to many defections from U.N.I.P. and seriously impaired the latter party's capability for mobilization, especially in Copperbelt Province. The split at the national level was mirrored by divisions at the local level and, on the Copperbelt, led to a great deal of violence when party branches and constituencies either divided or defected wholesale to U.P.P.[61] Indeed, U.N.I.P. lost many of its most efficient organisers and outspoken leaders. Furthermore, the great popularity of the U.P.P. leader, Simon Kapwepwe, among many Bemba-speaking people, presented U.N.I.P. with the very real possibility of losing much electoral support in Northern and Copperbelt provinces, thus threatening to make U.N.I.P. itself a regionally-defined party by default.

In addition to Kapwepwe, U.P.P.'s leaders included several prominent national Bemba-speaking U.N.I.P. figures. Yet for all the U.P.P.'s appearance of constituting a regional-linguistic group, the conflict was waged in terms of two large blocs rather than on simpler tribal lines; and since many Bemba speakers remained within U.N.I.P.

while some non-Bemba joined U.P.P., we have doubts about 'tribal-ism' as the source of disagreement. Two other significant influences need to be borne in mind. First, at the leadership level the split reflected differences about the role of the party which had their origins in the years of the nationalist struggle. In those earlier days, the younger, more educated, (often Lozi) element in U.N.I.P.'s leader-ship had emphasised the importance of unity and control from above as the basis of party organisation. In contrast, the older, more populist (often Bemba) leaders had emphasised mass participation and popular control. The U.P.P. now assumed that more populist approach. Thus while personality clashes meant that the division might be seen by some as a 'Bemba – Lozi' confrontation, there was an essential ideological undertone to it.[62]

Second, the U.P.P. attracted a variety of followers who felt frustrated by their lack of progress or promotion since independence. Thus a number of small businessmen, critical of ruinous competition from State retail chains, middle-level civil servants, local elected councillors, and party militants whose services during the anti-colo-nial struggle had seemingly been unrewarded after 1964, joined or flirted with U.P.P. and the party attracted several non-Bemba people among workers and local politicians.

The U.P.P. was thus in one sense an expression and consequence of competition for limited resources. While it is possibly convenient to view that party as an 'anti-modern' protest against a new modernising 'elite, and/or as a tribal party, it is perhaps safer therefore to view it as a protest by some disadvantaged groups (or those who perceived them-selves as disadvantaged) against the increasing dominance in national affairs of better educated politicians and the bureaucracy. That it was largely confined to a particular regional grouping represents perhaps a measure of the failure of its leadership to surmount such an image, rather than an indication of its intentions. Neither should the regional tendencies of U.P.P. allow us to ignore the very real protest which many Zambians felt at the time against certain government policies and the general direction of development. Development had not kept pace with the aspirations of the people, and indeed, its direction was frequently such as to bewilder and alienate members of the general public. The creation of jobs had been insufficient to absorb potential employment seekers. The distribution of benefits through the nation was uneven, the rural areas continuing to suffer relative disadvantage according to the colonial pattern, and many urban areas being re-latively disadvantaged in relation to the capital.

By 1971 the tendency to fragmentation arising out of dis-appointment and bitterness at the pace of development had to some extent become self-generating. Since access to individual employment and wealth, or to regional amenities and infrastructure, were frequently perceived as emanating from political position, political competition had become essential for self- and community advancement. Given that perception, patronage had become a necessary means of recruiting support or, conversely, of being represented in the distribution of benefits. The escalation of violence that followed the formation of the U.P.P. suggested the extent to which those who remained with U.N.I.P. now saw themselves as under attack. It also demonstrated the inability of the central U.N.I.P. leadership to control local-level activity. The by-elections which took place in December 1971 were also, in many respects, a hollow victory which further demonstrated the party's vulnerability. U.N.I.P. won eleven of the twelve seats contested. However, the A.N.C. retained its traditional stronghold in Southern Province, and the low poll suggested that U.N.I.P.'s victory was a result of voter abstention rather than change of heart. Furthermore, Kapwepwe's victory in Mufulira, against considerable odds and without campaigning personally, was the first occasion that U.N.I.P., which had enjoyed all the advantages, had been defeated in the Copperbelt in parliamentary elections on a universal franchise. Kapwepwe's victory represented the defection of a sizeable number of U.N.I.P. voters, and the failure of many U.N.I.P. voters to vote at all.[63]

Faced with a conflict they had failed to control, the government moved to limit political opposition by force and coercion. The formation of the U.P.P. was followed by widespread detentions of its leaders, so that, of the executive, only Kapwepwe himself was able to contest the by-elections that followed.[64] The detentions, which caused widespread bitterness, doubtless functioned to dissuade other U.N.I.P. leaders from defecting to U.P.P. or even expressing public sympathy for its personalities. In the course of the by-elections, however, U.N.I.P. leaders argued the introduction of a one-party state as a necessary counter to the rising tide of political violence.[65] Hitherto, the party had argued, with reasonable consistency, that the one-party state would be achieved in due course through the ballot box, when voters voted the A.N.C. out of existence. They had also rejected calls for legislation prohibiting the formation of opposition parties. By the end of 1971, however, U.N.I.P. leaders had shifted their position significantly, to argue the need to create a one-party state to overcome political disunity. The decision to legislate for the one-party state was thus justified in terms of the danger presented to national unity by the factionalism within the party. Speaking to the National Council in March 1972, Kaunda concluded:

The One-Party Democracy will help us to weed out political opportunists and people who have become professionals at manufacturing lies, spreading rumours, creating confusion and despondency and pretending to oppose what they inwardly welcome and exploit for their own personal benefits in the name of democracy which they have abused and desecrated. It has been fashionable in the past for any Party member . . . to threaten to quit, or indeed quit, the Party to join the opposition; for any civil servant . . . to threaten to quit . . .; indeed, for any religious leader . . . to render support to the opposition; for any businessman denied a licence or a loan on perfectly legal grounds to run to the opposition in the hope that if they formed the Government, he would be favoured. This era in which the politics of patronage has been a feature of life is gone.[66]

Factional conflict within U.N.I.P. and the formation of the U.P.P., in particular, thus constituted the immediate and conscious spur to the creation of the new system.

The introduction of the one-party state

The U.P.P. was banned and Kapwepwe and one hundred and twenty-three of its leading members detained on 4 February 1972. On the 25th, President Kaunda announced the Cabinet's decision to establish a one-party state by constitutional change.[67] The implementation of that decision occupied the greater part of 1972 and 1973. A National Commission under the chairmanship of the then Vice-President, Mainza Chona, reported in October on the changes necessary. Its report[68] and the government's White Paper[69] having been accepted by U.N.I.P.'s National Council in December, the National Assembly ushered in the one-party state on 4 December with a constitutional amendment that made U.N.I.P. the only legal party.[70] On 13 December, the Second Republic was inaugurated and President Kaunda sworn in as President.[71] A new constitution passed through the National Assembly the following August.[72] This, together with a new party constitution, were accepted by a special U.N.I.P. conference at the end of August, when a new Central Committee was elected unopposed and Kaunda endorsed as the party's presidential candidate.[73] Kaunda, in turn, announced appointments for the new posts of Secretary General and Prime Minister, as well as his own nominees to the Central Committee. Parliament was dissolved at the end of September and the first general elections in the one-party state followed in December.

Public debate on the constitution was limited,[74] the only serious opposition being expressed by the A.N.C., which refused the government's offer of representation on the Chona Commission and unsuccessfully challenged the government decision to introduce the

one-party state in the courts.[75] An attempt by former U.P.P. members
to form a new party in October 1972 was doomed from the outset,[76]
and following the inauguration of the one-party state, in January, the
government felt strong enough to release Mr. Kapwepwe and thirty-
five other detainees.[77] Nevertheless, the changes were accompanied
by a great deal of tension. The party's actions suggested considerable
preoccupation with the behaviour of local party officials, and concern
about party rather than public support. Party officials, in turn, directed a good deal of their attention to the perceived threat of continuing
U.P.P. influence, and thus to purging the party of 'U.P.P. elements'.
There were also serious disagreements within U.N.I.P. over certain
provisions of the one-party state.

The tenor of the Chona Commission's recommendations suggested
the 'liberal' influence of Zambia's new administrators and entrepreneurs, rather than the populist influence of the party. Thus the
report recommended the limitation of preventive detention; the
curtailment of both party and presidential power; the division of
presidential power and functions between an Executive President and
a Prime Minister with extensive powers of his own, including the
appointment of ministers; and the restriction of party activity, including the removal of party control over nomination for parliamentary
elections and responsibility for the electoral campaign.[78] The government, however, rejected all such proposals, and the President retained all the powers the office had previously enjoyed. Although the
office of Prime Minister was now introduced, — its incumbent being
responsible for government administration and leader of government
business in the National Assembly, — the President remained sole
executive. The separation of Central Committee and Cabinet, moreover, further enhanced his position. Furthermore, although the
Central Committee was elected by the party general conference, and
Parliament consisted of 125 members chosen ultimately by the
electorate, the 1973 constitution gave the President considerable
power to influence the complexion of each body through nomination
of additional members, three to the twenty elected members of the
Central Committee and ten to the National Assembly, though for the
latter he was prohibited from nominating anyone defeated in the
general election.[79] Furthermore, whereas the National Commission
recommended that a President be eligible to stand for a second five-
year term, after which he would not again be eligible to stand for
office until yet another five-year period had elapsed, the government
decided that there should be no such limitation.

There was also serious disagreement over the procedure for presidential election. The original proposal was for an electoral competition between three presidential candidates. The party objected to this,

however, on the grounds that it would divide both party and country on tribal lines, since there could be no party political differences between candidates. As a result, the constitution was modified to provide for one presidential candidate, elected by the party general conference, who would then be presented to the electorate for ratification. The change clearly reinforced party control over the presidency, although at the same time it provided for greater presidential control over the party.[80] The party made one further important gain which also reinforced presidential control. While the consitution of the re-public was silent on the matter, the new U.N.I.P. constitution stipulated the supremacy of the party over the government, and hence of the Central Committee over the Cabinet. Both Central Committee and Cabinet were charged with the implementation of National Council decisions, and in the event of serious disagreement between them the decision of the former would prevail.[81]

Finally, there emerged intense disagreement over the proposal to include a Leadership Code in the constitution, leading not only to significant modifications to the original proposals, but also to the decision at the June 1972 National Council to delay their introduction until after the elections.[82] The constitution, as passed in August 1973, set up a Leadership Committee to make regulations for the code, defined the offices affected, and provided for a Tribunal to deal with breaches and alleged breaches of the code. In the event, however, the code did not come into effect until 1976.

The disagreement about the Leadership Code must be placed in the context of the changes that had followed the economic reforms, and which had created a new business class which overlapped at all levels with the party hierarchy. Urban local-level party officials were to a large extent, as we have seen, embedded in a Zambian petty bourgeoisie, and on the Copperbelt Kaunda found himself forced to argue that the ordinary shopkeeper was not a capitalist.[83] Moreover, the definition of leadership encompassed a broad spectrum of the Zambian bureaucracy and parastatal management, among whom were many who now had some interest in the private sector.

There was thus undoubtedly a deep division within U.N.I.P. on the issue, which was fought out inconclusively at the National Council in March 1973.[84] The debate suggested that new alignments were already emerging within the party in the one-party state, with the new man-agerial element ranged alongside the old populist, petty-bourgeois elements within the party, which brought the whole principle into doubt.

Notwithstanding that the one-party state emerged as a device to ensure greater central control over factional conflict, the U.N.I.P. leadership argued that it would, at the same time, provide the in-

stitutional base for the unity and greater political participation which
the development process required. The one-party state, it was insisted, would widen the scope of leadership and vest power in the
masses. It would also eliminate the political violence which had
characterised the multi-party system.[85] The first test was therefore its
ability to integrate previously antagonistic elements into U.N.I.P.
itself. The credibility of the one-party system depended in large part
upon its ability to absorb the former opposition parties and to allow
for criticism within the single party.

The first step in this process was taken in June 1973, when
Nkumbula took his A.N.C. followers into U.N.I.P., at a much
publicised meeting at Choma attended by Kaunda and other U.N.I.P.
leaders. At that meeting the A.N.C. announced that all provincial,
district and area branches would immediately identify themselves
with U.N.I.P.[86]

The Choma Agreement constituted a significant personal victory
for Nkumbula. It legitimised his place in the one-party system, and to
a significant extent made the legitimacy of the one-party system itself
in the Southern Province dependent upon him. The agreement did
not, however, resolve the problems of all former opposition groups.
First, it did not include A.N.C's Western Province organisation (or
Nalumino Mundia, at that stage in detention). Second, the U.P.P.
conflict was too recent and too bitter to allow an early readmission of
that party's leaders or followers, and it was not surprising that it was
strongly resisted from within U.N.I.P. itself, at both the national and
the local level.[87] Hence the electoral system itself remained pivotal for
full participation.

Notes

1 See especially William Tordoff (ed.), *Politics in Zambia* (Manchester,
   Manchester University Press, 1974).
2 See, for example, a speech by President Kaunda at the Chifubu rally on
   the Copperbelt, 17 January 1965, reprinted in Colin Legum (ed.),
   Zambia: Independence and Beyond — The Speeches of Kenneth Kaunda
   (London, Thomas Nelson and Sons, 1966).
3 James Coleman and Carl Rosberg (eds.), *Political Parties and National
   Integration in Tropical Africa* (Berkeley and Los Angeles, University of
   California Press, 1964). See Conclusion.
4 Aristide Zolberg, *Creating Political Order: The Party States of West
   Africa* (Chicago, Rand McNally, 1966).
5 See, for example, Goran Hyden, *Political Development in Rural
   Tanzania* (Nairobi, East African Publishing House, 1969); Lionel Cliffe
   (ed.), *One Party Democracy* (Nairobi, East African Publishing House,
   1967); Geoff Lamb, *Peasant Politics* (London, Julian Friedman, 1974).

6 Henry Bienen, 'One Party Systems in Africa', in Samuel Huntington and
   Clement Moore (eds.), *Authoritarian Politics in Modern Society* (New
   York, Bask Books 1970).
   See also his 'Political Parties and Political Machines in Africa', in
   Michael Lofchie (ed.), *The State of the Nation, Constraints on Develop-
   ment in Independent Africa* (Berkeley, University of California Press,
   1971).
7 On factions see especially Steffen W. Schmidt, James C. Scott, Carl
   Lande and Laura Guasti (eds.), *Friends, Followers and Factions* (Berkeley,
   University of California Press, 1977); S.N. Eisenstadt·and Louis Roneger,
   'Patron-client Relations as a Model of Structuring Social Exchange',
   Comparative Studies in Society and History, 22, 1 (1980); Jeremy Boissevain, 'Of Men and Marbles: Notes Towards a Reconsideration of
   Factionalism' in M. Silverman and R. F. Salisbury (eds.), *A House Divided? Anthropological Studies of Factionalism*, Memorial University of
   Newfoundland, Social and Economic Papers, No. 9, 1977.
8 Thus restoring Frantz Fanon to a more central place on the stage. For an
   equally critical analysis from the liberal side see W. Arthur Lewis, *Politics in West Africa* (Oxford University Press, 1965).
9 Richard Sklar, 'Political Science and National Integration — A Radical
   Approach', *Journal of Modern African Studies*, V, 1 (1967).
10 See especially Richard Sandbrook, 'Patrons, Clients and Factions: New
   Dimensions of Conflict Analysis in Africa', *Canadian Journal of Political Science*, 5 (March 1972); also Crawford Young, 'Patterns of Social
   Conflict: State, Class and Ethnicity', *Daedalus* (Spring 1982) issued as
   Vol. III, No. 2 of the Proceedings of the American Academy of Arts and
   Sciences).
11 Colin Leys, 'Politics in Kenya: The Development of Peasant Society',
   British Journal of Political Science, 1 (July 1971); R Sklar, 'The Nature of
   Class Domination in Africa', *Journal of Modern African Studies*, 17, 4
   (1979). On the growth of inequality, see; for example, the I.L.O. Report
   on Zambia, *Narrowing the Gaps, Jobs and Skills Programme for Africa*
   (Addis Ababa, 1977), or the earlier I.L.O. Report on Kenya, *Incomes,
   Unemployment and Inequality*, (Geneva, I.L.O., 1972).
12 This also needs, of course, to be taken into account in any analysis of
   why parties have succumbed to the military, on which see, for example,
   Dorothy Nelkin, 'The Economic and Social Setting of Military Take-
   overs in Africa', *Journal of Asian and African Studies*, II (1967); S. E.
   Finer, 'The Statemanship of Arms', *Times Literary Supplement*, 17
   (1978); and Ruth First, *The Barrel of a Gun* (London, Penguin, 1971).
13 John Saul, 'Background to the Tanzanian Election 1970' in Lionel Cliffe
   and John Saul (eds.), *Socialism in Tanzania*, Vol. I (Nairobi, East African
   Publishing House, 1972).
14 Much of the literature on democracy and participation assumes a notion
   of the latter based on theories of competing élites. While we make some
   use of this idea in describing such competition between élites in Zambia,
   we have tried to avoid such an approach, which prejudices any analysis of
   a single-party system from the start. Instead, we distinguish between

mass participation and élite participation, the latter being seen from the perspective that it provides at different times and for different purposes, both a form of participation and a form of control by one class or group of classes over others. It is assumed that there is, to some extent, though not always, an inverse relation between control and participation over any one issue, though this may not hold as between different dimensions of a process.

15 See, for example, President Kaunda's Chifubu rally speech, *op.cit.*

16 *Report of the UN/ECA/FAO Economic Survey Mission on the Economic Development of Zambia* (The Seers Report), (Ndola, Falcon Press, 1964) p.1.

17 See Tordoff (ed.) (1974), *op.cit.*

18 *Times of Zambia*, 26 Feb. 1972.

19 By the then Vice-President, Mainza Chona, introducing the constitutional amendment into Parliament in December 1972. See *Daily Parliamentary Debates*, 6 Dec. 1972. See also his address to the University of Zambia Political Science Association on 6 July 1972 (University of Zambia, Mimeo, n.d.)

20 See the Seers Report, *op.cit.* For the response to UDI, see Richard L. Sklar, 'Zambia's Response to the Rhodesian Unilateral Declaration of Independence' in Tordoff (ed.) (1974), *op.cit.*

21 This emerges strongly from President Kaunda's Chifubu rally speech, *op.cit.* See also, for one rural reaction, Robert H. Bates, *Rural Responses to Industrialisation* (New Haven, Yale University Press, 1976).

22 *Report to the Government of Zambia on Incomes, Wages and Prices in Zambia: Policy and Machinery* (Turner Report) (Geneva I.L.O., 1969) p. 8.

23 Ian Scott, 'Middle Class Politics in Zambia', *African Affairs* 77, 308 1978).

24 On the economic reforms see Tordoff (ed.) (1974), *op.cit.*, *passim.*

25 Much debate surrounds the use of such class concepts. In part this derives from the tendency in much contemporary social science to substitute class concepts with those of stratification; in part, it arises out of neo-Marxist views of an international world market, in which the owning groups of underdeveloped countries are denied bourgeois status and regarded as a petty bourgeoisie because of their relatively insignificant stature in the world economic system. We have used the terms in a more orthodox fashion, using them to describe owners of the means of production involved in the capitalist market economy of Zambia. We regard the bourgeoise as those owning large or numerous businesses and employing regularly a quantum of labour; the petit bourgeoisie refers to small traders employing their own or family labour, or the occasional wage worker.

26 On the expansion of State participation and the growth of State capitalism see, *inter alia*, M.Williams, 'State Participation and the Zambian economy', *World Development* 10 (October 1973) pp. 43–53, and B. Turok, *State Capitalism: The Role of Parastatals* (University of Zambia, Mimeo, n.d. but 1979).

27 We deal more fully with these issues below. See Chapter 5.

28 Republic of Zambia, *Second National Development Plan 1972–1976* (SNDP), Ministry of Planning and National Guidelines, 1971, Lusaka, pp. 9–10. People in Zambia were conscious that in 1964 many people with a Standard Five schooling were able to assume civil-service posts of high responsibility. By the 1970's, Form II leavers could no longer be certain of finding any clerical work at all. The dissatisfaction felt at this process was therefore likely to be far greater than the figures indicated. Certainly, in the 1973 election campaign on the Copperbelt, candidates won a favourable response, even from people with little education, when they complained that planning had not ensured the provision of jobs appropriate to the educational attainments of the population. See also below, Chapter 5.

29 Turner Report, *op.cit.*, p. 9. In January 1968 the kwacha replaced the Zambian pound. Two kwacha were equivalent to one old pound, which was at par with sterling. After the British devaluation of 1958, one kwacha equalled 58p.

30 See, for example, Bates, *op.cit.* Also below, Chapters 6 and 7.

31 *Towards Complete Independence.* Speech by H. E. The President Dr. K. D. Kaunda, to the U.N.I.P. National Council held at Matero Hall Lusaka, 11 Aug. 1969, p. 44 (Lusaka, Zambia Information Services, n.d. but 1969).

32 For a full account of this period see Tordoff (ed.), 1974, *op.cit.* See also below, Chapter 5.

33 The subject dominates many studies of politics in Zambia. See, for example, Richard Hall, *The High Price of Principles* (Penguin, 1973); Jan Pettmen, *Zambia: Security and Conflict* (Sussex, Julian Freedman, 1974).

34 Robert Molteno, 'Cleavage and Conflict in Zambian Politics', William Tordoff (ed.) (1974), *op.cit.*

35 For a discussion of the basic thesis on uneven development, see Lenin, *The Development of Capitalism in Russia* (Moscow: Progress, 1956) and Trotsky, *History of the Russian Revolution*, Vol. I, Chapter I, (London, Sphere, 1967). The theory basically holds that, through external and internal forces, societies experience abrupt and discontinuous changes; that is, they do not necessarily pass through stages experienced by other countries and do not pass through them the same way. Development, therefore, is an uneven process, both internationally and internally. The unevenness of change produces a pattern of combined development in which different social forms coexist and *interact* within a particular society. How they interact, in any specific case, is a matter for empirical investigation.

36 See Andrew Roberts, *A History of the Bemba*, (London, Longmans, 1973).

37 See David C. Mulford, *Zambia: The Politics of Independence 1957–1964* (Oxford, Oxford University Press, 1967), Chapter 7. Also below, Chapter 6.

38 *Ibid.*

39 *Ibid.* Also below, Chapter 7.

40   We have utilised the notion of uneven development rather than the
      theory of social dualism, since the latter ignores the interaction and
      interdependence of the two sectors and, worse, ignores unevenness
      within each. Despite many criticisms (see Frank, *Capitalism and Under-
      development in Latin America* [Monthly Review Press, 1967], this static
      model continues to promote erroneous analysis of many underdeveloped
      countries, not least Zambia, which is often considered a paradigm case of
      dualism. See Anthony Martin, *Minding Their Own Business* (London,
      Hutchinson, 1972), as but one instance.

41   Hence the two broad groupings thrown up between 1967 and 1970, of the
      Committee of Twenty-four, associated with Northern Province
      Bemba-speaking politicians, and their opponents, the Committee of
      Fourteen. See *Times of Zambia*, 19 Apr. 1971.

42   Molteno quotes Simon Kapwepwe as saying in September 1970, that ' . . .
      you certainly cannot prove to be a national leader without sectional
      backing: to be a national leader usually you have got to start from the
      scratch, i.e. village, where you are born, district and then province up to
      national level . . . Even if you can be well known in Lusaka, without
      organising your village you would certainly stand to lose.' Quoted in
      Tordoff (ed.) (1974), *op.cit.*, p. 77.

43   Mulford, 1967, *op.cit.*, pp. 73–81 and Chapter III.

44   It is more accurate to state that it became confined to a language bloc
      among the Tonga-Ila people, since it held the Mumbwa area of Central
      Province where the same linguistic group constituted a majority.

45   William H. Riker has argued that 'overwhelming majorities' constitute
      chronically unstable forms of political coalition, since they have an
      inherent tendency to fragment given that the share-out of political spoils
      must necessarily be less than it would be for each unit of a smaller
      coalition. Riker argues that in such coalitions pressure builds up to *expel*
      certain groups rather than that dissatisfied groups secede of their own
      accord. In fact, there is some evidence that secessionist groups have been
      helped to leave U.N.I.P. by opposing factions, in defiance of Kaunda's
      attempts to preserve the coalition. But even if this were not so, Riker's
      thesis sheds light on the process of fragmentation in a patronage or spoils
      system where the ruling coalition is large. See his *The Theory of Political
      Coalitions* (Yale, Yale University Press, 1962).

46   Timothy K. Kandeke, 'The Development of Zambian Humanism as a
      socio-economic and political ideology in Zambia' (manuscript, Lusaka,
      undated). Kandeke notes that in 1965 U.N.I.P. leaders began a process of
      discussion with a view to formulating an ideology for the nation, and
      that in 1967, the President began to put forward his ideas in the form
      known as Humanism. See also his *Fundamentals of Zambian Human-
      ism* (Lusaka, Neczam, 1977).

47   Thus in one interpretation Humanism emerged as little more than an
      ideology of enlightened private enterprise and benevolent state capital-
      ism. See Justin B. Zulu, *Zambian Humanism: some major spiritual and
      economic challenges* (Lusaka, Neczam, 1970).

48 The ideology is strangely (for a social philosophy) rooted in moral and psychological explanations of social problems. Thus problems are often seen as arising from 'greed', 'selfishness', 'the animal in man', 'creating confusion', etc.

49 Thus it was 'Humanistic' to give people lifts in cars, to avoid abusing employees, to work hard, etc. See also Roderick Rainford, 'The Teaching of Humanism to Adult Students in the University Extra-Mural Programme', *Bulletin* No. 3 (1968), Institute of Social Research, University of Zambia. During the U.P.P. conflicts, the slogan 'Humanism is lies' was occasionally used on the Copperbelt. Opinion surveys undertaken among University of Zambia students in 1971 indicated a widespread rejection and/or suspicion of the ideology, and the observation was made by many respondents that the country's leaders did not practice what they preached.

50 This process did not end with the shifting of national leaders to government positions, but continued, for instance, in the 1968 elections in which 24 of the 37 new U.N.I.P. members of Parliament were recruited from the ranks of party officials. See Robert Molteno and Ian Scott, 'The 1968 General Election and the Political System' in Tordoff (ed.), 1974, *op.cit.*, especially Table 5.3.

51 Numerous instances of this were observed during the 1973 election campaign, as examples from Sinazongwe, Nkana, Zambesi and Livingstone, demonstrate, suggesting that the one-party state by itself would not ease this problem. One constituency official in Kanyama (Lusaka) Constituency, stated in an interview: 'The one-party state is destroying the party. We have never been so disunited and we are not able to do our work'. Interview, 4 Mar. 1973.

52 A survey of a sample of some 30 constituencies and branches in Ndola, Kitwe and Mufulira on the Copperbelt, undertaken in the Registry of Societies during the 1973 election period, indicated that there had been an overwhelming shift in the social composition of branches and constituencies. Before and immediately after independence, local party organisation tended to be run by workers (including miners) and the unemployed. In more recent years, that element had basically disappeared from the register of party officials to be replaced by white collar workers, supervisory level staff, salesmen, etc., as well as businessmen. The latter often occupied the key position of constituency or branch secretary. Our observation and interviews during the 1973 election tended to confirm this impression and to indicate that, whereas many had worked full time for the party (often without pay) during the struggle for independence, the party had now become a part-time occupation, confined to occasional meetings after work (and with a certain amount of time at such gatherings devoted to a discussion of business matters). We are grateful to our colleague, Dr. Ian Scott, for confirming that a large proportion of M.P.s elected in 1973 were formerly teachers. This fact makes the absence of current teachers from the ranks of candidates and winners even more noticeable, and gives some indication of the extent to which political leaders had moved from such occupations into more

remunerative sectors. This degree of individual mobility had
significantly altered the character of U.N.I.P. since independence.

53 Scott, *op.cit*; T. Rasmussen, 'Political Competition and One-Party
Dominance in Zambia', *Journal of Modern African Studies*, 7, 3 (1969).

54 Act No. 47 of 1966, Gazette Supplement, 22 Sept. 1966. The amendment
followed closely a similar provision enacted earlier in 1966 in Kenya
under similar circumstances. See C. Gertzel, *The Politics of Independent
Kenya* (London, Heinemann, 1971).

55 Tordoff (ed.), 1974, *op.cit.*, p. 26.

56 *Times of Zambia*, 19 and 20 Aug. 1968, and 17 Feb. 1971. On both
occasions the new 'Code of Behaviour' precluded any U.N.I.P. M.P.
speaking on any parliamentary motion without the permission of the
Chief Whip; and prohibited any minister from issuing a statement without presidential approval; or making statements on any subject except
Cabinet-approved policies.

57 On the economic reforms, see Martin, *op.cit*. On the extension of pres-
idential authority, see C. Gertzel, *The Political Process in Zambia:
Documents and Readings, Vol. II The Presidential System* (University of
Zambia, 1973), Introduction and pp. 12–15.

58 Cabinet Office Circular 101/12/11. *Zambia Daily Mail* 27 Aug. and 3
Sept. 1969.

59 William Tordoff and Robert Molteno, 'Government and Administration'
in Tordoff (ed.), 1974, op.cit. Also Cherry Gertzel, *District Administration in Zambia*, University of Zambia, Seminar Paper, 1971. The pres-
identially appointed Governors were more the representatives of the
centre than of their area. Many observers felt in 1973 that decentralisation had increased control sufficiently to ensure the defeat at the local
level of the U.P.P.

60 U.N.I.P. *Constitution*, Nov. 1970 (mimeo). In the Central Committee
election of 1967, the Bemba-speaking wing of U.N.I.P. had won most of
the seats on the committee. And since party positions were linked to
Cabinet office, this represented a sweeping victory for one faction. The
1971 party constitution, on the other hand, enshrined a balance of representation between areas of the country, ensuring also some representation for minorities which had previously been ignored in the
apportionment of portfolios. While this was welcomed by many as a
more equitable solution to inter-party competition, to the Bemba it
meant that decisions made in committees deprived them of victories
won in open elections. The faction's leaders on several occasions stated
that the new system was undemocratic, and so it is likely that, just as it
satisfied previously unrepresented groups, it alienated and finally drove
out many Bemba. Dissatisfaction however, was not confined to the
Bemba, and it is likely that, but for the promise held out by the new
constitution, other groups might have flirted with the U.P.P. In the
event, Kapwepwe was disappointed that few other leaders decided to
follow him — Bemba or non-Bemba. The detention of U.P.P. leaders
undoubtedly influenced this too.
See Tordoff (ed.), 1974, *op.cit.*, p. 139.

61 See below, Chapter 5.

62 In 1960 a U.N.I.P. pamphlet on Solidarity written by Munu Sipalo, then Secretary General of the party, a former member of the Study Group and one of the key Lozi nationalists, had claimed:

> U.N.I.P. is not a faction, not a group, not a wing, it is an institution rooted like a tree in the centre around which men group themselves as best they can. It is a fundamental and self-evident thing like life, liberty and the pursuit of happiness or like a National Flag . . . It is in fact the synonym of patriotism (Nationalism) which is another name for U.N.I.P. . . . On this basis therefore it is inconceivable that any self respecting man should not belong to . . . U.N.I.P. . . . U.N.I.P. is in a sense a political church which requires regular attendance and has a creed which epitomises the 'modernising' approach.

For the early conflict between modernist and populist, see Robert Rotberg, *The Rise of Nationalism in Central Africa: The Making of Malawi and Zambia, 1873–1964* and Fergus MacPherson, *Kenneth Kaunda of Zambia: the times and the man*. For a more recent clash see *Daily Parliamentary Debates* 26 Jan. 1972, c. 364–7. Sipalo had long since moved out of the leadership but the Wina brothers remained key figures at the centre.

63 See C. Gertzel, *et al*, 'Zambia's Final Experience of Inter-Party Elections: the By-elections of December 1971', *Kroniek Van Afrika*, 2, 2 (1972).

64 See *ibid.*

65 For example, *Times of Zambia*, 7 Nov. and 4 Dec. 1971. The issue had been debated at the National Council in October. See *Times of Zambia* 5 Oct. 1971.

66 Opening Address to U.N.I.P. National Council at Mulungushi Hall by President K. D. Kaunda, *Background* 8/72, Information Services, Lusaka, p. 4.

67 *Times of Zambia*, 5 and 26 Feb. 1972.

68 *Report of the National Commission on the Establishment of a One Party Participatory Democracy in Zambia* (Lusaka, Government Printer, October 1972), (The Chona Report).

69 *Government Paper No. 1 of 1972*, November 1972. Report of the National Commission on the Establishment of a One Party Participatory Democracy in Zambia. Summary of Recommendations accepted by the Government (Lusaka, Government Printer, 1972).

70 *Daily Parliamentary Debates*, 4 Dec. 1972.

71 *Times of Zambia*, 14 Dec. 1972.

72 Second reading, *Daily Parliamentary Debates*, 2 Aug. 1973. A draft bill for a new constitution published in May 1973 (N.A.B. 28/1973, 30 May 1973) was withdrawn to be replaced by N.A.B. 30/1973, published 4 July 1973.

73 *Times of Zambia*, 23–8 Aug. 1973; *Power to the People*, Addresses to and resolutions of the Seventh (Extraordinary) General Conference of the U.N.I.P., Mulungushi Rock, 25–6 Aug. 1973.

74   Press reports of the Chona Commission's public hearings suggesting also
     it was restricted to the more educated in society.
75   *Times of Zambia*, 29 Feb. and 5 Aug. 1972.
76   *Zambia Daily Mail*, 2 Oct. 1973.
77   *The Times*, 2 Jan. 1973.
78   *Chona Report*, paras 41–57, 82–6.
79   David Gwyn Morgan, 'Zambia's one Party State Constitution', *Public
     Law*, Spring 1976. In 1973, there was in fact no election for the Central
     Committee, since a slate of 20 individuals was put forward and accepted
     unopposed. It was widely understood that the President had been the
     ultimate selector of that slate.
80   This conclusion is based on observation over the period of the party
     conference. But see also Morgan, *op.cit.*, p. 50.
81   Chapter 11, article 12 (3) of the Constitution of U.N.I.P. states that,
     'should any decision of the Central Committee conflict with any deci-
     sion of the Cabinet on any matter of government or party policy the
     decision of the Central Committee shall prevail'.
82   *Times of Zambia*, 6 July 1973. For the proposed code, see Kaunda, *A
     Nation of Equals*, The Kabwe Declaration, 1–3 December 1972, pp. 31–
     45. The original proposal for a code went back to 1967, and Kaunda,
     Humanism Part I (p. 23). Subsequently, in November 1970, Kaunda had
     proposed a specific code in *Take up the Challenge* (p. 53), and established
     a sub-committee to work out a machinery for implementation. (*Times of
     Zambia*, 10 Nov. 1970). See also *Chona Report* paras. 170–9.
83   At Kitwe's Chimwemwe location, 30th Sept. 1973, at the rally at which
     he announced the dissolution of Parliament.
84   Report of National Council, June 1973, which agreed to postpone the
     introduction of the Code until after the general elections. See also Chap-
     ter 3 below.
85   The dangers of political violence also being very real at the beginning of
     1972, when, for example, there was a wave of petrol bombings on the
     Copperbelt. *Sunday Times of Zambia*, 23 Jan. 1973.
86   *Times of Zambia*, 28 June 1973; *Sunday Times of Zambia*, 1 July 1973.
87   See, for example, *Times of Zambia*, 23 Jan. and 13, 23 and 25 Sept. 1973.

Elections in the one-party state

Introduction

This essay examines the electoral process in the Zambian one-party state in the 'seventies. Elections in Africa had, by that time, it is true, become largely peripheral to the main issues of policy and power in the independent state. Nevertheless, regular elections still took place in a number of one-party states, fulfilling a variety of functions beyond that of legitimating the regime in power. Contested elections within the very different single-party systems of Tanzania and Kenya, for example, had served to change political personnel without changing the regime. The relevance of elections in such systems had come to be more in what they revealed about the exercise of control and the level of consciousness of the voters, than in their capacity to change governments or policy.

It is with the balance of control and participation in mind, therefore, that we consider elections in the Zambian one-party state, and the general elections held in 1973 and 1978.[1] Those two elections differed in certain important respects. The first was the size of the poll, which in 1973 dropped dramatically to 39.4 per cent, less than half that of the previous general election in 1968, and the lowest of any held since 1962. In 1978, the turn-out increased considerably, when it averaged 66.7 per cent. It was still below that of 1968, however, and confirmed the continued decline in electoral turn-out since independence.[2] The second difference concerned the presidential election, and the attempt in 1978 of independent candidates to contest the party's official nomination. That attempt provoked a constitutional amendment altering the qualifications for presidential candidates, and in the process increasing central party control.[3] In the election itself there was also a small but highly significant increase in the 'No' vote. Yet in spite of these differences and altered economic and foreign policy contexts,[4] the most notable aspect of those elections was the degree of similarity and continuity they displayed. The balance of control and participation within the electoral process remained remarkably the same. Both were conducted with a minimum of violence. Both saw a high turnover of M.P.s, bringing a significant number of newcomers to Parliament. In what follows, we focus primarily on the 1973 elections, since as the first under the one-party system they constituted a significant watershed in Zambia's political development. At the same time, however, we shall maintain a comparative perspective so that such changes as did emerge in 1978 may be located within the broader framework of the electoral system.[5]

Electoral procedures and regulations in the one-party state

The 1973 constitution increased the number of parliamentary constituencies from 105 to 125. Candidates had to be Zambian citizens over twenty-one years of age, able to speak and write English, and members of the party who had not been formerly convicted of a criminal offence. All Zambian citizens over the age of eighteen were eligible to vote. There were two distinct stages to the parliamentary elections, the first of which, the primaries, was restricted to the party. Candidates at this primary stage were required to lodge a deposit of K25 (which was refundable) and to have their nominations supported by nine registered voters. Voting was by an electoral college consisting of all party officials at regional, constituency and branch level in the parliamentary constituency concerned. The names of the three candidates with the highest vote in each primary election were then forwarded to the Central Committee for confirmation or rejection, the committee having the power to veto any individual whose candidacy was considered to be 'inimical to the interests of the state'. In the event of such a veto being exercised, the candidate with the next highest number of votes moved up to third place. The three with the highest votes in the primary then proceeded to the general election, for which they required a K50 deposit (not in this case refundable) and again the support of nine registered voters.[6]

The conduct of both the primary and the general election campaigns were the responsibility of the party. At the national level, the Central Committee's Election Committee was in control. At the level of the constituency, regional officials under the District Governor were responsible for the organization and conduct of meetings, at which candidates shared the platform to speak on a list of topics selected by the party. The poll and the count remained the responsibility of the Office of the Director of Elections.[7]

The presidential election was held simultaneously with the general election, at the same polling stations, although with separate ballot boxes. Prior to the general election, a general conference of U.N.I.P. was required to elect a president for the party who became the sole candidate in the presidential election, voters being required to vote Yes or No to the party's choice.

The requirement that parliamentary candidates be U.N.I.P. members constitutionally narrowed the choice in that respect, since previously independent as well as opposition candidates had been free to stand. In practice, however, the new system offered Zambian voters a much greater opportunity for electoral participation than had hitherto applied. A critical change concerned the removal of party discipline that had applied in the multi-party state, both over would-be candidates and over the party's supporters in the electorate. In previous elections parliamentary candidates had been chosen by the national party executive, where presidential control had been the determining factor. Although constitutionally any Zambian citizen had been free to stand, in practice few independents had ever done so. Moreover U.N.I.P.'s dominant position had meant that many constituencies had been uncontested. Under the new constitution, the party relaxed its control. The result was an extension of participation at three levels. First, a much greater opportunity for those wishing to contest parliamentary seats led to a significant increase in the number of candidates. In 1973, 532 and in 1978, 762 nomination papers were filed prior to the primaries. And whereas in 1968 30 of 105 constituencies had had only a single candidate who was elected unopposed, in 1973 only 14, and in 1978 only 6 of 125 seats were uncontested in the general election.[8] Second, the voter was now free to vote without reference to party and from among as many as three candidates. The ability of the individual candidate to represent his constituents effectively thus became more explicitly a criterion for selection. Third, so far as the party officials were concerned, the primary election provided an additional opportunity for participation in candidate selection.

Important limitations were, however, clearly imposed upon the voters' choice, and party control was manifest in three ways. First, voters were unable to reject the party programme, to which all candidates were required to subscribe. Party policy was not at issue. Second, the party monitored the selection of candidates both through the party primary and the Central Committee's ultimate power of veto. Third, the party selected the sole presidential candidate, who was then presented to the electorate for ratification or rejection. While it was clearly possible for the electorate to reject the party's presidential choice (in which case the party was constitutionally required to present another candidate in a new election), the choice offered them was restricted to Yes and No. Furthermore, in 1978 the party demonstrated its unwillingness to permit a presidential contest, even within the party.[9] Thus in some sense, greater participation was afforded local party officials and members of the public as potential candidates and voters. None the less, the single-party system also saw a consolidation of central party control.

Party control at the local level: the electoral college

Analysis of the dynamics of participation and control in the electoral
system must begin with the local party officials who, by virtue both of
their role as an Electoral College and their assumption of responsibility for the election campaign, acquired the capacity, in 1973,
to exert a significant influence upon the outcome of the elections. As
an Electoral College, they were responsible for the selection of three
candidates to stand for the general election from among all those who
placed their names in nomination. As the local party organisation,
they supervised the election campaign. To the extent that a larger
number of primary contests were held in 1978 than in 1973 — 100 as
against 78 — the role of lower party officials in the elections was
arguably greater in the more recent contest. The average number of
primary voters per constituency was also greater in 1978 — 522 as
against 413 in 1973 — suggesting an increased rate of participation
among officials.[10] But in both elections, lower party officials exerted
an important impact on candidate selection through the primaries.
The high casualty rate among former A.N.C. leaders in 1973, and in
both elections among candidates too long absent from the region
where they stood, demonstrated the difficulties that faced candidates
without a secure base in the local party apparatus. In 1973, four
former A.N.C. M.P.s in Central Province and four in Southern Province, for example, were eliminated in the primaries. In the Eastern
Province the former Solicitor General (at that time a civil service
rather than a political post) lost in the primary, and only by virtue of
being subsequently promoted through the disqualification of an
opponent was he able to go on to win the election. In 1978 twelve
incumbents were ousted at the primary stage, presumably because
they were regarded as ineffective representatives of their constituencies, and five former ministers and three District Governors
also lost out in the primaries. Local party officials, therefore, undoubtedly enjoyed a significant, if not absolute, influence over the
final outcome in the elections. Only those candidates with strong
central support had a chance of success in this situation.[11]

Local-level party influence in 1973 was enhanced by the party
reorganisation and registration of branches that preceded the elections, as necessitated by the disarray of the party machinery at that
time and the requirements of the primary poll. At the beginning of
1973, U.N.I.P. was a very disorganised party. Few branches had the
three constitutionally prescribed bodies: main body, women's wing
and youth wing. Many had disintegrated, with positions vacant
(through withdrawal from the party, or departure from the district, or
death) and membership extending little further than the office bearers

themselves. Some branches had operated informally for long periods without official registration, while others existed only on paper. The need to compile registers for the primary forced the party, therefore, to put its house in order.

After the June National Council, a drive began to recruit new members, set up new branches, create youth and women's wings and ensure that officials were properly registered and party organisation operational.[12] The objective was party consolidation, but the exercise also provided an opportunity for individual party officials to influence the coming elections through their selection of branches for registration. It also made it possible for potential candidates to organise voters into branches which might then be expected to support them in the primary polls. As the registration proceeded, it became clear that many people interpreted the reorganisation as a method of ensuring a voice for themselves in the decision as to who would contest the parliamentary seats.[13]

In the six-month period up to the end of September 1973, approximately 6,000 new branches were registered with the Registrar of Societies,[14] amounting to an 152.4 per cent increase in the total number of registered U.N.I.P. branches within the country (see Table 2.1). Some had undoubtedly existed in the past, while others represented the addition of women's and youth wings to existing bodies. Nevertheless, the majority were new. This represented, therefore, a significant expansion in the party presence, and in the number of men and women at the local level who acquired a voice in the local party process.

Such a proliferation of new branches was to be expected in Southern and Western provinces where the opposition parties had hitherto been dominant. The equally large figures for the two most urban provinces (Central and Copperbelt) were, however, more surprising, even allowing for their rapid growth in population. Until the formation of U.P.P., the party on the Copperbelt had been efficient and militant compared with other areas; the figures given in Table 2.1, however, indicate that it had experienced little growth. The fact that this area had been a focus for many of the factional conflicts within U.N.I.P. had had an adverse effect on the willingness of local notables and potential local leaders to participate. It is also possible, given that individual mobility and the creation of the petty bourgeoisie was greatest in the urban areas, that the two urban provinces reflected the greatest loss of former party activists to the private and parastatal sectors and subsequently to 'retirement' from party position.[15] In other words, it is possible that the more 'it paid to belong to U.N.I.P.', the less it paid to work for the party. Whatever the reasons, the need for so extensive a pre-primary registration of branches indicated a marked decline in party organisation since 1964.

Table 2.1   Formation of new party branches in six months
prior to 1973 elections

Province	Existing branches Feb. 1973	New branches Feb.–Sept. 1973	Total Sept. 1973	Percentage Increase	Branches per 1000 population Feb. 1973	Branches per 1000 population Sept. 1973
Central	371	1167	1538	314.6	0.43	1.77
Copperbelt	304	1019	1323	335.2	0.30	1.30
Eastern	510	1074	1584	210.6	0.93	2.87
Luapula	531	664	1175	121.3	1.46	3.23
Northern	1114	224	1338	20.1	1.88	2.26
North Western	614	248	862	40.4	2.44	3.42
Southern	363	729	1092	200.8	0.67	2.03
Western	256	1087	1343	424.6	0.56	2.34
Total	4063	6212	10255	152.4		

Source. Office of the Registrar of Societies, Lusaka, Ministry of Home Affairs.
File Index Feb. 1973 and latest returns to 30 September 1973, *Monthly Digest
of Statistics*, Vol. IX, No. 6, June, 1975.

The potential clearly existed for local party notables to influence
the registration of branches. Yet although irregularities occurred, for
the most part they had little impact on election results. More
significant was the conflict that developed amongst lower level party
officials themselves. Party branches and constituencies frequently
stood opposed to one another as sponsors of different candidates
whom they hoped might, if successful, operate the patronage mechanism in their favour. In not a few cases, branch or constituency officers
served as election agents and unofficial campaigners for a particular
candidate, bringing the division out into the open. The resulting
conflict was frequently perceived in totalistic terms, and as a consequence was severely disruptive of party work, hampering the presidential campaign on which the party was assumed to be united. In a
Kitwe contest, for example, where one U.N.I.P. constituency leader
was a candidate and a second was agent for a rival, the campaign
became so vituperative that the constituency committee ceased to
function, meeting only when the District Governor called it together.
In the opinion of the latter, the officials could no longer 'look each
other in the eye';[16] indeed on one occasion three constituency officials
came to blows in a District Governor's office and had to be physically
separated by the Governor and his aides. Part of the difficulty was the
lack of any clear demarcation between legal and illegal campaigning
and the failure to establish what constituted legitimate and illegitimate procedure. The persistence of this lack of demarcation yielded
very similar features in the second election of 1978 when, as G.

Maipose shows, bribery and other attempts at influence were pre-valent.[17] In both 1973 and 1978, then, the opportunity for the local party official to be both election agent and campaign referee created serious difficulties for the party. While such roles enabled the ex-tension of party control in the local area, the resulting divisions limited its effectiveness in mobilising support for the electoral pro-cess itself.

In view of the greater opportunity now enjoyed by party officials to influence the choice of candidates, it may be of value to try to gauge the extent to which public opinion, as demonstrated by the election results, followed that of local party leaders. This may be approached by analysing the extent of congruence between the rankings of the top three successful candidates in the primaries and their positions in the general elections. An assessment of this sort can only be tentative, since the incidence of local party participation at the primary stage varied considerably. The provinces of Western and Northern in 1973 and Luapula, Northern and Western in 1978 had fewer primaries than other provinces. In addition, the percentage of voters in the general elections who had also voted in the primary varied from province to province, in accord with both the percentage poll and the prevalence of local party branches. Finally, because the congruence of rankings was necessarily distorted by the Central Committee's vetoing of primary winners, provinces experiencing a high degree of such vetoing cannot be adequately compared with those where vetoing was mini-mal or absent. Taking all of these qualifications into account and focusing on provinces experiencing relatively little incidence of vetoing, it is still possible to note in 1973 a particularly high degree of congruence between the ranking of candidates in the primary and general elections in Luapula and a striking lack of congruence in some of the sixteen constituencies in Southern Province.[18] In the latter case, where former A.N.C. M.P.s fared particularly badly in the primaries, voters in the general elections put into office candidates who had ranked third in primary contests in six constituencies and in two others those who had been second. Such lack of congruence between the ranking of candidates in primary and general elections was par-ticularly striking given the general apathy among voters in Southern Province, where the poll in the general election was only 29.2 per cent and where about 11 per cent of the voters in the general election were probably lower level officials who had voted in the primary. The low poll itself in part reflected the fact that many of the choices of the populace had already been eliminated by the primaries. None the less, though few voted, they still managed to override the preferences of lower party officials in about 60 per cent of the constituencies in which primaries were held. That pattern of voting represented a lack of support, if not for U.N.I.P., then at least for the U.N.I.P. leadership within the province. It is of interest, however, that in 1978 the congruence in rankings between primaries and general elections was similarly high in Southern Province as elsewhere.[19]

Party control from the centre: the role of the Central Committee

While a measure of control was exercised by local party officials over the mass of the population (albeit sometimes rather ineffectively), control over the local party organisation and, more generally, over the electorate was, in turn, more clearly exercised by the central organs of the party, particularly by the Central Committee. The influence of the Central Committee was threefold: first, the committee was ultimately responsible for the organisation and supervision of the campaign, and especially for the conduct of the presidential election; second, it was constitutionally required to approve or disapprove of candidates successful in the primaries; and third, it was generally believed that its members intervened in support of particular candidates in a number of constituencies across the country.

Central Committee support for particular candidates was the subject of widespread accusations during both elections, in respect of which it was often difficult to separate allegations from fact. The course of the elections in 1973 left little doubt that in a number of cases pressure was exerted upon particular candidates not to contest, though whether in all cases this was directed from the Central Committee was not clear. Thus, in one constituency where the local chiefs openly instructed people not to run against the sitting Cabinet Minister, he was returned unopposed. In another constituency, a prospective candidate was told that it was his patriotic duty to allow the candidature of a minister to succeed without opposition. On the Copperbelt, an outstanding local party loyalist was informed that duty required support for the local Minister of State rather than opposition to him; he ignored the advice and subsequently lost the election.[20] In Lusaka, there were frequent expressions of anger over the decision of a junior civil servant to stand against the Prime Minister; the opponent's house was even set on fire. In yet another constituency, the District Governor openly supported the campaign of a sitting minister, forcing his opponents to address numerous protests and petitions to the governor of the neighbouring district; in this case no action was taken by the centre. In Sinjembala, in Western Province, where the successful candidate was elected unopposed, he was subsequently unseated by an election petition brought by a would-be candidate who claimed that he had been unfairly prevented from presenting his nomination papers by regional party officials. In the subsequent by-election, the petitioner went on to win the election.[21]

In 1978 there were many similar situations. There were numerous allegations against candidates who claimed, on occasion with support of senior government or party officials, to be 'official' party candidates in the name of Freedom House or State House. Many allegations were also made of regional party officials campaigning for particular candidates and even attempting publicly to discredit others. Two particularly notorious cases involved the District Governor of Mansa, who was subsequently transferred to a neighbouring district because of personal involvement or interference in the campaign, and the District Governor of Lusaka Rural, who was named in the High Court as having offered substantial bribes to persuade an individual to drop allegations against the sitting M.P. for the local constituency. A total of twenty petitions against malpractice in the elections were ultimately filed in the High Court; only 6, however, were successful.[22]

While many allegations of pressure or patronage proved difficult to establish, they nevertheless produced great bitterness between groups. The most controversial case in 1973 involved Livingstone, the only seat in Southern Province held by U.N.I.P. in the two previous elections. The constituency was contested by a senior civil servant, Milimo Punabantu, and a successful businessman, former parliamentarian and Zambia's first Minister of Finance, Arthur Wina. The former was Tonga-speaking, the latter Lozi. In a town fairly evenly divided between Tonga- and Lozi-speaking people, the campaign quickly polarised around the question of rivalry between the two groups, arousing bitter allegations from both sides of outside pressure upon other would-be candidates to withdraw and thus ensure that neither side split its vote. Whatever the validity of the various claims, it was clear that the election created bitterness among party officials and the general public, so that long afterwards there were disputes, for example, over the language to be used at political meetings and in the schools. Livingstone's experience thus illustrated a central problem: that whether allegations were true or false was less important than that they exacerbated existing sectional cleavages in many constituencies and greatly divided and weakened the local party, as well as dividing the electorate. Equally, while there was little evidence to substantiate interference on the part of the Central Committee or its members, the disputes nevertheless created some suspicion towards that body, or some members of it, on the part of many local party activists. And this, in turn, further weakened the unity and stability of the party.

Article 75 of the Zambian Constitution obliged the Central Committee to review all candidates who had passed through the primaries.

In 1973 the Central Committee disqualified twenty-six candidates at this stage, sixteen of them in Eastern and Northern provinces. In 1978 thirty candidates in twenty-five constituencies were disqualified, though in the case of two Lusaka candidates, the Central Committee decision was subsequently reversed. Six of them were sitting M.P.s.[23] No reasons for disqualifications were required or given in either election, and local interpretations varied greatly. In 1973 there was evidence in some cases of former corrupt behaviour on the part of a particular candidate. A more prevalent explanation related to suspected sympathies for the former U.P.P. Nevertheless, not all those disqualified could be regarded as having been corrupt or displaying U.P.P. sympathies. In fact, other candidates against whom a suspicion of corruption existed were permitted to continue to the general elections; and while some of those disqualified, particularly on the Copperbelt, might have been regarded as recalcitrants, a few others similarly distrusted by local officials were permitted to go forward.

Similar generalisations can be made in respect of Central Committee disqualifications in 1978, which were concentrated in Northern, Luapula and Copperbelt provinces. In contrast to 1973, Eastern Province was exempt. In common with the earlier election, Southern and North Western provinces remained largely free of this form of intervention. The concentration of 1978 disqualifications in the Bemba-speaking provinces no doubt encouraged the popular view that they were essentially directed at U.P.P. sympathisers. However, in a number of cases, and perhaps particularly as regards sitting M.P.s in Luapula and Southern provinces, disqualifications seemed to be intended in part to prevent the return of parliamentarians who had been particularly and vociferously critical of the executive during the previous Parliament and to discourage the formation of an opposition bloc in the National Assembly.[24]

In assessing the rationale behind the Central Committee vetoes, particularly in 1973, consideration of the opponents of those disqualified makes it clear also that, in many cases, disqualification assisted the election of a candidate likely to have been favoured by the centre who appeared to be challenged by a strong opponent. Table 2.2 indicates that most of those who won in constituencies where disqualifications occurred in 1973 were candidates of national or local prominence who could be assumed to have had strong links with, and were likely to be regarded with favour by, the centre. Tables 2.3 and 2.4 show that in the fifteen constituencies where 'notables' were standing and disqualifications occurred, six were won, at the primary stage, by candidates later disqualified. Three of the eventual fifteen winners finished third or fourth in the primaries. In all, sixteen of the twenty-five constituencies where disqualifications occurred had

Table 2.2 The effect of disqualification – winners in constituencies where candidates were disqualified, 1973

Winner where a candidate disqualified	Province								
	CeP	CoP	EP	LP	NP	NWP	SP	WP	Total
Cabinet minister					1				1
Minister of state[a]		1	4		1			2	8
M.P.	1		1		1				3
Local notable[b]		1	1					1	3
Local councillor	1						1		2
Other[c]		1	2		2				5
Unknown		1			2				3
Total	2	4	8	0	7	0	1	3	25

Notes:
a. Includes a sitting M.P. who had been minister of state until appointed High Commissioner to London.
b. Includes a prominent lawyer in Copperbelt Province, the former Solicitor General in Eastern Province and a prominent businessman, long-time party worker and U.N.I.P. regional trustee in Western Province.
c. Includes two teachers.

Table 2.3 Position of disqualified candidates in the primary elections, 1973 and 1978

Position of disqualified candidate in primary	Province																	
	CeP		CoP		EP		LP		NP		NWP		SP		WP		Total	
	73	78	73	78	73	78	73	78	73	78	73	78	73	78	73	78	73	78[a]
First		1		2	4				1	1			1				6	4
Second		1	2	3	1	2				2					1	1	4	9
Third[a]	1	1	1		2	2			2	4				1		1	6	9
No primary[b]	1		1		2	3			4	3					2		10	6
Total	2	3	4	5	9	7			7	10			1	1	3	2	26	28

Notes:
a. Candidate in Northern Province in 1973 tied for third place; no run-off because of disqualification.
b. Two of the candidates disqualified in Northern Province in 1978 were in a single constituency where there was no primary.
c. Thirty candidates were initially disqualified in 1978, but two were subsequently reinstated.

candidates who were ministers, ministers of state or sitting M.P.s, and a seventeenth was one where a former high-level civil servant was promoted and won the election. In the ten constituencies where no primaries occurred, the disqualifications resulted in five candidates (three ministers of state), an M.P. and a 'local notable') being returned unopposed; three of these subsequently became cabinet ministers.[25] Thus, while disqualifications were far from the sole determinant of the outcome of the final election, they were nevertheless extremely influential.

Table 2.4   Position in primary of ultimate winner for constituencies where candidates were disqualified, 1973 and 1978

Position of winner in primary	CeP		CoP		EP		LP		NP		NWP		SP		WP		Total	
	73	78	73	78	73	78	73	78	73	78	73	78	73	78	73	78	73	78[a]
First	1			1	3	2			2	2	3		1		1	1	8	9
Second			1	1	2				1	1	1						4	3
Third			1			1			1							1	1	3
Promoted			1	1	1	1					1		1				2	4
No primary	1			1	2				3	4	2				2		10	5
Total	2	3	4	4	8				7	7	7		1	1	3	2	25	24

Note:

a. Candidates were initially disqualified in 25 constituencies in 1978, but 2 candidates in one Lusaka constituency were subsequently reinstated.

In 1978, however, the role of disqualifications in easing the victory of 'notables' appears to have been much less than in 1973. Although in three constituencies in which disqualifications occurred cabinet ministers were ultimately elected — a notable case being that where the Prime Minister Lisulo was a candidate — and in four others sitting M.P.s were ultimately returned, winners in the large majority of the twenty-four constituencies where vetoing occurred were first-time M.P.s. This was, of course, partly a consequence of the fact that some sitting M.P.s themselves suffered disqualification. Even so, there was relatively little evidence in 1978 to suggest disqualification to favour, if not ensure, the election of candidates with strong ties with the 'centre'. It would seem rather that vetoed candidates were considered by some criteria objectionable in themselves, and that the vetoing occurred in many cases regardless of the perceived chances of such individuals ultimately being elected. In contrast to 1973, two-thirds of vetoed candidates in 1978 had been placed either second or third in the primaries. In almost half of all constituencies where disqualifications occurred and primaries were held in 1978, the ultimate victor had won the primary as well.

There were several cases in both 1973 and 1978 where disqualification ensured the elimination of candidates who would almost certainly have won had they contested the general elections — even though favoured candidates did not always profit from the exercise.

This appeared to be particularly true of contests involving sitting M.P.s in Luapula, Northern and Southern provinces in 1978. A critical case in 1973 was Kitwe, where the local Mayor, Harry Lupili, and a former District Governor, Francis Kapansa, were eliminated after overwhelming primary victories. Both were extremely popular and strong candidates, and the former had been certain to win. Although both were alleged by their local opponents to have U.P.P. sympathies,[26] they enjoyed very considerable support within U.N.I.P. and angry officials expressed vociferous contempt for the decision when addressed by Central Committee members in Kitwe.[27] For a period after the disqualifications, many party officials boycotted election meetings in Kitwe, a number of which were called off. It was clear that to many party officials the disqualifications constituted unwelcome central interference and affected their performance in campaigning for votes. Yet in 1978, when both Lupili and Kapansa contested the same constituencies, interestingly, neither received above 20 per cent in the primary; while it was by no means clear why this was so, it possibly suggested the decline of the so-called 'U.P.P. element' within the local U.N.I.P. organisation.

A final element of Central Committee control over the elections followed from its direct responsibility for the conduct of the presidential campaign, in which it sought directly and specifically to influence voters to vote for President Kaunda. In 1973 directives from the centre made it clear that all party officials were to be actively engaged in the presidential campaign, by establishing official campaign committees to educate voters in the presidential ballot and by ensuring that voters got to the polls. Central Committee members touring the provinces emphasised this campaign, and much of the time at election meetings was spent on the presidential as opposed to the parliamentary election.

The structure of the elections in the one-party system meant that it was precisely in the presidential election that voters had an opportunity to make a general point about the performance of the government as a whole. As a result, a very real fear existed among party leaders that, despite Kaunda's clear popularity among the mass of the people, opponents of the system would use the opportunity to dissent by voting 'No'. Aware of that possibility, a number of regional and district party officials in 1973 deliberately used the presidential election as the basis of a demand for national unity, the threat to which was suggested by allegations of plots hatched 'by enemies of the nation' to unseat the President. In this way, the party assumed the mobilising role which the absence of an opposition party had otherwise destroyed, and it was clear that many officials were far more comfortable with this aspect of the campaign than with the parliamentary elections. Hence the campaign against secret enemies was seen as necessary for national stability and enabled the party further to exercise control over the population as a whole. Nevertheless, while the high vote for the President suggested the success of this strategy in both elections, the low poll in 1973 reflected badly on local party efforts and on U.N.I.P. popularity in general. The 89 per cent 'Yes' vote in that election represented only 39.4 per cent of registered voters, a result which disturbed many officials. It suggested that the anger unleashed by local officials through factional squabbles over candidates, added to the displeasure expressed over the disqualification of popular candidates, had adversely affected the vote-getting efforts of the party, to some extent independently of actual voter opinions regarding the President. Only four constituencies returned a majority of 'No' votes in 1973 — Malole in Northern Province and Pemba, Magoye and Bwengwa in Southern; but even so the overall reaction of many party leaders was one of disappointment.

In 1978, however, the party was forced to assert much more direct control to prevent a very deliberate attempt by critics of the government to use the presidential election to oppose the party leadership. The 1978 election occurred in the midst of severe economic difficulties, causing inevitable discontent amongst those most affected, and rumours of efforts to mobilise such discontent were rife in the early part of that year. In due course it became clear that both Nkumbula and Kapwepwe intended to contest the presidential election alongside Kaunda, and seek the party's nomination. A third candidate was a Lusaka businessman, Robert Chiluwe. Faced with early indications that the President would have rivals, the National Council of June 1978 endorsed Kaunda's nomination several months prior to the party's general conference which had final constitutional authority for selecting a presidential candidate. U.N.I.P.'s leadership thus made clear that their full support would be given to Kaunda. The Secretary General of the party, Mainza Chona, remarked that 'the people who were intending to challenge President Kaunda were making a mockery of Zambia's democracy'. He added that there was no vacancy for the presidency because the post was already occupied and advised local leaders to ensure that the delegates they selected for the general conference were loyal to and would vote for Kaunda.[28]

Apparently wary, however, of leaving the matter to any possible chance, the party went further. On the day Kapwepwe announced his intention to stand against Kaunda, the party announced that constitutional amendments would be introduced to alter the requirements of a presidential candidate. Only formally announced a week prior to the general conference, these changes included the stipulation that a candidate be a paid up member of U.N.I.P. for a five-year period previous to filing nomination papers, must be a disciplined person with no criminal record and must be supported by twenty delegates from each province in the country. In addition, a candidate's nomination was to be subject to the approval of the U.N.I.P. National Council.

In the event, the President announced Kapwepwe's disqualification by virtue of his not having been a U.N.I.P. member for five years prior to the endorsement of the new amendment by the general conference. The other aspirant candidates, Nkumbula and Chiluwe, failed to obtain the required number of sponsors.[29] Increased control from the centre thus effectively stifled any opposition in the presidential contest. In the presidential campaign itself, mobilising efforts by the Central Committee when touring constituencies were, if anything, more intense than in 1973. Similarly, as in the earlier election, some leaders argued that a 'No' vote was equivalent to a call for chaos, a 'Yes' vote a mandate for continuity in peace and stability.[30] While election results revealed that the 'Yes' vote remained strong, the majority affirming Kaunda's continued leadership dropped, however, to 80.7 per cent.

The electorate: participation in 1973

The response of the electorate in 1973 was necessarily crucial to the legitimacy of the new one-party system. In this regard, discussion of voter participation must proceed against the fact that the poll was the lowest ever experienced in a Zambian election. Only 39.4 per cent of registered voters went to the polls in 1973, as compared with 82.5 per cent in 1968. The lowest provincial poll was in Western Province where only 22.0 per cent of the electorate voted. The highest, 54.0 per cent in Luapula, nevertheless represented a sharp fall against the 1968 vote. Table 2.5 shows that there had been a steady fall in electoral turn-out across the country as a whole since the independence elections of 1964, with a partial upturn only in 1978. The decline in 1973 was, however, dramatic, in many cases falling below the turn-out for the 1970 local government elections. The great majority of voters clearly chose not to vote. This applied not only to the general election but to the primaries as well, which were characterised by a similarly low turn-out. Of the 94,921 voters on the primary registers, only 27,663 voted: roughly 30 per cent.

The poll was the culmination of a campaign characterised by a welcome absence of violence but also by limited public involvement. Election meetings for the most part were poorly attended, and with the removal of competitive party politics seemed to have gone also the old cut and thrust of a political campaign. In many areas there was

Table 2.5 Gross percentage polls by province in Zambian elections since independence[a]

| Election year | Province | | | | | | | | |
	CeP	CoP	EP	LP	NP	NWP	SP	WP	Overall
1964	93.6	95.1	96.0	96.5	94.9	96.3	94.9	85.3	94.8
1968	82.0	91.4	85.3	91.0	86.0	79.8	81.1	62.1	82.5
1969 referendum	60.2	84.6	78.8	92.7	83.8	51.0	51.7	38.4	69.6
1970 local govt.	48.2	61.0	48.7	—	—	30.5	44.0	43.8	43.8
1973	36.3	46.7	48.8	54.0	38.4	37.8	29.2	22.0	39.4
1978[b]	69.9	71.7	70.0	70.4	68.6	72.5	59.8	44.5	66.7

Notes:

a. Figures for 1964, 1968 and 1970 are for contested constituencies/wards only. Those for 1973 and 1978 are for the presidential elections and thus cover all constituencies. The referendum was, of course, held in all constituencies.

b. Central Province included Lusaka in all elections until 1978 when figures were published separately to reflect the new provincial status of the capital. We have combined them here under the Central Province label.

Source: For 1964 calculated from Northern Rhodesia Government Elections Office, *Analysis of Polling, Northern Rhodesia Elections 1964*, Table II, 28 January 1964; for 1968, calculated from Parliamentary Elections Office, *Analysis of Polling, Zambia General Elections, 1968*; for 1969, Elections Office, *Referendum, Tuesday, June 17, 1969; Summary of Results*, Director of Elections, Lusaka; for 1970, U.N.I.P., *Results of the first Presidential and General Elections under the One Party Participatory Democracy Constitution*, Lusaka, Zambia, 5 December 1973; for 1973, calculated from Elections Office, *Presidential Elections, 1973, Summary of Results by Provinces*, Lusaka 1973; and for 1978, Elections Office, *Presidential and Parliamentary Elections Results 1978*, Lusaka, May 1979.

little to indicate that a general election was in progress, especially by comparison with the atmosphere of earlier elections and with the referendum of 1969.[31]

A variety of explanations for the low poll were offered by party and other observers. Party officials argued in the first place that many voters no longer saw the point of an election, given that under the one-party state U.N.I.P. no longer faced the possibility of defeat; and undoubtedly this was a factor to take into account. Moreover, many people, they suggested, found it inconceivable that President Kaunda could be defeated, and hence felt no need to make the often arduous journey to the polling station. Such attitudes were in fact frequently apparent among those content with U.N.I.P. leadership, who had voted in the past only to keep A.N.C. out. Zambians, moreover, had faced regular elections since 1964. A few districts had had an election of one kind or another every year since independence and might have been forgiven for growing tired of them. Hence an apathy about elections was not difficult to explain.[32]

In the second place, party leaders at both national and local level argued strongly that the low poll was a consequence of a number of practical difficulties, including long distances from the polling stations for people without transport, lost voters' cards, and a certain confusion as to where to vote. Again, there was some truth in this criticism. The last registration of voters prior to the 1973 elections had been in 1969; subsequently many voters had moved to another locality and in order to vote faced a journey to a distant polling station.[33] Party officials did not, as they had done in the past, provide transport for U.N.I.P. supporters, so that distance also undoubtedly affected the voting trend.

While such practical problems contributed to the low poll, they were, however, an insufficient explanation for the limited public participation that characterised the elections as a whole. Rather, it was the case that limited popular participation was, to a significant extent, the result of the party's failure to adapt to a changed electoral situation. The party had failed to provide adequate communication between candidates and voters, or between rulers and ruled. As a result, members of U.N.I.P. as well as of the public were frequently unaware of the procedures to be followed, or, in a number of cases, the candidates among whom they were to choose.[34]

The party's administrative inadequacies emerged at an early stage, during the preparation of the electoral college registers. Party records were in disarray, and the often frantic registration of branches in the months before the elections did not make the task of local party officials any easier. Overlapping party and parliamentary constituency boundaries on occasion presented an insuperable problem to the local officials as they attempted to compile their registers, many of which subsequently proved to be incomplete. Whereas the Director of Elections had estimated a possible 200,000 eligible voters in the primary elections, the final registration was 94,921, suggesting that either party branches were fewer than the party claimed or officials were unable to compile complete registers.

The inadequacies of the party as a mobilising force were, in many respects, a function of its nature as an organisation. In many areas the party had, as we have seen, acquired a petty bourgeois character which may well have alienated many ordinary people. Such alienation could only have been increased by the fact that many election meetings comprised audiences of party officials and local notables rather than the mass of the voters, who tended (in urban areas at least) to be involved only in weekend meetings.[35] In addition, the party's failure to recruit new generations into its membership often meant that the older men who dominated it were unable to mobilise the support of the younger and frequently better educated voters. This was true even of the party's youth wings, which tended to be led by men long past youth. Moreover, in those areas where opposition to U.N.I.P. had been strong before the introduction of the one-party state, local-level U.N.I.P. officials were often unwilling to absorb former opposition supporters into the party. Attempts at mass recruitment to the party, when these did occur, often served to produce alienation from the leadership. Card checks at bus stations and markets introduced elements of coercion so that party membership would not be a criterion of interested and enthusiastic participation; one more factor, perhaps, in explaining the low poll in the context of a one-party system.[36] Finally, account must be taken of the belief in some quarters that the one-party system had been imposed from the top.[37] Although apathy was clearly important in determining the low level of voter turn-out, the abstention was to some extent therefore an expression of protest.

Yet the extent to which the low poll was such a form of negative participation, registering a protest vote against either candidates or party, is difficult to assess. A further elaboration of the nature of voter participation may, however, provide greater insight into the matter.

The changed electoral situation in the one-party state resulted in an increased focus upon local issues and the demand, especially in rural areas, that M.P.s should be of local origin and acquainted with the problems of the district. The notion of the 'outsider' gained increasing salience, as past M.P.s were criticised for their alleged neglect of their constituents. '*Tabumoneka*', 'We have not seen you here', was a cry heard frequently. At more than one meeting in more than one constituency and more than one province, someone in the audience stood up to ask the candidates: 'Why should we vote for you? You will go off to Lusaka and make money. We will be left here, the same as before'.[38] Even so, increased emphasis upon past neglect and the desirability of local ties did not universally result in the election of local candidates, though it did contribute to the defeat of a number of national figures who had in recent years, often because of ministerial responsibility, spent little time in their constituencies or home areas.

The sharper focus upon local issues and locality tended to parochialise conflict and to intensify lines of cleavage other than those along regional or linguistic lines. In a number of constituencies this resulted in an increased emphasis upon ethnic identity at the local level. Note has already been made of problems that emerged in Livingstone, where conflict between Tonga- and Lozi-speaking residents was exacerbated by the elections. Ethnic rivalry was also evident in the confrontation between Eastern Province and Bemba-speakers on the Copperbelt, where the basis for such rivalry was ultimately economic. It was not only in urban areas, however, that this issue become more pronounced. Zambezi District, for example, manifested serious ethnic tensions in the course of the elections. The district includes a number of ethnic groups, the largest of them the Lunda, concentrated in the east, and the Luvale, concentrated in the west. Those two elements of local society had in the past engaged in continuing rivalry for control of the district, in a contest that had left a legacy of bitterness. In 1973 that old rivalry was revived in the contest for parliamentary office in which party was no longer the determining factor. Constituencies in Zambezi were not the only ones affected in this way. There were many others as well where local leaders sought to ensure that there was a candidate from their own people. A case in point was Sinazongwe, in Southern Province, where three chiefs' areas each produced a candidate to seek to ensure that their own area would be assured a place at the centre and thus a share in the distribution of resources. In this way, while large regional blocs lost something of their old importance, the parochial focus of the new system gave a greater salience to far smaller divisions, many hitherto forgotten, but now accorded a new 'non-traditional' character in contests manifestly concerned with patronage.

The retreat to locality and the emphasis upon parochial issues high-lighted local perceptions of neglect, so that the low poll might be interpreted in some measure as a generalised protest at the apparent failure of government policies to achieve expected levels of development. The difficulties created by the closure of the Rhodesian border in January 1973 had played their part in building up a further sense of grievance among voters.[39] In urban areas this reflected a general protest at the economic hardships arising from the increasing rate of inflation and the household commodity shortages that were integral to the urban scene. In the rural areas a similar sense of grievance derived from perceptions of rural deprivation and the failure of rural development, contributing to the feeling that little purpose was served in voting. The polls thus reflected a negative public pronouncement upon government's achievements, the shortcomings of which were borne out by the mid-term review of the Second National Development Plan when it appeared a year later. Underlying the so-called apathy of the voters was a widely-held sense of economic neglect and economic hardship.[40] For all this, some of those who did vote also took the opportunity to exercise what may be construed as a protest. Thus three cabinet ministers and nine ministers of state lost their seats in 1973, demonstrating a degree of independence rare among the electorate in African one-party systems as voters sought new personalities who might be more responsive to their own needs.

One minister of state was defeated by the Mayor of Lusaka in Kanyama constituency; interviews indicated that some, at least, regarded his experience of local government as more important than his opponent's national stature in providing desired development in the constituency. In Eastern Province, similarly, a candidate with long experience in local politics and the co-operative movement of the area was given a large majority over a minister of state. Local needs and protest against perceived neglect might thus be as adequately expressed through the ballot box as through abstention.

One final and important influence upon the voters was suggested by the distribution of the 'No' vote, both between and within provinces; this was the influence of past political loyalties, especially to the two former major opposition leaders, Simon Kapwepwe and Harry Nkumbula. Because the presidential ballot marked the only occasion when voters had the opportunity to think nationally and to register support for or opposition against the government, the 'No' vote may be interpreted as an indication of dissatisfaction with U.N.I.P.s' policies and past performance, and abstention may be interpreted in the same way.

An overwhelming majority of those voting, 88.8 per cent, voted 'Yes' in the presidential election, and only 11.2 per cent 'No', which may fairly be interpreted as an indication of strong support for President Kaunda from those who went to the polls. The presidential vote varied a great deal, however, between constituencies and provinces, from 98.7 per cent 'Yes' in Luapula Province to 62.2 per cent in Southern. Between districts and parliamentary constituencies, the range was even greater. Thus in Western Province the 'No' vote ranged from 4.1 to 45.3 per cent; in Southern Province from 18.4 to 80.2 per cent; and in Northern Province from 0.6 to 50.9 per cent. At the same time, a significant feature of the presidential election was a correlation between a high 'No' vote and a past tradition of opposition to U.N.I.P. This was clear enough in Southern and Western provinces, which recorded 37.8 and 22.6 per cent 'No' votes respectively; and in this respect it is necessary to bear in mind the reluctance of local-level U.N.I.P. officials to open the party to former opposition followers. Two further features of the polls, however, need to be taken into account. First, the spread of the 'No' vote within provinces, other than Eastern, Luapula and North Western, was sufficient to cast doubts on the notion of a provincial stance. Second, the 'No' vote was also high, 14.9 per cent, in Northern Province, one of U.N.I.P.'s traditional strongholds. Indeed, in Malole constituency the 'No' vote was 50.9 per cent. Furthermore, the highest 'No' polls in Northern Province were linked with comparatively higher polls for the general election. Some participation in that province was thus related to the articulation of opposition.

The Northern Province had not, in the crisis of 1969-72, supported the U.P.P. Nevertheless, that crisis had cost the region its strongest leaders, and had brought a good deal of public condemnation of Bemba-speaking people from Northern Province for their alleged associations with that party. In the past, the provincial party organisation had always been a powerful pressure group within U.N.I.P., claiming a privileged position on the basis of its past nationalist and political record. Now it had largely lost that position along with its former leaders, and not surprisingly the sense of lost position was strongest in the Chinsali region, the heartland of Bemba country and also Kapwepwe's home. Constituencies in Northern Province which had the highest 'No' vote were precisely those in and around this heartland. Chinsali, Shiwa Ng'andu, Kasama, Lukashya and Malole all cast a high 'No' vote, and voters in all but Chinsali deposed incumbent M.P.s who were long-standing U.N.I.P. men, professional politicians and party organisers of long association with the U.N.I.P. that had rejected Kapwepwe. Hence the internal U.N.I.P. conflict, which had cost the party much of its earlier vitality, could be seen to remain influential, now expressed in an opposition to the party in power. This did not necessarily mean a rejection of the one-party system as such; but it did mean a rejection of those in power and indicated continuing loyalty to Kapwepwe as a former national and regional leader. A similar coincidence of expressed opposition to U.N.I.P. and close association with a former opposition leader, in this case Nkumbula of the A.N.C., was to be detected beneath the distribution of the 'No' vote in Southern Province.

So far as the electorate was concerned, therefore, in 1973 the one-party state neither superseded old political loyalties nor destroyed the personal standing of either of the country's two major opposition leaders. The response of the electorate was an indication of the inability of U.N.I.P., in the short term, to overcome past cleavages, or absorb former opposition leaders and ensure them a place in the new system, and thus win the support of their followers. In this respect, the outcome of the elections was in no sense peripheral to the main issues and courses of politics.

The electorate: participation in 1978

In 1978 the poll at 66.7 per cent was considerably higher than in 1973. Yet while the voters were more effectively mobilised, divided loyalties remained. Indeed, the attempt of the two former opposition leaders, Kapwepwe and Nkumbula, to stand for the presidency against Kaunda formalised not merely a continuing but also a renewed critique. There was some evidence, moreover, that their would-be supporters actively attempted to persuade voters to turn out to record a 'No' vote against the President. If so, part, though probably a minor part, of the explanation for the higher poll in 1978 was that Kaunda's opponents advocated active rejection as a substitute for boycott of the election. It was certainly the case that the 'No' vote was higher in 1978 than in 1973, especially in Northern and Southern provinces. There were three constituencies in the former and seven in the latter (plus one in Central Province) where Kaunda was rejected by a majority. Admittedly in some instances a majority 'No' vote occurred in constituencies which also experienced polls of under 50 per cent. But in three Northern Province cases the poll was higher than the national average. In Malole where the 'No' vote was 62.3 per cent, the poll was 72 per cent.

Mobilisation of opposition remained, however, only a small part of the explanation for the higher poll, and indeed it is probable that opposition continued to be expressed in some measure by voters staying away from the polls. In Luapula, for example, which experienced a high proportion of all Central Committee disqualifications, the increase in the poll was markedly less than in other provinces (see Table 2.6). At the same time, the percentage in favour of Kaunda as President dropped more drastically in Luapula than in any other province.

Table 2.6   Percentage gross poll and 'yes' vote in the presidential elections of 1973 and 1978

Province	Poll			'Yes' vote		
	1973	1978	Difference	1973	1978	Difference
Central	36.3	69.9	+ 33.6	89.8	84.9	− 4.9
Copperbelt	46.7	71.7	+ 25.0	88.6	80.3	− 8.3
Eastern	48.8	70.0	+ 21.2	97.8	96.4	− 1.4
Luapula	54.0	70.4	+ 16.4	98.7	82.0	− 16.7
Northern	38.4	68.6	+ 30.2	85.1	74.2	− 10.9
Northwestern	37.8	72.5	+ 34.7	97.2	96.0	− 1.2
Southern	29.2	59.8	+ 30.6	62.2	51.2	− 11.0
Western	22.0	44.5	+ 22.5	77.4	80.1	+ 2.7
Overall	39.4	66.7	+ 27.3	88.8	80.7	− 8.1

Source. Calculated from *Presidential and Parliamentary General Elections Results* 1973 and 1978, Republic of Zambia, Elections Office, Lusaka. Gross poll figures refer to votes cast in the presidential elections.

But while in some cases non-voting was undoubtedly a measure of protest against the regime, a certain proportion of non-voting can also be attributed to continuing apathy among the electorate. As in 1973, many considered the election, particularly of the President, a foregone conclusion. Many remained unconvinced of the need to vote in a single-party system. Taking account of apathy and active boycott as continuing elements, what needs rather to be explained when comparing the 1973 and 1978 polls is the marked increase in voting in the latter. There are a number of factors which must be regarded as contributing to this increase.

One was a more concerted attempt at what was termed 'voter education'. In 1973, it is true, an active campaign had been conducted to get out the vote, particularly for the presidential election, with members of the Central Committee being assigned to the various provinces to address public gatherings. And indeed Kaunda himself had visited each province shortly before the election, if ostensibly on official business unrelated to the campaign. Even so, it is arguable that the effort of the party hierarchy to mobilise voters was even more energetic in 1978.[41] The campaign was conducted through widespread and frequent media advertisement, public meetings addressed by Central Committee members and routine advocacy of a 'Yes' vote by all parliamentary candidates.

The party's voter education efforts must, however, be regarded as having been a relatively minor contribution to the higher poll. More significant was the simple opening of more than 600 additional polling stations which served to reduce the distance and difficulty of many in reaching the polls and casting their votes. Many still had to travel long distances and, as in 1973, there were numerous cases where promised transport did not materialise.[42] But improvement in the basic institutional structure of voting must surely have assisted in achieving a higher poll.

Perhaps the most important factor behind that higher poll was the change in the general political atmosphere wrought by Zambia's role in the struggle for independence in Zimbabwe, and more specifically the fact that Zambia itself was under real threat from the Rhodesian forces. Bombings and incursions throughout the year must surely have had the consequence of drawing the Zambian people together, temporarily overriding internal difficulties in the need to confront an external aggressor. The need to impose a curfew in 1977 in certain parts of the country undoubtedly magnified the sense of danger and justified the government's call for national unity. It is possible that the percentage poll would have been lower in other circumstances. Indeed, it is even possible that there might have been a higher presidential 'No' vote but for the security situation. As it was, the electorate clearly considered Kaunda's leadership essential in the current circumstances.[43]

As in 1973, however, voters continued to place great emphasis in their choice of candidate upon their trust that an individual would speak up for local needs. Focus on local issues and locality again led to an atomisation of cleavage, the exaggeration of lines of cleavage in the local arena. Thus Maipose has described how popular considerations relegated Samfya Central constituency to the mainland Kabende, Samfya North to the Ngumbo and Samfya South to the Bisas of the Bangwelu swamps. In Samfya Central constituency, the electorate accordingly rejected a candidate much more experienced and educated than the ultimate victor, because the former belonged to an ethno-regional sub-grouping other than the one to which local people considered the constituency should 'properly' belong.[44]

Conclusion

The general elections in 1973 and 1978 both demonstrated the complex interaction of party control and political participation in the one-party state. The system, it is clear, permitted a wide-reaching control over recalcitrant elements, which minimised conflict at the national level. In so doing, however, it necessarily institutionalised a situation in which no radical alternatives (of whatever ideological hue) could be formally posed against its policies. In this sense, party control was greatly increased over the political process, the complexion of Parliament and over mass dissent. In 1978 the possibility of introducing opposition from within via the presidential contest was swiftly checked through the introduction of constitutional amendments, in the process central control being significantly tightened.

At the same time, however, local leadership was able to exert a greater influence than in the past over the pattern of recruitment to central office, and the electorate was able to reject leaders whom they saw as unresponsive to their needs. In this latter regard, the casualty rate in both elections among incumbent parliamentarians was unusually high for any electoral system. This local rejection of national leaders may fairly be interpreted as a protest against what was perceived as relative deprivation; it was, moreover, the stronger where the electorate retained strong ties with former opposition leaders. In this sense a significant element of participation was evident. Such participation was, however, at the local level, and the elections were to a significant extent about the state of the locality rather than the state of the nation. The outcome at the local level was the parochialisation of cleavage. U.N.I.P., moreover, proved unable to absorb the former opposition and to create a new consensus within the framework of the one-party state at grass-roots level. Thus the most distinctive feature of the election in 1973 was U.N.I.P.'s inability to mobilise the electorate to a more positive participation in the new system. The election was characterised less by mass participation among the electorate than by élite participation among the candidates. In 1978 mass participation increased, but so did central control, as evidenced by the manœuvres to prevent any formal opposition to Kaunda in the presidential contest and the Central Committee's disqualification of incumbent M.P.s. In that election also, competition among candidates for office continued to be more intense than was active participation by the voters. It therefore becomes important to consider the candidates themselves, and the kind of individuals thus voted into power.

Notes

1   In addition to the two general elections, Zambia also held local government elections in 1975; a number of by-elections were necessitated by successful election appeals; and there were party elections at the local level in 1977 and 1980. For a critique that highlights the peripheral nature of African elections, see Goran Hyden and Colin Leys, 'Elections and Politics in Single-Party Systems: the case of Kenya and Tanzania', *British Journal of Political Science*, 2, 4 (1972). For an attempt to review such functions as elections now performed in contemporary Africa, see Naomi Chazan, 'African Voters at the polls: a re-examination of the role of elections in African politics'. *Journal of Commonwealth and Comparative Politics*, XVII (1979) pp. 136–58.

2   See below, Table 2.5.

3   *Times of Zambia*, 2 and 9 Aug. and 10 Oct. 1978.

4   See below, Chapter 4.

5   This chapter is based on field research carried out by both authors in the period 1973–75, and especially during the election campaign of 1973. It also draws on similar field research carried out by Cherry Gertzel at the same time. We are grateful to G. S. Maipose, and Bornwell Chikulo for access to their work on the 1978 election.

6   For the details of the electoral procedures, see United National Independence Party *Manual of Rules and Regulations Governing the 1973 General Elections*, issued by the Central Committee, n.d. but 1973.
    See also The Electoral Act 1973, and the Constitution of Zambia Act 1973, 75 (3).

7   *Manual of Rules, op.cit.* In the past, the Electoral Commission had given a good deal of guidance and help to candidates, e.g. by the production of *The Candidates Guide* (Parliamentary Elections Office, Lusaka, November 1968). Such assistance was now the responsibility of U.N.I.P. The commission thus had fewer responsibilities than in the past, although it remained central to the electoral process itself.

8   For the results in both elections, see Elections Office, Lusaka, *Presidential and Parliamentary General Elections Results*, 1973, (1974) and 1978 (May 1979). In 1978, one of the unopposed seats, that for Mongu, originally had four contestants. One was disqualified and the other two apparently dropped out, leaving D. Lisulo unopposed. It should be noted,

in addition, that in Mwansabombwe Constituency in Luapula, the incumbent M.P. was unopposed at the primary stage, but was disqualified by the Central Committee; subsequently nominations were reopened and two contestants came forward.

9   G. S. Maipose, 'Institutionalization of One-Party Participatory Democracy in Zambia: a Case Study of the Electoral Process During the 1978 Presidential and Parliamentary General Elections' (unpublished paper, University of Zambia, 1980). This paper provides valuable material from one of the few researchers who observed the 1978 elections.

10 This pattern varied considerably from region to region. In Luapula, primary voting suffered a severe drop in 1978. In Southern Province, in contrast, there was an increase from 383 per constituency in 1973 to 724 in 1978. Whether the overall figures reveal an increased rate of party enthusiasm or a stronger local party apparatus in 1978, however, cannot be categorically stated on the basis of the figures alone.

Average Votes per Constituency by Province in the 1973 and 1978 Primary Elections

Province	*Average Votes per Constituency*	
	1973	*1978*
Central	496	694
Copperbelt	357	462
Eastern	343	543
Luapula	733	380
Northern	451	333
Northwestern	366	604
Southern	383	724
Western	346	372
National average	413	522

11 Election results 1973 and 1978 in Maipose, *op.cit.* The importance of the local party as a screening mechanism is difficult to overstate. Although better educated candidates did well in the elections, it is clear that they did so particularly where they could avoid a primary or had sufficient support within the local party. In one case, a candidate with high qualifications was not merely rejected in the primary, but frequently told during the campaign that he was 'alien' in his dress and not be trusted. He informed an interviewer that the election was biased against non-party people and that those elected would be ineffective because they would not be independent. This somewhat embittered view reflects clearly the control function of the local level politicians.

12 See *Times of Zambia*, 6 June 1973, Report to the National Council; also speech by Mr. A. Milner, as Secretary General to the Government, at N.I.P.A., June 1973. The party reorganisation was co-ordinated by regional party officials, although in a number of districts civil servants were called in to assist.

13 One candidate eliminated in the primary felt that the election was 'arranged for the party boys and girls. Unless you formed your own

branches, you could not get through the primary . . .' Interview 7 Nov. 1973. This view is undoubtedly exaggerated and easily ascribed to the disappointment of defeat. But it is clear that without some base in the local party organisation, candidates had had little hope of proceeding to the general elections.

14 Returns from District Secretaries to the office of the Registrar of Societies as of 30 September 1973. Since a number of District Secretaries were late in sending in returns from their respective districts, this figure must be regarded as a conservative reflection of the actual number of new branches formed and registered prior to the election.

15 See above, Chapter 1, and below, Chapter 5.

16 Meeting with candidates and regional officials, Kitwe, 13 Nov. 1973. Interview, 16 Nov. 1973. See below, Chapter 5.

17 Maipose, *op.cit.*, pp. 23–4.

18 Based on calculation of coefficients of correlation for the ranking of each individual in the primary with their ranking in the general election for various provinces.

19 The higher degree of congruence between preferences expressed in 1978 through the primaries and through the general election in Southern Province presumably reflects greater support for lower level U.N.I.P. leadership in the province by the voting public. This may have been in consequence either of U.N.I.P. leadership coming more in tune with the sympathies of the general electorate, or a greater acceptance on the part of the Southern Province population of U.N.I.P. as legitimately and effectively representing their interests.

20 Interview, 9 Nov. 1973.

21 The comments on the Lusaka scene are based on observation of campaign meetings in Munali Constituency. The Prime Minister's opponent was quite open in voicing his complaints as to how he perceived the campaign to have been conducted. As for Sinjembela see *Times of Zambia*, 1 June 1974.

22 Maipose, *op.cit.*, p. 22 and footnote 34.

23 The six M.P.s were F. Matanda, J. Kapilikisha, A. C. Mulanshoka, A. Wina, V. Kayope and P. Chanshi.

24 In this regard it is perhaps of more than passing interest that in early 1974, one of the 1978 victims of Central Committee veto casually identified to one of the authors a small group of M.P.s with whom he considered himself in solidarity in opposition to the executive. Four of this small group were among those vetoed along with himself in 1978. See also Chapter 4 below.

25 Mr. Rajah Kunda became Minister of Commerce, Mr. Unia Mwila was appointed Minister for Northern Province, and Mr. Sylvester Tembo was reappointed as a Minister of State immediately after the elections, and later promoted to Cabinet rank as a provincial minister.

26 Interviews, 10, 12 and 17 Nov. 1973. See also Chapter 5. We wish to make it clear that we are not commenting on the veracity of these allegations, but noting the conflict they reflected and served to perpetuate. Lupili was a relative of Kapwepwe.

27   Meeting at Buchi Hall, Kitwe, 14 Nov. 1973 addressed by three Central
      Committee members. The meeting was raucous and at times disrespect-
      ful of the three central leaders. By the end, however, it was clear that
      most officials, although they remained displeased, were willing to accept
      the explanations offered by the Central Committee members.

28   *Times of Zambia*, 22 Aug. 1978; 17 Aug. 1978, as referred to in Maipose,
      op.cit., p. 14. For procedure for presidential party nomination and elec-
      tion, see U.N.I.P. *Constitution*, 1973, 58, and 1979, 50.

29   Nkumbula claimed that his disqualification was due in part to the fact
      that some of his agents had been picked up by the police in order to
      'avoid trouble'. Maipose, *op.cit.*, p. 16 and 17 and footnote 23.

30   *Ibid.*, p. 25.

31   See David, C. Mulford, *The Northern Rhodesia General Election 1962*
      (Nairobi, Oxford University Press, 1964); Molteno and Scott, in Tordoff
      (ed.), 1974, *op.cit.* Assessment of the 1973 campaign is based on attend-
      ance at meetings across the country as reported by a number of observers.

32   Even in 1968, registration of voters had often been hindered by the fact
      that many people felt that they had already voted in 1964 and did not
      understand why they were required to do so again — a problem of voter
      education encountered in the Lusaka area by one of the present authors.

33   It is impossible to estimate the relative weights which should be
      assigned to apathy, voter alienation, party disorganisation, lack of voter
      education and the lack of a voters' registration drive before the elections
      among explanations of the low poll. But it is clear that the failure to
      create a new electoral roll must have reduced the turn-out considerably,
      although by how much is not certain. Psephologists calculate a wastage
      of about 6 per cent over a year after collection of data in Britain. (See
      Richard Rose, [ed.] *Electoral Behaviour: a Contemporary Handbook* (New
      York, Free Press, 1974) p.494; and David Butler and Dennis Kavanagh,
      The British General Election of October 1974, Nuffield College Series of
      Election Studies 10, (London, Macmillan, 1975) pp. 333–4). If the same
      formula applied over the four years from 1969 to 1973 and to Zambia as
      to Britain, this could imply an 'effective' electorate over 25 per cent
      smaller than the notional electorate of the electoral roll. Given the rapid
      shift of population from rural to urban areas which has characterised
      Zambia since 1964, it is very likely that urban electoral rolls under-
      represented potential voters, while the vote in the rural areas was not as
      low as it appeared, since many on the electoral roll had relocated to the
      towns. The 1978 totals of registered voters indicate only marginal
      changes compared with 1973 for the five provinces off the line of rail. Of
      the other three, the electorate of Southern Province grew by 17.3 per
      cent, that of Copperbelt Province by 27.3 per cent, and of Central and
      Lusaka by 31.7 per cent. At the same time, it would be unwise to give too
      much weight to such a 'technical' explanation alone; all observers of
      both elections were impressed by poor party organisation, voter aliena-
      tion and apathy — as was the party itself. We are indebted to Ralph
      Young for his comments and advice on this problem.

34 The party was aware of this, certainly at the level of the Central Committee. See U.N.I.P.'s *Post Mortem* on the elections. Also *Daily Parliamentary Debates*, 22 Jan. 1974, col. 286, for the criticisms of one of the successful candidates on the Copperbelt.

35 The general pattern of the campaign in many areas was for candidates to address party officials, businessmen, trade unionists, etc., during the week, and then speak to large mass meetings at the weekend when people would presumably be free from work. It is difficult to suggest any possible alternative to this system, but it did mean that much of the effort of the campaign was directed at those most closely integrated into the new political system, rather than at those most needed to legitimate it.

36 Maipose, *op.cit.*, p. 35.

37 One of the authors took part in a television programme about the election on the eve of the primary vote during which viewers were invited to phone questions in to the studio. Several who did insisted that the system had been imposed on the people and would therefore not be worth participating in. Clearly the message of the government that such a system sought to blend stability with democracy had not been successfully communicated.

38 A comment made at an election meeting in Kaoma. See also *Zambia Daily Mail*, 30 Oct. 1973, for a report of complaint from Mazabuka voters that once an M.P. was elected he forgot his constituents.

39 In Kanyama (Lusaka) on polling day, several party officials who spent the day urging people to go to the polls were angrily rebuffed. Some of the refusals were on the grounds that high prices and commodity shortages plus lack of housing and better wages convinced them that they would achieve nothing by voting. 'What must we vote for? For no soap, no cooking oil, no candles?', said one. See also *Times of Zambia*, 28 June 1973; *Sunday Times of Zambia*, 1 July 1973.

40 This was borne out time and time again in the course of the elections by the responses at meetings as well as by chance remarks in conversation. That it was not a new feeling is indicated in the case studies of Western and Luapula provinces below.

41 B. Chikulo, 'Elections in a One-Party Democracy', in B. Turok (ed.), *Development in Zambia* (London, Zed Press, 1979), p. 210.

42 Maipose, *op.cit.*, p. 51.

43 This was undoubtedly the opinion of a significant number of observers in Zambia in 1978.

44 Maipose, *op.cit.*, p. 34.

The rise to political prominence of the Zambian business class

Introduction

One of the most important features of the 1973 election was the extent to which it marked the emergence of a substantial number of M.P.s with business interests. Zambia's indigenous bourgeoisie was still small, and many of those elected in 1973 who had such business interests were actually small-scale operators and best located within the petty bourgeoisie. Even so, members of Zambia's emergent capitalist class were present in strength in the 1974–78 Parliament, and the pattern was generally sustained in 1978. The entry of members of this class into legislative bodies in fairly substantial numbers was not simply a function of their increasing economic entrenchment or maturity. Indeed, their presence was if anything greater than the economic strength of the class would suggest. Rather, it would appear that the structural change to a single-party system was particularly conducive to the rather dramatic entry of indigenous capital into this part of the political system.

The process of candidate selection under the one-party system was itself of primary importance in producing the disproportionate representation of indigenous property owners in the elections of the 'seventies. The multi-party system had ensured that each party selected one candidate for each constituency it contested. While some inevitably had business interests and connections, it was stature within the party and a record of loyalty and service which had counted for most. In the single-party system, however, when any member was free to stand providing he or she could obtain sufficient sponsors, the grip of the party centre on the nature of candidates was necessarily weakened and the opportunities for would-be candidates to offer themselves for election considerably increased. This becomes perfectly clear when we consider the sharp increase in the level of competition under the new system. Whereas seats had seldom been contested by more than two candidates under the multi-party structure, the average number filing nomination papers in 1973 was 4.3 per constituency and 6.1 in 1978. As Table 3.1 indicates, though there was considerable variation between constituencies and between provinces, there was consistently higher than average participation along the line of rail between Livingstone and the Copperbelt and an increase for all areas in the 1978 averages, notably so in the case of Eastern and Western provinces.

Table 3.1 Constituencies with various numbers of candidates 1973 and 1978 (primaries)

Number of candidates in constituency	Province																	
	CeP[a]		CoP		EP		LP		NP		NWP		SP		WP		Total	
	73	78	73	78	73	78	73	78	73	78	73	78	73	78	73	78	73	78
1		1			3		2	1		2	1	1			3		9	5
2	4	2	2	1	3			1	7	1	2	1	1		3	1	22	7
3	1		2		2	2	2	3	3	3	1	3	1	1	4	1	16	13
4	5	2	3	2	2	1	2		4	1	5		3	2	4	4	28	12
5	1	2	6	3	2	2	4	2	3	6		2	3	1	1	2	20	20
6	2	1	2	1	2	4	1	4		1	1	2	4	5		5	12	23
7	3	5	2	2		1			1	3		1	2				8	12
8	2			3	1	2	1	1					1	4		1	5	11
9	1				1	3											2	3
10		3	1	3						1				1		1	1	9
11			1											2			1	2
12		1		2									1				1	3
13		1		1	1													3
14				1														1
18		1																1
Total	19	19	19	19	16	16	12	12	18	18	10	10	16	16	15	15	125	125
Average	4.9	7.2	5.2	7.9	3.9	6.7	4.2	4.5	3.4	4.7	3.4	4.1	5.6	6.9	2.8	5.3	4.3	6.1

Note:

a. By 1978 an additional provincial administrative division had been created for Lusaka; but for purposes of comparison, the new Central and Lusaka provinces are combined and treated simply as Central Province.

There were several reasons why change should have favoured the increased presence of businessmen[1] in the political system. In contrast with the period before 1973, the new system tended to favour candidates with strong local connections; and indeed, a majority of candidates in 1973 and 1978 stood in their home districts. To the extent that businessmen had acquired local prestige through their economic activities, they were particularly well placed as 'local notables'. And to the extent that their local status, derived from class position, could be regarded by them as a measure of their potential political importance, it is not surprising that they should be so well represented among those coming forward as candidates. The requirement of a deposit at both the primary and general elections stages further assisted their entry into electoral politics, since in either case, deposits represented sums that the vast majority of the population could not hope to raise. Finally, the requirement of English literacy on the part of candidates, while not benefiting businessmen exclusively, inevitably biased the class composition of aspirants against the peasantry and working class.

Incumbents and the election

A comprehensive analysis of the class background of successful candidates in the elections of the 'seventies is difficult. Because of the racial structure of colonial society, indigenous Zambians had in the past been largely restricted in terms of class mobility. Indeed this was one of the issues which served to galvanise the nationalist movement. Those who became professional freedom fighters, who came to earn their income from party work, tended to come from the ranks of workers, particularly white collar workers. A great many were teachers at one point in their careers, though in the early days a considerable number were also drawn from the ranks of trade union leadership. But once having become professional politicians, their class character becomes less clearly identifiable; indeed, they might even be regarded as having moved outside the class structure. It was from this group that political parties had tended to recruit parliamentary candidates in the first elections following independence. When they reached outside this sphere, as was true for example of about a third of the 'new' (non-incumbent) U.N.I.P. candidates in 1968,[2] they turned primarily to white-collar workers or professionals — civil servants, diplomats, teachers and lecturers. When these were elected, they in turn tended — for the most part — to become professional politicians. Very few M.P.s continued to work in their former occupations or practice in their professions after gaining parliamentary office.

Thus, as elections have proceeded in Zambia, the largest category of candidates has invariably been one difficult to specify in class terms — the incumbent M.P. In time, victorious candidates have continued to 'lose' their original class positions, at least as workers. On the other hand, as will be elaborated subsequently, M.P.s have found it perfectly compatible with their parliamentary duties to operate, or take up shares in, business enterprise and thus to join the owning class.

The background of M.P.s elected under the single-party system in 1973 showed some important similarities with that of previously-elected parliamentarians, but also some dramatic differences.[3] As in previous elections, and notwithstanding the high turnover in M.P.s, the largest single category of victors was that of incumbents, who represented 34 per cent of those elected in 1973 and 38 per cent in 1978. Incumbent M.P.s had a particularly high rate of success, 60 per cent of those who stood winning their contests in 1973, though with a drop to 49 per cent in 1978. The rate of success in 1973 was especially high for those who had been in office since 1964 (68 per cent) as against those who had been parliamentarians for only a single term (56 per cent).

Table 3.2   Performance of M.P.s, ministers of state and ministers, by province, 1973.

| | | | a. | Performance of M.P.s | | | | |
| | | | | *Province* | | | | |
	CeP	CoP	EP	LP	NP	NWP	SP	WP	Total
Won	4	6	8	4	5	4	4	8	43
Lost general election	5	0	2	3	8	1	1	1	21
Lost primary	3	0	0	0	0	1	4	0	8
Total	12	6	10	7	13	6	9	9	72

| | | | b. | Performance of ministers of state | | | | |
| | | | | *Province* | | | | |
	CeP	CoP	EP	LP	NP	NWP	SP	WP	Total
Won	0	3	5	1	1	1	0	2	13
Lost general election	3	0	2	1	4	0	0	0	10
Total	3	3	7	2	5	1	0	2	23

| | | | c. | Performance of ministers | | | | |
| | | | | *Province* | | | | |
	CeP	CoP	EP	LP	NP	NWP	SP	WP	Total
Won	1	2	1	0	1	2	0	2	9
Lost general election	0	0	0	1	2	0	0	0	3
Total	1	2	1	1	3	2	0	2	12

Tables 3.2 and 3.3 give breakdowns by province for the performance of incumbent M.P.s taken as a whole, incumbent ministers of state and incumbent ministers. In both elections, at least three-quarters of ministers who contested seats were re-elected. The success of ministers of state (who figured as a category much more in the 1973 election than in that of 1978, the position by the latter date being much less used) was rather less. In 1973 only 56 per cent of those who stood were

re-elected. Four defeated ministers of state were from Northern Province; the success rate of contending incumbents as a whole in the province was only 38 per cent. Central Province also saw the defeat of three ministers of state, as well as five incumbent M.P.s.

Table 3.3   Performance of M.P.s, ministers of state and ministers, by province, 1978

a. Performance of M.P.s[a]

	CeP	CoP	EP	LP	NP	NWP	SP	WP	Total
Won	10	5	7	4	6	2	8	6	48
Lost general election	3	2	5	3	4	4	5	5	31
Lost primary	1	3	2	2	3		1		12
Disqualified	1			2	2		1		6
Total	15	10	14	11	15	6	15	11	97
Did not stand	4	9	2	1	1	3	3	1	27

b. Performance of ministers of state

	CeP	CoP	EP	LP	NP	NWP	SP	WP	Total
Won	1	1	1		1			1	5
Lost general election		1							1
Lost primary							1		1
Total	1	2	1		1		1	1	7

c. Performance of ministers

	CeP	CoP	EP	LP	NP	NWP	SP	WP	Total
Won	2		1	2	2	2	2	1	12
Lost general election		1				1		1	3
Total	2		2	2	3	2	2	2	15

Note:

a. One M.P. from North Western Province who successfully passed through the primary but dropped out before the general election has not been included in the table.

In 1978 the casualty rate among incumbent M.P.s who chose to stand was particularly high in North Western Province. But it was also 50 per cent or more in Copperbelt, Eastern, Luapula and Northern provinces (in the latter two after discounting disqualifications). The number of 'old' M.P.s who still held seats after the election was particularly low in Northwestern and Copperbelt provinces, in consequence both of defeat and decision not to stand. In Copperbelt Province, nearly half of M.P.s elected in 1973 chose not to contest in 1978.

Background of non-incumbent candidates

If previously the recruitment of new U.N.I.P. candidates had been largely from the ranks of professional politicians, this was much less so from 1973. Holders of official party positions were obliged to resign prior to placing their names in nomination, and this, in combination with the lack of official party sponsorship, dissuaded most from taking the risk. Only nine District Governors or Regional Secretaries stood in 1973, representing less than 2 per cent of all candidates. Interestingly, four of these had business interests, offering some cushion of income outside their jobs. In contrast, well over half of U.N.I.P.'s non-incumbent candidates in 1968 had been professional politicians, and 17 per cent had been current Regional Secretaries. In respect of winners, party regional officials had constituted about 19 per cent of U.N.I.P.'s 'new' M.P.s in 1968 whereas in 1973 the figure was 2.4 per cent. An additional 32 per cent of U.N.I.P.'s 'new' M.P.s in 1968 had been assistants to ministers of state, political assistants or former Regional Secretaries.[4] Very few candidates in 1973 could be so classified and it would appear that none was successful.

On the other hand, a large number of new M.P.s in 1973 were drawn from those occupations from which the ranks of professional politicians were 'traditionally' recruited in Zambia: civil servants and other white-collar workers. In 1968 teachers, headmasters, lecturers and diplomats had constituted 18.4 per cent of non-incumbent candidates (both A.N.C. and U.N.I.P. included) and 20 per cent of new M.P.s.[5] In 1973 the figures were about 19 and 35 per cent respectively. Indeed the figures for 1973 indicate that this group formed an extremely important part of the new Parliament and enjoyed a high rate of success in the contest. Among the civil servants, the most successful were those who had been working at the provincial or national, rather than district, level. Over 40 per cent of the former were elected as against fewer than 20 per cent of the latter.

Overall in 1973, success seemed to come more frequently to those at higher and more prestigious positions, perhaps indicating the electorate's preference for those they perceived to be most skilled, educated, experienced and most likely to have useful contacts at the national level. An important new category of candidate was that of management or executive officials, mostly from the parastatal sector. Though few in number, their presence indicated not just the emergence of a new stratum within the population, but the interest of some among this stratum in parliamentary participation. They constituted 2.4 per cent of all non-incumbent candidates and 3.7 per cent of all new M.P.s.

In total, wage and salaried employees constituted at least a third of all non-incumbent candidates in 1973 and about half of all new M.P.s. Yet this is hardly to say that they were representatives of the mass of the working class. As indicated, the bulk were white-collar workers and some, both in the civil service and in the parastatal and private sectors, essentially managerial personnel. Very few manual workers were among the candidates, and only one worker below the supervisory level was known to have been among the winners. Neither did officers in the trade-union movement figure strongly in the 1973 election, in this respect perhaps following a trend throughout the period since independence of declining trade-union influence in parliamentary politics. And where present, the electorate showed little enthusiasm for their selection. Of five national-level trade-unionists who stood for Parliament in 1973, only one, the President of the Mine Workers Union, was elected.

Businessmen and the election

This pattern of parliamentary representatives coming in substantial numbers from the ranks of the professional politicians, white-collar workers and particularly from high level or managerial personnel hardly marks Zambia as unique among capitalist political economies. In a sense it reflects an increasing approximation in Zambia to western patterns. But of course it also reflects changing class patterns and the emergence and consolidation of indigenous elements within the capitalist economy in positions of management and supervision. Nowhere was the changing class character of Zambian society more profoundly indicated, however, than in the political presence of property owners, since an extremely important set of candidates, not entirely new to the national legislature, but certainly present now in much greater numbers, were those with business interests: with shops, construction companies, commercial farms and the like. Businessmen had previously figured as contestants in Zambia's elections. In 1962, 21 per cent of the candidates put up by U.N.I.P. had had businesses or farms.[6] In 1968 seven of the candidates put forward by A.N.C. were shopkeepers, while five were farmers.[7] But the 'seventies saw a dramatic increase.

In 1973 at least a quarter of all new, non-incumbent candidates were solely classifiable as businessmen. Since background information on all candidates was not available, this must be regarded as a

Table 3.4   Occupation/position of candidates at the time of the 1973 election

Occupation or position	Number	%	Number with bus. interests	% with bus. interests	% of non-incumbents	Est. % of non-incumbents (unknowns removed)
Incumbent M.P.	72	13.5	28	38.9	—	—
Wage or salaried employee	139	26.1	16	11.5	30.2	42.9
Business interest only	119	22.4	119	100.0	25.9	36.7
Professional	8	1.5	2	25.0	1.7	2.5
Chief	6	1.1	1	16.7	1.3	1.9
Progressive farmer	12	2.3	—	—	2.6	3.7
Subsistence farmer	4	0.8	—	—	0.9	1.2
Retired or unemployed	17	3.2	—	—	3.7	5.2
Unknown but was local govt. officer	19	3.6	—	—	4.1	5.9
Unknown	136	25.6	—	—	29.6	—
Total	532	100.1	166		100.0	100.0

Those with business interests as % of all nominees   31.2
Those with business interests as % of all non-incumbent candidates   30.0
Those with business interests as % of all non-incumbent candidates after
   unknowns redistributed among other categories   42.6

minimal estimate, the actual total being undoubtedly higher. One estimate of that actual total is 37 per cent, arrived at on the basis of the assumption that the distribution of 'unknowns' was roughly similar to known backgrounds (disregarding the category of M.P. for which all cases were known). In addition, however, there were a number of others, classed as wage and salaried employees, professionals and chiefs, who also had business interests. This overlap is important and we will return to it later; for the moment it is sufficient to note that a minimum of 30 per cent of all non-incumbent candidates had business interests, although it is possible that the actual percentage was as high as 43 per cent.[7]

Candidates with business interests did reasonably well in the election. Among new M.P.s (i.e. non-incumbents) a minimum of 42 per cent had business interests, the estimate of the actual percentage being as high as 47 per cent. In a quarter of the cases involved, business interests were combined with the holding of a wage or salaried position. Indeed, those who combined employment with business holding enjoyed a particularly high rate of success in the parliamentary contest.

Table 3.5　Occupation/position of M.P.s elected in 1973

Occupation or position	Number	%	Number with bus. interests	% of non-incumbents	Est. % of non-incumbents; unknowns removed
Incumbent M.P.	43	34.4	19	—	—
Wage or salaried employee	39	31.2	9	47.6	53.4
Business interest only	25	20.0	25	30.5	34.2
Professional	3	2.4	—	3.7	4.1
Chief	2	1.6	—	2.4	2.7
Progressive farmer	—	—	—	—	—
Subsistence farmer	—	—	—	—	—
Retired or unemployed	1	0.8	—	1.2	1.4
Unknown but constituency official	1	0.8	—	1.2	1.4
Unknown but was local govt. officer	2	1.6	—	2.4	2.7
Unknown	9	7.2	—	11.0	—
Total	125	100.0	53	100.0	99.9

Those with business interests as % of all winners　42.4
as % of all non-incumbent winners　41.5
as % of all non-incumbent winners, unknowns redistributed　46.6
as % of all incumbent winners 44.2

Non-incumbents with business interests represented something less than a third of all those who won parliamentary contests in 1973 (see Appendix I) and their election was a significant measure of the entry of indigenous owners into the national legislature. But these did not exhaust the total number of successful candidates with business interests, for as Table 3.5 indicates, nineteen of the M.P.s re-elected in 1973 could also be classed as businessmen. Indeed M.P.s with business interests enjoyed an even higher rate of success than incumbents as a whole. In total, incumbents and 'new' M.P.s taken together, at least fifty-three, or more than 40 per cent, had business interests of some sort.[8]

While it proved impossible to categorise all business interests by type and size of concern, eighteen of the winners were known to have owned large, very large[9] or multiple enterprises, and five others were large landowners or commercial farmers. Together these constituted 43 per cent of those elected who had business interests. These larger scale businessmen enjoyed a fairly high rate of success, about 47 per cent of all nominees in the category being elected. Relative to the numbers of Zambians owning or having shares in such large establishments, they were highly over-represented in the Parliament elected in 1973.

Background data available for candidates in the 1978 election suggests that tendencies observed in 1973 continued. Relying solely on data of property ownership in the mid-'seventies, 34 per cent of winners could be identified as having had business interests; undoubtedly the actual figure was much higher. Of the forty-three winners so identified, twenty were incumbents and twenty-three new M.P.s, indicating a continuing process of entry of indigenous owners into Parliament. M.P.s elected in 1978 included five with state land farms, two of these among the largest African commercial farmers in the nation. At least twenty-three held shares in locally-registered and, for the most part, indigenously-owned and controlled enterprises. Two others held shares in local subsidiaries of multinational corporations. Of the remainder, most were shopkeepers; yet it was significant that, as in 1973, a proportion of those with business interests who were elected (estimated as over 40 per cent) were or had been involved in particularly substantial or multiple ventures.

Alongside the high incidence of businessmen among winners in 1978 was the low incidence, as in 1973, of workers, trade-union leaders and peasant farmers. Thus Maipose has characterised the Assembly elected in 1978 as 'swamped' by members in business or holding public executive and administrative posts.[10]

In neither the 1973 nor 1978 elections could indigenous owners be regarded as having made a collective and organised bid for political power. In some sense indeed, the single-party system hindered class associations and groups seeking explicit representation for their particular interests, prohibiting as it did the competition among ideologically distinct political parties and compelling all to subscribe, however nominally, to a general populist orientation. Characteristically, candidates vied independently for office, legitimating the attempt with the claim that they would look out for the general interests of their constituents.[11] In some cases businessmen were posed against one another in the same contest. Even so, it was widely considered among businessmen that, if elected, one of their number would speak to the interests of the business community if for no other reason than that such an individual had experienced the difficulties attending business enterprise within the Zambian economy.[12] The party's perception of them as representing an important political interest group is suggested also by the fact that some campaign meetings were organised exclusively and specifically for local businessmen. Taken as a whole, therefore, the composition of candidates and elected M.P.s in 1973 and 1978 provides compelling evidence that indigenous property owners were highly active politically at the national level. In an important sense the election of 1973 thus marked a change in the relative political force of particular class groups. The election of 1978 reinforced the direction and degree of this change.

The state and the growth of indigenous enterprise

It is clear that the high proportion of businessmen/M.P.s in the 'seventies reflected an important change in Zambia's class structure. But it is also clear that the shift in class position of parliamentarians was disproportionate to the growth of indigenous capital within the economy. In some ways the strength of business's presence in Parliament was a measure of a peculiarly close relation between the state and indigenous ownership, which bears closer examination. For the growth of indigenous capital or the number of indigenous capitalists was itself partly a function of assistance given this class by the colonial as well as post-colonial state.[13]

A large number of petty commercial enterprises, but also some larger ventures, were initiated by Africans prior to independence. One Luapulan established a chain of retail outlets across Luapula and Northern provinces.[14] As early as 1945 small-scale capitalist agriculture had emerged in Southern Province, researchers having found forty-six Africans who sold 100 or more bags of maize annually.[15] This emergent or aspirant owning class was proffered some assistance by the colonial government. An 'Improved Farmer' scheme in Southern Province served through a bonus system to transfer a portion of the surplus created by peasant farmers to the more 'advanced' African farmer who subscribed to certain rules of cropping and had a higher output.[16] One of the few successful elements of a development scheme for Northern and Luapula provinces which ran from 1959 to 1961 was a loans programme to shopkeepers.[17] However, for the most part, the growth of indigenous enterprise was more in spite of government policy than because of it.

The momentum of accumulation established early on under colonialism continued, albeit slowly, following independence. Ministry of Agriculture reports identified up to 289 farmers operating on land held under customary tenure (and thus presumably Africans) as commercial farmers in 1967, selling maize worth K1200 or more per year or growing tobacco or selling dairy products to the Dairy Produce Board.[18] A small number of Africans began to purchase farms formerly occupied by settlers who had left the country. A few firms in transport, construction and commerce began to be registered as local companies by African shareholders. In 1966 19 per cent of all trading and 54 per cent of all liquor licences were held by Africans.[19] As during the colonial period, some assistance was given to indigenous owners by the state in the form of loan facilities. Farm purchases were assisted by the Land Bank and later by the Credit Organisation of Zambia. Entrepreneurs in commerce, the services and small-scale manufacturing were assisted by a loans programme under the Industrial Development Corporation; but the recipients were relatively few (155 during 1966 and 1967) and the amounts received were relatively small (averaging £1300).[20]

It was only with the economic reforms, presented in three stages in 1968, 1969 and 1970, that state assistance to indigenous capital became substantial — and indeed that the state could be seen as actively sponsoring the growth of indigenous entrepreneurship. The reforms altered the level of dominance enjoyed by foreign capital and settlers in the Zambian economy, primarily through a policy of state take-overs. But towards the general end of indigenising ownership, they also stipulated that certain sectors and certain scales of enterprise should be reserved for citizens.[21] The consequence could be seen by the mid-'seventies in an important increase in indigenous participation in the economy.

Foreign and state capital constituted overwhelmingly the dominant actor within the economy, holding virtually all of the large-scale enterprises and dwarfing the participation of private Zambian capital. Indeed, even resident non-Zambian individuals probably remained more economically important than private Zambians. Of the eighty-four construction and engineering firms with 100 or more employees in 1973, only three were owned by indigenous Zambians as compared with twenty-five by foreign companies and twenty-nine by non-Zambian residents. Of the eighty-nine manufacturing firms with 100 or more employees in the same year, only two had a majority share held by African Zambians; twenty-nine were owned by the government as parastatals or statutory bodies.[22] And of seventy firms in six manufacturing sub-sectors with 50 to 100 employees, only three had majority ownership by African Zambians.[23]

Even so, indigenous owners had made strides, particularly in those areas protected by provisions under the economic reforms. Over 90 per cent of retail and liquor licences were taken out by African Zambians by the early 'seventies,[24] and 70 per cent of local transport companies registered in 1975 were majority owned by Africans.[25] Overall during 1975, 38 per cent of all newly-registered firms had a majority of shareholding by African Zambians, while a further 5 per cent had half their shares indigenously owned — comprising a combined total of 182 companies. In agriculture, some 356 individual Africans held state land under freehold or leasehold title, 263 of these holding more than 50 acres.[26]

The vast majority of the new indigenous owning class could best be regarded as petty bourgeois, owning small enterprises, most frequently in commerce, and utilising a large component of family labour. But a growing number could be classified as small capitalists, employing wage labour. Studies of Luapula merchants and Southern Province farmers in the mid-'seventies found their average number of employees to be five and nine repectively.[27] Finally, a small but significant group could be identified by the mid-'seventies as a true bourgeoisie, owning large and complex operations or a share in a number of operations, necessarily divorced from the labour process and even perhaps from the management of some of their holdings. By the mid-'seventies, for instance, it was possible to identify ninety-one individuals who held shares in at least three locally registered companies or two companies and a farm.[28] Their small numbers in the population underline the extent of their over-representation in the Parliament of 1973. By 1978, for which our data is much more sketchy, there were undoubtedly a larger number in this top layer of the indigenous owning class. The economic crisis which continued throughout most of the 'seventies saw the demise of many marginal indigenous enterprises, but interestingly not the cessation of acquisition of medium- and large-scale firms by indigenous capital. It is rather probable that the middle and late 'seventies witnessed increased accumulation and consolidation on the part of the largest operators within the ranks of indigenous owners, though certainly even some of these were vulnerable to collapse as creditors called up their loans. Indeed, it is important to note that the increasing formation of indigenously-owned enterprises had, as its counterpart, a pronounced reluctance to invest on the part of foreign capital. Only 1 per cent of new firms registered in 1975 were owned by foreign companies. Thus the precariousness of indigenous capital must be emphasised as much as the fact that its presence has increased.

What is important here is the extent to which the increased movement into Parliament of these Zambian businessmen enhanced the potential for their increased influence over policy. While the Zambian political system is one where policy is formally introduced almost exclusively by the government, parliamentarians through debate could influence the degree to which policy would gain legitimacy. The political importance of businessmen, however, is not to be measured or inferred merely from their presence in Parliament. The issue is more complex and involves the highly intimate relation of indigenous capital and the state, evident in the extent to which high position in the party or state has served as a point for entry into the ranks of indigenous owners. The number of incumbents re-elected in 1973 who had business interests illustrates this point. In some cases, the holding of business interests preceded entry into Parliament, as it necessarily did for those 'new' M.P.s with business interests elected in 1973. But in other cases, the acquisition of business interests followed the move into the ranks of the professional politicians. The point can be made not only in respect of incumbent parliamentarians but also the more specific group of government ministers (some of whom were nominated rather than elected parliamentarians). Of all those who held Cabinet office from 1964 to 1976, half had farms or business interest in 1976; another 10 per cent had small holdings of less than 100 acres on state land.[29] Again, many acquired such interests after the acquisition of public office.

The dynamics of this process of accumulation while in or following occupation of public or party office are complex and will not be treated here in full.[30] Sometimes elements of corruption were involved. Probably more frequently high level position of itself afforded experience, useful contacts, and, in respect of position within the top layers of the civil service and parastatals, high salaries from which savings could be accumulated. There is also evidence that those with party and high level state position had benefitted from a particularly marked level of access to state loan facilities.[31]

But whatever the precise mechanism or mix of mechanisms, what is striking is the extent to which position within the state apparatus had served as a *locus* for recruitment into the indigenous owning class, particularly in respect of its uppermost level. Of the ninety-one individuals who might be characterised as a true bourgeoisie in the mid-'seventies, at least 36 per cent had held or continued to hold positions in the upper levels of the party, government or public enterprise.[32] And the public clearly perceives this relationship to exist. Popular wisdom in Zambia abounds with stories of this minister, or that parliamentarian, Central Committee member, disgraced official, parastatal head, etc., having acquired this business or that, to the extent that one is surprised to find a high level official not accredited with the title of 'big businessman'. Much in the telling is exaggerated, but it also contains elements of truth.

The relationship between indigenous owners and the state thus grows and becomes increasingly complex through a two-way process. On the one hand it occurs through the entry of businessmen into

Parliament and local councils through election; on the other hand it has involved the acquisition of business interests by those in party and state positions and often the exit from such positions to exclusive location within the capitalist class.

The expression of business interests

The political consequence of this two-way process could be seen with particular clarity from the mid-'seventies, when the growing strength of the indigenous business lobby was reinforced not only by the growing acquisition of business interests by incumbents of high level state positions, but also by the strongly increased presence of businessmen within Parliament. It could be argued that in combination these two changes led to a political impact somewhat disproportionate to the economic position of indigenous enterprise. Yet at the same time, persistent petitioning of the government by the organisations of indigenous petty capital (in particular the Zambia African Traders Association and later the Zambia National Council of Commerce and Industry) had been largely ineffective because of the clear economic weakness of this group in the first decade of independence.[33] The increasing participation of larger scale indigenous capital within the economy, if still limited, was by the mid-'seventies, however, sufficient to make its political demands credible; this was all the more so given that these demands were not simply made by a body external to the state, but also from within.[34]

Thus it would appear that, from the mid-'seventies, pressure exerted both inside and outside of legislative institutions has increasingly served to postpone or obstruct the implementation of policy presented as 'socialist' or to modify it in such a way that it either has come to enhance the interests of indigenous owners or constitute a much reduced threat to that class. A case in point involved Zambia's Leadership Code, initially put forward as a means of preventing a political ruling clique from organising itself as an economic class and controlling the political as well as the economic and social destiny of the country.[35] The provisions of the 1970 version had held that no leader should receive two or more salaries, hold directorships or shares in private companies or undertake individual business ventures. Reservations had been expressed from the outset by some of those classifiable as leaders who would necessarily be affected by the code; several M.P.s with business interests argued in Parliament for revision or postponement of the measure. Modifications were subsequently introduced so that by 1974, provision was made for a leader continuing to carry on a business, own or occupy land or receive emoluments from business interests, on condition that he or she agreed not to receive a salary for public office and that the President affirmed the case as meriting an exemption. In the event Kaunda allowed exemptions for a number of Cabinet and Central Committee members both in 1975 and subsequently.[36] Inspection of the Company Register in 1975 and 1976 suggested, furthermore, that many top level leaders not only maintained their former business interests but also entered into new ventures subsequent to the implementation of the code.

A second case where indigenous owners voiced a stand involved the proposed introduction of works' councils in industry, to be constituted two-thirds of employees and one-third of management and to be consulted about as well as participate in the formulation of company schemes relating to health and welfare of employees, housing, pensions, recreation facilities and other amenities. In a notable expression of class solidarity, indigenous capital joined with representatives of foreign and resident expatriate capital in a 'businessmen's steering committee' to protest against the proposal in a report issued in 1975. Zambian workers, they said, were not capable of participating in decision-making within firms, and management, whether of private or parastatal enterprise, should remain in 'competent' hands. The import of the move was not lost on the editor of the *Times of Zambia* who wrote that, 'for the first time the country appears to have a class of Zambians and residents speaking articulately against the revolutionary measures of the party. They are Zambia's businessmen.'[37] The Presidents wrath was aroused by the protest, but it nevertheless had the effect of stalling implementation of the councils. Moreover, the final provision stipulated that councils need only be introduced in firms with 100 or more employees, rather than twenty-five as originally proposed, thus greatly reducing their impact. When the issue of equity participation in industry was subsequently raised, a number of prominent indigenous owners were adamant in rejecting it, one characterising the notion as 'absolute rubbish'.[38] The chairman of a Special Commission on Equity Participation concluded after hearing representations from the business community that the proposal could well discourage foreign investment.[39]

Criticisms were also made by indigenous capital concerning Zambia's foreign policy stance, and particularly concerning continued adherence to the border closure with Rhodesia. Several M.P.s with business interests spoke on the point in Parliament. While the government did not in fact capitulate, it faced continuing discontent on the matter, stimulated by the business community who made use of the prevailing state of economic crisis to advocate a change clearly compatible with their own interests. In 1978, when announcing his intention to challenge Kaunda for the presidency, Kapwepwe noted that one of his priorities, if elected, would be to reopen the border.[40]

It would appear, then, that during the 'seventies a politically conscious and active indigenous owning class emerged in Zambia, symbolised and necessarily reinforced by the increased presence of businessmen in the National Assembly. The pressure of this class had an observable impact on policy, though it was not able to displace all elements of the populist programme enacted following independence and espoused by Kaunda. To some extent the need for the government to attend to the compelling hardship of other groups — the rural peasants, the workers and unemployed in the towns — prevented all the claims of indigenous capital being granted. Moreover, Zambia's position as a front-line state, and the external threat under which the nation suffered, served to bind the population in the recognition of the need for unity and minimal policy upheaval; though, significantly, with Zimbabwe's independence, criticism from some quarters of the indigenous business community again increased. Formulation of policy is a function of the balance of class (and other) social forces. For the moment the indigenous bourgeoisie was still limited in its capacity to challenge the state or to influence policy, retaining as it did a degree of political dependence on the party apparatus for its access to the state. Nevertheless, under the one-party system, it had come increasingly to assert its class interests, and the pattern of development provided little indication that this process of assertion would not continue and grow.

Notes

1   The term 'businessmen' as used here is not intended as a synonym for capitalists or bourgeoisie. It is rather used in a broad sense, to refer to all those who own businesses as private individuals or are shareholders in registered companies. Businesses or business interests include small-scale retail establishments, such as groceries, and larger enterprises, such as shops, restaurants, bars, filling stations, insurance or advertising agencies, commercial farms, manufacturing firms, construction and transport companies. The term 'businessmen', therefore, does not distinguish between size of enterprise owned, type of operation or product, nor type of labour used — whether family or non-family, waged or unwaged. Obviously important distinctions do exist within the broad category of businessmen so defined, precisely on the basis of size of enterprise and type of labour used, as reflected in the concepts petty bourgeoisie and bourgeoisie. Such distinctions will be referred to and elaborated upon in the text. However, we have found it useful in the general categorisation of the background of M.P.s to lump all those with business interests into an initial, single category of businessmen.

2 Robert Molteno and Ian Scott, *op.cit.*, p. 170.

3 Data on candidates had to be gathered from a number of independent sources. In the case of the 1973 elections, most important was data obtained in interviews of candidates carried out by all three authors. We are grateful to former colleagues and students of the University of Zambia who made available to us biographical data which they had also collected in the course of that election. We are grateful also for assistance received from R. Molteno, I. Scott, the then Director of Elections Mr. M. Mitchell and his staff, journalists of Z.A.N.A., A.I.S., the *Times of Zambia* and the *Zambia Daily Mail*, and party officials. Data was also obtained from published sources including *Who's Who in Zambia*, Kelvin C. Mlenga (ed.), 1968, Zambia Publishing Co. Ltd., Lusaka; 'Party and Government Personnel', *Times of Zambia*, 7 Aug. 1973; *Election Results* for 1964, 1968, 1970 and various by-elections of 1967, 1968, 1970 and 1971; Government of the Republic of Zambia, *Background*, a periodic publication of the Zambia Information Services; and many of the various books cited in other footnotes. Data collected for the 1973 election was also utilised in analysis of the background of 1978 candidates, since many of the same individuals stood in both elections. It was supplemented by the writers' information on ownership of local companies registered 1970-75 and by information supplied by B. Chikulo, G. Maipose and C. Gertzel, who is also grateful to the Director of Elections, Mr. T. Mbewe, for assistance. Though the information as obtained was found highly reliable, it was not available for all candidates nominated, being most complete for those finally elected, and displaying most gaps for those excluded in the primaries and by disqualification.

4 Molteno and Scott, *op.cit.*, p. 170.

5 *Ibid*, pp. 170, 173.

6 According to Mulford, the proportion of candidates put up by the A.N.C. in this election who were either businessmen or farmers was 14 per cent, by the U.F.P. 39 per cent, and by the Liberals 18 per cent. He cautioned, however, that his background information on candidates was not infallible and was primarily intended as a guide (Mulford, *The Northern Rhodesia General Election 1962*, Nairobi, Oxford University Press, 1964, pp. 101 and 102.)

7 Molteno and Scott, *op.cit.*, p. 173. Unfortunately, they do not provide similar details about U.N.I.P. candidates.

8 Candidates with business interests were elected throughout the country, in all of its provinces. Approximately half emerged from contests in line-of-rail provinces (Central, Copperbelt and Southern). But this constitutes only slight overrepresentation of the urban provinces, since 43 per cent of all constituencies are located in these three provinces. It should perhaps be pointed out, however, that candidates elected from rural constituencies in many cases had business interests in town, this having been particularly true of those with large or very large enterprises.

9 It is not possible to be precise about such distinctions (here indicated primarily on the basis of size); but generally we consider 'large' to refer to an enterprise which utilises labour outside the family, with perhaps at

least 10 permanent workers. Such an enterprise, it would be assumed, would require a sizable outlay of initial capital and some management skill. Quantity of output or turnover would also necessarily enter into a comprehensive definition, but for purposes here we will offer no precise figures. By a 'very large' enterprise is meant, very roughly, the sort that multi-national capital might be interested in associating itself with.

10   G.S. Maipose, *op.cit.*, p. 58. Maipose also refers to the underrepresentation of rural residents, who were estimated to constitute only 25.6 per cent of all M.P.s elected in 1978.

11   Such apparently independent pursuit of office by candidates with business interests is, of course, not untypical of practices in most capitalist societies and of much less ambiguous cases of bourgeois hegemony.

12   See below, Chapter 6; a survey by one of the authors of Southern Province African commercial farmers in 1975 found this attitude to be a prevalent one among that group of 'businessmen' as well.

13   For a further discussion of some of these points see C. Baylies and M. Szeftel, 'The Rise of a Zambian Capitalist Class in the 1970s', *The Journal of Southern African Studies*, 8, 2 (1982).

14   Interview, No. 88, Luapula sample; from a set of interviews conducted by one of the authors in 1974.

15   W. Allen, M. Gluckman, D.U. Peters, C.G. Trapnel, *et al*, *Land Holding and Land Usage Among the Plateau Tonga of Mazabuka District: A Reconnaissance Survey, 1945*, Rhodes-Livingstone Papers, No. 14 (Manchester University Press, 1948), pp. 166–7.

16   See C.E. Johnson, *African Farming Improvement in the Plateau Tonga Maize Areas of Northern Rhodesia*, Department of Agriculture, Northern Rhodesia, Agricultural Bulletin No. 11 (Lusaka, Government Printer, 1956).

17   Government of Northern Rhodesia, *Report on Intensive Rural Development in the Northern and Luapula Provinces of Northern Rhodesia, 1959–1961* (Lusaka, Government Printer, 1961); Magnus Halcrow, Development Commissioner, *Recent Advances in the Northern and Luapula Provinces of Northern Rhodesia* (Lusaka, Government Printer, 1959).

18   Republic of Zambia, *Agricultural and Pastoral Production, 1967* (Lusaka, Government Printer, 1968), 1.

19   Figures are based on examination of applications for trade and liquor licences published in the *Government Gazette* for 1966. Precise figures are difficult to give because some licences were awarded to businesses rather than individuals, but the estimates given here are reasonably accurate.

20   Indeco, *Seventh Annual Report, 1966*, p. 23; *Eighth Annual Report, 1967*, p. 35; *Business and Economy*, July, 1967, pp. 33, 34.

21   The third phase of the reforms specified that by January 1972 only solely Zambian- or state-owned companies would be permitted in the transport sector, and that all mining and Public Works contracts worth less than K100,000 would be granted to Zambian contractors; in commerce, only a few specialised areas of trade were to remain open to non-citizens.

22 Government ownership as used here refers to at least 50 per cent government share participation. Figures are based on data obtained from the Company Register, Lusaka.

23 The 6 sub-sectors were food, beverages and tobacco; textiles, wearing apparel and leather; wood, wood products and furniture; paper, paper products, printing and publishing; chemicals, rubber and plastics; and non-metallic mineral products. Derived from *Industry Monographs*, Nos. 1–6, Lusaka, Central Statistical Office, August 1975–March 1976.

24 From applications for such licences as published in the *Goverment Gazette*, Lusaka; note should be taken that some Zambians fronted for non-Zambians in applying for licences.

25 Figures are based on a classification of local companies registered in 1975 by sector and type/nationality of owner. From the Company Register, Lusaka.

26 Derived from data included on cadastral strip maps produced by the government's Land Use Services Division, listing acreages and owners of demarcated farms. State land refers to that category of land initially set aside by the Crown for alienation to settlers as private property. Most lies in a thin strip along the line of rail. Other land remains under customary tenure.

27 Based on surveys conducted by one of the authors in 1974 and 1975. Some of those employed were undoubtedly relatives of the owner. The samples in fact comprised a range of enterprises from petty bourgeois to small capitalist, the largest where all labour was waged being the latter. C. Baylies, 'The State and Class Formation in Zambia' (unpublished Ph.D. thesis, University of Wisconsin, 1978).

28 Based on research in the Company Register, Ministry of Commerce, Lusaka, undertaken jointly by the authors during 1975 and 1976. This involved collection of information about some 2,500 companies incorporated locally from 1929. Information about directors, shareholders, sectoral distribution, access to loan capital and historical evaluation was collected for each firm. Almost all companies registered from the beginning of 1972 to the end of August 1976 were surveyed in this way. Information on farm ownership was derived from cadastral strip maps.

29 Estimates of business interests of government personnel are derived from the Company Register and cadastral strip maps for the period. It must be stressed that such figures are minimum estimates since we did not use the Register of Business Names and since, of course, we had no check on possible nominees covering for such personnel.

30 See Baylies and Szeftel, *op.cit.*, for a fuller discussion of this issue.

31 Inspection of two lists of Industrial Finance Company loan recipients, for example (one for the country as a whole and covering the last six months of 1973; the other covering recipients in the Lusaka area to the end of 1975) indicated that at least 36 per cent were either prominent U.N.I.P. members, high level civil servants or parastatal personnel. The figures represent minimum estimates since it was not possible to obtain information about all names on the lists.

32   Another 7 per cent had been, or continued to be, members of the learned professions.

33   See C. Baylies, 'Zambia's Economic Reforms and their Aftermath: The State and the Growth of Indigenous Capital', *The Journal of Commonwealth and Comparative Politics*, XX, 3 (1982).

34   It must of course be emphasised that neither the representation of indigenous capital's interests in Parliament nor on the part of capital-holding policy-makers was always direct or self-conscious. Yet to the extent that property holdings influence one's orientation, class position is bound to influence or place constraints on policy advocated or formulated.

35   K. Kaunda, 'Take up the Challenge . . .', Speeches made by His Excellency the President to the U.N.I.P. National Council, Lusaka, 7–10 Nov. 1970 (Lusaka, Zambia Information Services, 1970), p. 35. See also above, Chapter 1.

36   K. Kaunda, 'The "Watershed" Speech', Address by His Excellency the President to the U.N.I.P. National Council 30 June–3 July 1975 (Lusaka, Zambia Information Services, 1975), p. 12. *Times of Zambia*, 4 Nov. 1980, reported that 12 M.P.s had been allowed to retain their business interests on exercising the option not to receive their National Assembly salaries.

37   *Ibid.*, 29 Aug. 1975.

38   *Ibid.*, 14 Nov. 1977.

39   R. Fincham and G. Zulu, 'Labour and Participation in Zambia', in B. Turok (ed.), *Development in Zambia* (London, Zed Press, 1979), whose article includes an evaluation of the operation of works councils.

40   Maipose, *op.cit.*, p. 12; *Economist*, 14 Aug. 1978.

Dissent and authority in the Zambian one-party state 1973–80

Introduction

The introduction of the one-party state in 1973 did not provide a final solution to party conflict in Zambia. On the contrary, the political debate continued to present U.N.I.P. with the same problems of conflict management that the one-party state had been designed to overcome. The first dispute arose over the relationship between party and Parliament when parliamentarians claimed the right on behalf of their constituents to oppose the policies of the party to which they all now belonged. The issues went beyond Parliament, however, for they concerned the legitimacy of opposition and the limits of control within the one-party state, issues on which the 1973 constitution had been largely silent. This essay, therefore, considers the nature of dissent and the assertion of authority in the one-party state between 1973 and 1981.[1]

Although the period is short, these years were of fundamental importance in the evolution of the one-party state. The government came under increasing attack over its conduct of affairs, leading in October 1980 to the arrest of a number of prominent Zambians allegedly involved in a conspiracy and subsequent charges of treason against some of them.[2] Moreover, during the same period there was mounting tension within the labour movement, which culminated, also in 1980, in a confrontation between U.N.I.P. and the unions which presented the party with its most serious crisis since independence. Faced with such challenges, U.N.I.P. asserted the principle of party supremacy, extended party control over government, and in the process moved Zambia closer to a party-state. The result, notwithstanding the continued emphasis upon participatory democracy, was the further concentration of power in the presidency. Presidential authority was sustained, however, less by the party than by the state.

We must also bear in mind that the transition to the one-party state was made at a time of increasing external threat and internal economic crisis, both of which produced fundamental disagreement as to the appropriate response. The growth of dissent thus reflected a crisis of confidence in government, for an understanding of which we must look briefly, in the first place, at the circumstances against which it emerged.

External threat and internal economic crisis in the 'seventies

Zambia's security, as a front-line state, was directly affected by the escalation after 1970 of the liberation struggle, first against the Portuguese and then against Rhodesia. Until 1975, the most serious security problems were on Zambia's Angolan and Mozambique borders, arising from the increased conflict in those territories.[3] The Portuguese coup in Lisbon in 1974, however, and the Angolan and Mozambique independence that followed, shifted the central focus of the conflict to Rhodesia and to the Zimbabweans' struggle for majority rule, which subsequently dominated Zambia's southern African policy until 1980.[4] The continuing struggle in Angola spilled over into the Western Province, and although Jonas Savimbi's forces were not allowed, once Zambia accepted the M.P.L.A. regime, to remain in Zambia, her border remained at serious risk.[5] The greater dangers after 1976, however, were from Rhodesia, and arose from Zambia's support, along with the other front-line states, for full-scale armed struggle against the Rhodesian regime, and Kaunda's provision of operational bases for Joshua Nkomo's Z.A.P.U. wing of the Zimbabwe liberation movement. That support brought Zambia under increasing Rhodesian attack, with the result that from 1977 to 1980 the country was subjected to a succession of bombing raids and military incursions, which on occasion struck into the centre of Lusaka itself.[6] Zambia became essentially a country at war, but unable to hit back. There were also diplomatic repercussions arising out of Kaunda's involvement in the early attempts to negotiate a settlement on Rhodesia with South Africa, and his original support for Savimbi's U.N.I.T.A., which threatened Zambia's standing in the O.A.U. when that body in 1976 recognised the M.P.L.A. as the legitimate government in Angola.[7]

Finally, the southern African conflict had serious economic consequences. It led to increased defence spending,[8] and it created serious transport and communications problems. Much of Zambia's earlier success in re-routing exports and imports away from the south (following her introduction of sanctions against Rhodesia in 1965),[9] which had been achieved at considerable cost, was lost as a result of the increased conflict of the 'seventies. The Angolan war closed the Benguela Railway at a time when Lobito Bay had become one of the country's major import and export ports, and after Zambia's own closure of the Rhodesian border in January 1973 had significantly reduced the government's room for manœuvre. The hoped-for improved communications through independent Mozambique failed to materialise when that country closed its border with Rhodesia in 1976, and the new Tazara railway linking Zambia with Dar es Salaam, which began operations in 1976, quickly ran into difficulties. Thus from 1976, Zambia faced acute interruptions to her export of copper and imports of essential goods, the full significance of which was borne home in October 1978, when the government was forced to reopen the Rhodesian route to allow much-needed supplies of fertiliser to reach the country.[10]

The causes of the economic crisis that engulfed Zambia after 1973 lay also in the world energy crisis and economic recession. Whereas in 1973, the cost of Zambia's oil imports was K17.7m, by 1980 it had increased to K122.9m, and import costs had escalated for all sectors of the economy. The slump in world copper prices in the mid-'seventies had severe consequences for the country's budgetary position, her balance of payments and her foreign exchange reserves. Whereas in 1974, copper and cobalt provided more than 90 per cent of the country's foreign exchange and 54 per cent of government income, between 1977 and 1979 they provided nothing. In 1974, copper generated one-third of the country's G.D.P., in 1977, 11 per cent. The mines by that time faced acute financial difficulties, were borrowing heavily, and running at a loss. Production costs had risen faster than those of Zambia's competitors, reflecting in part the severe internal constraints that the industry faced. Thus, notwithstanding some recovery in prices, the mining industry remained, at the beginning of the 'eighties, in severe difficulties. The depression in the mining industry, in turn, had repercussions on the service and manufacturing sectors, and the increased price of imported materials and spare parts constituted an additional constraint. As a result, the industrial sector as a whole operated far below capacity.[11] Finally, the country's economic difficulties were compounded in 1978 by a severe drought, which resulted in two years of poor harvests and made large maize imports necessary at a time of severe balance of payments problems.[12]

The proportions of the economic crisis that engulfed Zambia were thus enormous. Between 1974 and 1979, G.D.P. declined by 46 per cent in real terms, capital expenditure fell 65 per cent and successive budgets suffered draconian cuts. Total collapse of the economy was averted in 1978 only by the intervention of the International Monetary Fund, although a temporary recovery in copper prices in the late 'seventies provided some relief.[13]

The social consequences of the recession were equally serious. First, notwithstanding attempts by the government and the mining companies to avoid redundancies, jobs were at risk in both public and private sector, and wage employment declined by 2.4 per cent between 1975 and 1980, from 393,490 to 384,090. Employment in mining and manufacturing was essentially the same in 1979 as it had been in 1972, although urban population had increased by 45 per cent, and although the decline appeared by 1979 to have been halted, unemployment remained severe.[14] Second, urban workers suffered a decline in the real value of wages. Third, shortages of basic commodities, including cooking oil, flour, soap, candles and meat became a regular feature of life, and public services deteriorated as government expenditure was cut. Living standards therefore fell and estimates in the late 'seventies suggested that 25 per cent of urban households were living below basic minimum needs of food and income.[15] Fourth, there was a more fundamental deterioration in the rural areas, especially in the more distant provinces off the railway, with an estimated 80 per cent of rural households now lacking resources to satisfy minimum needs.[16]

Lastly, urban unemployment and rural stagnation both contributed to the escalation of social violence and crime, while scarcity and economic crisis were accompanied by increasing corruption, which by 1980 was acknowledged to have become 'apparent in all aspects of public life'.[17] Industrial unrest also grew, culminating in January 1981 in an eight-day strike on the Copperbelt which raised memories of the strikes of 1935 and 1940.[18]

The economic crisis and the social repercussions were of fundamental importance in the growth of political dissent after December 1973. Not all Zambia's difficulties could be explained as the consequence of her dependency upon the international economic system or her defence of freedom in southern Africa. The decline in the terms of trade against the rural sector had begun, as we have seen earlier, in the first six years of independence, at a time of economic expansion.[19] The country's agricultural failures reflected grossly inadequate investment in agriculture.[20] Successive administrative reforms had failed to ensure the administrative capacity to implement government rural development policies, for example those concerned with village productivity.[21] Hence, as the economic crisis grew, so did criticism of government policy, initiated by U.N.I.P. backbenchers who used parliamentary privilege to assert their independence of the party in the one-party state. The question of dissent is thus most effectively approached by looking first at the parliamentary debate, and then at the wider conflict of which it was a part.

Parliament and the articulation of bourgeois dissent

The formal powers and procedures of the Zambian Parliament remained the same in the Second Republic as they had been in the
first.[22] The composition of the National Assembly however, was,
changed in certain important respects. M.P.s, to a far greater degree
than in the past, were local men returned from constituencies to
which they belonged by birth, although not all of them had lately been
resident there. A much smaller number than in the past were professional party organisers who had worked their way up through the
party hierarchy to a parliamentary seat. Many of them had been
teachers at some stage of their careers, and over 40 per cent had
business interests of one kind or another. The newcomers to
Parliament were generally better educated than their predecessors and
included a number of independent professional men, including six
lawyers and several former civil servants. Among the backbenchers
there were also men with past ministerial experience and a national
reputation. Overall, the new Parliament had within its ranks, therefore, a good deal more professional and administrative expertise than
its predecessors, particularly on the backbench.[23]

Backbenchers also now had greater opportunities for independent
debate than in the past. The Chona Commission had recommended,
and the government had agreed, that in the one-party state M.P.s (but
not ministers) should be free to speak and vote as they liked on any
issue that came to the National Assembly.[24] On that basis, M.P.s
claimed the right to challenge party policy in arenas external to the
party, insisting that this was consistent with their responsibilities to
their consitutuents and also in the interests of national unity.[25]
Although a majority of them were new to Parliament, backbenchers
quickly acquired the confidence bred by membership of a national
institution, and they demonstrated on occasions considerable courage
in their insistence upon their right to criticise party and government.

There was little to indicate that Parliament as a result exerted any
significant control over the executive. Parliamentarians persuaded
government on a number of occasions to modify its position, but they
did not effect any major change of policy. In this respect the National
Assembly might be seen as a 'residual legislature', enjoying little
authority of its own.[26] Backbenchers could not prevent government
from governing. Moreover, party control over Parliament was
ultimately ensured by the Central Committee's power to veto prospective candidates, which was exercised in 1978 as it had been in
1973.[27]

The significance of the National Assembly lay, however, less in its
control of the executive than in the opportunities it provided for an

independent forum where political debate could be conducted outside the structures of the party, and especially the National Council, the highest policy-making body in the party in the intervals between general conferences.[28] Backbenchers argued that Parliament was independent of the National Council, and, as Arthur Wina put it in 1974,

... in my parliamentary experience nothing that comes before this House is subject to the authority outside it except in the case of financial Bills ... other than that this House is independent of any influence from any quarter ...[29]

What was at issue, therefore, was the authority of the party and its capacity to control the policy debate. The National Council consisted of all regional party officials, District Governors, Central Committee members, the President of the Zambia Congress of Trade Unions, and the M.P.s, of whom twenty-three were ministers and eight ministers of state. Even were the backbenchers to vote as a block within the National Council — an unlikely event — they therefore remained a minority. Moreover, the National Council in practice provided a very limited forum for intra-party debate. It met only twice a year (and from 1979 only once). Its meetings rarely lasted more than two or three days, and a good deal of that time was customarily taken up by the presidential address and Central Committee reports. Not unnaturally, the M.P.s saw the National Assembly, therefore, as offering them a more advantageous platform for debate, and in the early months of the first one-party Parliament they used it to make extensive criticisms of their own party policy.

The result was the first extension of party control in the Second Republic. In the party's view, while the House was legally supreme and nothing could become law without its consent, nevertheless, the National Council was 'politically' supreme, and the source of the policy decisions and programmes which M.P.s might question, but not oppose.[30] Backbench criticism was seen as a challenge to party control and, following Kaunda's own powerful criticism of the backbench debate, the National Council resolved, at its April 1974 meeting, that the party's disciplinary rules should extend to M.P.s' statements in Parliament, and that

no M.P. shall engage in activities which are a breach of Party disciplinary Code, and anyone abusing [parliamentary] privileges and immunities for personal aggrandisement or with intent to divide the nation shall be disciplined by the Party.[31]

A year later, it endorsed the President's decision that party disciplinary rules should be incorporated into Parliament's Standing Order, with the result that M.P.s became guilty of a breach of party rules if their debate in Parliament brought the name of the party into ridicule or contempt. Whether such breach of the rules had occurred, would be decided by the party. The freedom accorded the backbencher in the one-party state to speak and vote as he wished on any issue was therefore circumscribed by party control.[32]

The issue was not, however, so easily resolved, for the relationship between the M.P. and the party had itself been modified by the introduction of the one-party state. While party membership was constitutionally required, the M.P. was now, in practice, having received Central Committee approval, a good deal less dependent upon the party for election than had been the case in the past. The turnover of M.P.s in the second general election demonstrated their ultimate dependence on the electorate rather than the party. U.N.I.P., moreover, became increasingly vulnerable to criticism after 1975, in the face of the suspension of a succession of party officials and leaders for alleged corruption and the government's continued inability to overcome the economic crisis.[33] Whether or not M.P.s were disciplined by the party, they therefore remained undeterred by the threat, with the result that the National Assembly assumed a prominence it had rarely enjoyed in the past for the public expression of criticism of the party.

Three major strands could be identified in the resulting debate. First, backbenchers drew attention to constituency needs and demands. They asked a great many more questions than in previous parliaments about a wide range of constituents' needs, and they questioned government decisions in terms of their impact on their constituencies. In this way, they exploited U.N.I.P.'s populist tradition to challenge government, as for example in 1974, when they successfully opposed government legislation to extend control over commercial fishing, on the grounds that it imposed unnecessary restrictions on the ordinary village fishermen.[34]

Second, M.P.s criticised government implementation of policy. They charged the administration with tribalism, nepotism and inefficiency, and the Cabinet with failure to act in the face of economic crisis.[35] They pointed to political appointments as a source of administrative weakness. They used the Public Accounts Committee (of which Arthur Wina was the first chairman) to probe into government financial laxity; and although their efforts in that committee to enforce accountability seemed no more successful than those of their predecessors,[36] the newly-established Parliamentary Committee on Parastatals forced greater presidential attention to the growing problems of management in that sector.[37] Their criticisms extended also to the party and to party functionaries, whose weakness they considered to be a major cause of the failure of rural development.[38]

Third, backbenchers questioned policy itself. Although on this they presented a wide spectrum of opinions not always consistently held,[39] two themes persisted. First, while no one supported the principle of apartheid, a number of M.P.s urged the modification of Zambia's stand against the minority regimes in the interests of economic recovery, and the re-opening of southern trade routes. 'Morality', one M.P. suggested in 1975, 'cannot be the basis on which we conduct a successful foreign policy.'[40] Second, the party's socialist strategy came under attack on two grounds: on the one hand, it was argued that the government's equivocal position on foreign private investment blocked the massive foreign assistance believed to be necessary to revive the economy.

The Party and Government's shift to socialism [is] scaring away would be investors and if not relaxed the economy would collapse . . .[41]

On the other hand, socialist measures were opposed in defence of the Zambian private sector.[42]

By 1979, some of the most articulate of the backbenchers from the first Parliament had gone, either vetted out by the Central Committee, or having retired; and some of those who remained were now appointed to ministerial office. As a result, while the occupational background of M.P.s in the second Parliament was generally similar, there was probably less professional experience on the backbench and the personalities had to a significant extent changed. Nevertheless, there was a remarkable continuity in the debate, in which backbenchers doggedly pursued government mismanagement and party decline, until in April 1981 they were charged by Kaunda with acting as an 'opposition'.[43]

The charge of opposition was consistently denied, and it would indeed be difficult to identify an organised opposition on the backbench. To some extent there was a tendency to informal provincial groupings, and the emphasis upon grass roots' needs reflected perceptions of past and continued provincial neglect, including provincial dissatisfaction with the distribution of national office in the one-party state. The charges by M.P.s in Luapulan and Northern provinces of rural neglect demonstrably reflected this concern, and it was not unimportant that of the thirty-three M.P.s who voted against the government in the first division in the House in 1974, eight were from Northern Province and four from Luapula.[44] Nevertheless, although there was considerable speculation at the potential power of the fifty-odd Bemba-speaking M.P.s, the latter did not emerge as a solid block in the first or second Parliament and they lacked leaders of national standing. The central party leadership was, moreover, prepared to accommodate such populist, provincial-focused criticism as it had done in the past by a careful balance of provincial representation in the central government and the Central Committee. This meant, however, as backbenchers were not slow to point out, that it was the party in the one-party state that was responsible for the continuing identification of dissent with provincial and ethnic cleavages.[45]

The increased presence of businessmen in the National Assembly was reflected in the consistent demands for greater support for the private sector, more generous credit policy, and opposition to the extension of the public sector.[46] Support for private enterprise and for the reopening of the southern route went hand-in-hand, so that the debate on that issue also undoubtedly reflected the increased presence of the Zambian entrepreneurial class. Zambia's business community was hard hit by the transport crisis, which throughout the 'seventies resulted in severe shortages of raw materials and spare parts for machinery as well as foreign exchange. The same business and new commercial farmers were the most critical of Zambia's socialist strategies. Once again, however, it was not always so easy to draw the lines of dissent. The concern over economic decline was shared by the population as a whole. The criticisms of the Angolan crisis in January 1976 reflected a widespread bewilderment among Zambians as a whole that the country, which had supported the liberation movements at considerable cost to herself for more than a decade, should now be under attack from other African states.[47] Moreover, provincial interests could divide businessmen, and there were potential conflicts of interest between the petty bourgeois elements and those with larger entrepreneurial interests. More significant was the extent to which the private sector was represented on the front as well as the backbench, so that the influence of that sector must be acknowledged as more complex than that of a backbench lobby.

The potential alignments and the conflict of interests underlying the debate emerge more clearly if we consider the most trenchant criticisms of these years, which came from backbenchers who must be identified less in terms of provincial interests than by their standing as part of Zambia's new bourgeoisie. Among that group we include some of the larger businessmen, the independent professional men and former civil servants. These were all educated men, all property owners, enjoying status and prestige by virtue of their occupation or profession. While they did not all come from the same province, a majority were Bemba-speaking. More important, they were urban in their experience (although not necessarily representing urban constituencies) and cosmopolitan in their orientation (and so viewed Zambia's situation in global rather than parochial terms). They all had long and close U.N.I.P. connections, although they had not all held party office, and they did not belong to the category of professional party organisers.

The position held by this group was most clearly stated in October 1977, in a debate on President Kaunda's address to an emergency session of Parliament, called to discuss the growing economic crisis. At the end of that debate, a Select Committee was set up 'to reexamine the country's political, economic and social structures and to recommend action for economic recovery'.[48] Its *Report* provided the closest to an alternative to official U.N.I.P. policy that had been offered up to that date.[49] Many of its recommendations accorded with the government's own position: for example on the need to diversify the economy, to shift the emphasis to production over consumption, and to concentrate on rural development. On three issues, however, they diverged: on their preference for greater private-sector activity and the more direct involvement of that sector in economic planning; on the reduction of capital expenditure on welfare services as a contribution to the reduction of government expenditure; and on the reduction in the number of political posts funded by the party. The report placed the responsibility for Zambia's economic crisis squarely on the country's 'political superstructures' which were seen as a 'serious constraint on efficiency'.[50] It recommended fundamental changes in the party machinery, and especially the role of the Central Committee.[51]

These views were clearly not restricted to the backbench. The committee was chaired by the then Minister of Finance (himself a backbencher at the beginning of the Parliament until his appointment as Minister in 1976, and who had also held ministerial office in previous U.N.I.P. governments). It included three other ministers, one of them also a member of the Central Committee. The evidence given to the committee, furthermore, had come from a cross-section of senior civil servants and national politicians.[52] Its recommendations, therefore, might safely be said to reflect the views of a wide spectrum of Zambia's bureaucrats and politicians, inside as well as outside the government system, as well as the business class.

The growth of dissent within Parliament revealed conflicting views on policy and new political alignments within government and party. The doubts about party policy thus went a good deal further than the backbench, and by 1980 could persuade at least one minister to charge that U.N.I.P. was on the verge of disintegration.[53] The limited implementation of the Leadership Code,[54] the concessions to the private sector in both the Industrial Development Act and the budget of 1977,[55] as well as the fate of the proposals for industrial democracy,[56] all suggest that these new alignments must be placed in the context of the growing presence of indigenous capitalists, which was the subject of the last chapter. Nevertheless, dissent reflected complex social as well as economic forces, and the opposition was based upon a concern related to more than economics. Criticism arose also out of a belief in the need for an efficient, professional bureaucracy, divorced from politics, and therefore opposition to party dominance over the civil service. In part, this reflected the fears of Zambian bureaucrats for the loss of their privileges, but it also reflected a preference for the diffusion rather than the concentration of power and a vehement rejection of arbitrary rule.[57] These were the ideas of social democrats. Dissent also spilled over into the Church, which became alarmed in 1978 and 1979 at Kaunda's increasing use of the language of Marxism-Leninism and his closer association with the Marxist parties of independent Angola and Mozambique.[58] Some of the most cogent comment on corruption and other social ills and in defence of a liberal democratic society was produced by *The National Mirror*, published by the Catholic Church's *Multimedia* organisation, whose board of governors was chaired by one of the most articulate of the backbench critics.[59] The views of the emerging bourgeoisie were not, therefore, without influence across a broad spectrum of a society concerned at the crisis the country faced.[60]

Labour and the articulation of working class discontent

Dissent was not only, however, a consequence of the growth of a bourgeoisie. It reflected also the reaction of labour to the economic crisis. Organised labour had very little representation in either parliament and in the confrontation between labour and the party that ultimately occurred in 1980, M.P.s played an important mediating role.[61] Nevertheless, because few M.P.s were drawn from the working class, and notwithstanding that the Zambia Congress of Trade Unions (Z.C.T.U.) was represented in the National Council, it was the Supreme Council of the Z.C.T.U. that provided the forum for the articulation of working-class interests, with the result that the role of the labour movement and its relationship with the party also became a source of disagreement in the one-party state.

The resulting conflict has to be set against the background of the impact on urban society, on the one hand of the economic crisis, and on the other of government's policies for recovery. While the economic decline was a national crisis that affected all sections of society, there was no doubt of the increasing severity of the hardships that faced urban Zambians, and especially those in the lower income groups, from 1975 to 1980.[62] The most serious problem was the loss of employment, which in the same period declined by 2.4 per cent from 393,490 to 384,090.[63] Although construction, manufacturing and mining were all hard hit, the greatest threat was that experienced by the mining industry (which provided 14.16 per cent of formal sector employment), as the companies were forced to introduce cost-cutting measures that ultimately affected jobs.[64] In the early stages of the crisis, government policy ensured that public-sector employees were not dismissed (and thus exacerbated problems of over-employment and non-profitable operations in the parastatal sector).[65] Under the Employment (Special Provisions) Regulations of 1975, moreover, no employer could declare employees redundant without the consent of the Ministry of Labour.[66] In spite of this, redundancies grew: 4,858 in 1975, 9,066 in 1976, 8,217 in 1977.[67] At the beginning of the 1980s, therefore, at a time when government's strategy for rural development had failed to persuade urban unemployed back to the land, the problem of unemployment remained central to the conditions of the urban working class.[68] Over the same period, urban dwellers had also faced deteriorating services and steadily-rising prices, demonstrated by the rise in the low income price index from 71.6 in 1970 to 192.3 in 1979.[69] In addition, they had to content with persistent shortages of a range of basic commodities, which produced among other consequences a rapidly expanding black market.

Successive economic measures introduced by government in the search for recovery themselves imposed further hardships. Devaluation in 1976 and again in 1978 under the I.M.F. Agreement might have been necessary for the recovery of the mining industry, but it contributed significantly to a further spiralling of the cost of living. The I.M.F. Agreement, moreover, imposed other conditions on the Zambian government which meant further budgetary constraints and austerity measures, the two most contentious being those of subsidies and wage restraint.[70] On the first, one significant factor contributing to Zambia's economic difficulties related to those government subsidies, especially on maize and fertiliser, which had been designed to keep down the cost of foodstuffs to the urban consumer and which had grown rapidly since the late 'sixties.[71] Government was forced in the 'seventies to review that policy, and not without great difficulty such subsidies were reduced (although not eliminated) between 1976 and 1980. The consequence was significant increases in the price of mealie meal, the staple diet of most Zambians, and other basic consumer items.[72] At the same time, government permitted only minimal wage increases and the I.M.F. Agreement required a total wage freeze for the public sector at the same time as devaluation produced a further increase in the cost of living.[73]

Urban discontent in the face of these changes had first been manifested in November 1974 when government attempted, without prior warning, to introduce major price increases on a number of commodities including bread and cooking oil. The public reaction was immediate and hostile, resulting in vigorous demonstrations on the

Copperbelt and in Lusaka. The Z.C.T.U. announced that the consequence of the price increases must be a demand for wage increases
which they would support. A week later the increases were revoked.[74]
Urban tension did not, however, abate, as the response to subsequent
price increases showed.[75]

Such urban discontent has to be placed in the context of a society in
which industrial action had always carried with it the threat of political opposition. In this respect, the most serious problems were on the
Copperbelt, where the 1973 elections had indicated a significant loss
of support for U.N.I.P.[76] The province remained subject to intense
intra-party tension, increased in 1978 by U.N.I.P.'s refusal to allow
Kapwepwe to contest the presidency. In the second general election,
the province recorded a substantial 'No' vote (19.7 per cent) in a high
poll.[77] At the same time, the province remained under-represented at
the centre, to the extent that there were no longer any long-standing
Copperbelt leaders of national stature in either the Central Committee or Cabinet. Copperbelt M.P.s were now local rather than
national leaders, and there was a vacuum at the centre so far as the
Copperbelt was concerned. In the late 'seventies, therefore, the potential for political dissent on the Copperbelt went beyond the miners
and involved urban labour as a whole.

The dilemma that faced government in relation to labour had not
changed since independence. Government policies for economic recovery were unlikely to succeed without the support of organised
labour, and especially their acquiescence in a period of abstinence in
the interests of increased production. The party lacked the means,
however, to ensure that support. They argued that workers, as members of the party, must support party policy, notwithstanding the
hardships it might impose in the short term, and that labour leaders,
as members of the National Council, must ensure that they did. Thus,
when the National Council in 1975 made the reduction of subsidies
and the increase of prices a party policy, the Z.C.T.U. was considered
to share responsibility for its implementation.[78] Union leaders, on the
other hand, faced with their own constituency, insisted that they had
a responsibility to question party policy on behalf of their members
and denied that this was inconsistent with their membership of the
party.

It was this issue that lay at the centre of the growing tension
between labour and the party in the 'seventies. The first clash
occurred in 1975, when, after the Z.C.T.U. had attacked the price
increases, Kaunda reminded them that the decision on prices and
subsidies was also theirs, and that, as members of the party, they must
follow the party line:

The Z.C.T.U. as a people's organisation is also responsible to the party and comes under the discipline of the Party. It is the duty of the Z.C.T.U. to pursue the Party's programmes and to implement Party policies because the Party is supreme over the Z.C.T.U. and other national institutions.[79]

As with the M.P.s, however, the matter was not so easily resolved. Labour leaders did not derive their authority from U.N.I.P. but from labour, and they had an organisational base independent of the party. It was also the case that their own leadership was often in question within the unions, where they faced continuing problems of communication with the rank and file, and where head office frequently could not control the grass roots.[80] Nevertheless, union membership grew enormously in these years, so that by 1980 it was about 367,000 — double that of the party.[81] The Z.C.T.U. itself emerged as a more cohesive and articulate body. Under the leadership of its young chairman, Fred Chiluba, elected in 1974, and its Secretary General, Newstead Zimba, a trade unionist of considerable experience, it increasingly took issue with government policy on general economic grounds as well as in support of workers' demands.

Government's ability, not only to hold wage increases to a maximum of 5 per cent but also to impose higher prices for basic foodstuffs as it did in 1976 and 1978, has to be evaluated against the increased use of authoritarian measures to control those demands.[82] At the same time, the emergence of an articulate labour leadership, prepared to challenge government on major issues of economic policy, was a crucial aspect of dissent in the one-party state. Union leaders were not unaware of the magnitude of the economic crisis, nor unwilling to co-operate in the implementation of policies for recovery. There was in fact a good deal of effective consultation between labour and government at least until 1978.[83] In 1977, the National Council extended Z.C.T.U. representation to both District and Provincial Political and Development committees, suggesting increased recognition of its role in the party.[84] Nevertheless, labour leaders could not ignore the restlessness of their own constituents, and they were increasingly critical of government's handling of the economic situation. Their concerns were essentially the same as those raised in the parliamentary debate. They considered that much of the country's economic crisis could be attributed to government mismanagement, and they were not unsuccessful in their efforts to uncover corruption.[85] They approached economic policy as managers rather than as socialists, preferring the development of an efficient mixed economy rather than an inefficient state capitalism, if that would ensure greater employment opportunities for Zambians.[86] They were also cautious in relation to the implementation of industrial participatory democracy, lest it have an adverse effect on employment,[87] and in due course were accused of making common cause with the employers. They were 'social democrats' rather than radicals. Nevertheless, their criticism of party and government was less in defence of employers than in opposition to a development strategy that made greater demands upon low-income workers than upon the top, and which resulted in increased income inequality. Moreover, they justified their criticism on the grounds that the increasing income gap revealed 'a capitalist way of life which is opposed to the philosophy of humanism'.[89] Their case was for a wages and incomes policy that reflected workers' needs, and from 1978 they supported the demands for a wage increase, which lay at the heart of urban working-class discontent.[90]

The government was itself engaged from 1975 in an attempt to enunciate a wages and incomes policy that took into account the country's growing problem of unemployment, as well as changing economic conditions, and which would provide a basic strategy for the Third National Development Plan. In 1975, they had invited an International Labour Organisation (I.L.O.) mission to carry out a Basic Needs Survey,[91] and in 1978 engaged Professor Turner to make a second wages, incomes and prices report.[92] They were also sensitive to the growing problem of Zambia's poor, and in 1975 promised a new poverty datum line, which for low-income workers symbolised the wage question. Nevertheless, throughout the 'seventies the government also, as we have seen, enforced a 5 per cent limit on wage increases, and the 1978 I.M.F. Agreement resulted in a total freeze in the public sector.[93] Moreover, with the exception of the Mwanakatwe Report in 1975, which provided the most generous pay increases to the lowest-paid government employees, little had been done to reduce income inequality.[94] The I.L.O. report's recommendations for structural change were overtaken by the severe expenditure cuts of 1976, and the 20 per cent devaluation in July of that year, and no action appeared to be taken on them.[95] The Turner Report, completed in 1979, became the subject of fierce criticism, and the government recommendations for wage increases which emerged out of it were challenged by labour leaders as inadequate.[96] Moreover, the confusion over their implementation led to a considerable increase in industrial unrest in 1979.[97] The mood of labour, especially on the Copperbelt, was therefore uneasy at the beginning of 1980.

It was against this background that the confrontation between labour and the party occurred at the end of that year. In August 1980, the government introduced into Parliament legislation to provide for a new structure of decentralised administration.[98] The proposals had far-reaching implications for political participation in the one-party state as well as for government administration, and they came under severe scrutiny from M.P.s, in the face of which they were on the 21 August deferred at the government's request.[99] Two proposals in particular drew criticism. First, the method of election of the new District Councillors, which was confined to party members and which critics argued, not without justification, infringed the constitutional right of Zambian citizens to vote.[100] Second, on the Copperbelt the consequences of decentralisation included the integration of the mine townships into the urban local authorities, and therefore the merger of the mines' social and welfare services with those of the urban authorities. The miners' services were, however, superior to those provided by the local authorities, and miners had consistently rejected earlier proposals for integration, as recently as 1975.[101] It was not therefore surprising that the Mineworkers Union (M.U.Z.) now opposed the decentralisation proposals, or that the miners threatened to go on strike if they were imposed.[102] The Z.C.T.U. supported M.U.Z. on the basis not only of the adverse effects the new structure would have on the miners, but also on the ground that proposed decentralisation would result in a costly and cumbersome bureaucracy that the country could not afford.[103] Furthermore, they pointed out that it had not been discussed at the party's general conference.[104]

The subsequent clash grew out of that disagreement. The government rejected the Z.C.T.U. argument, and the party, notwithstanding the deferral of the legislation, proceeded with party elections in anticipation that the new administration would be introduced in due course. Both M.U.Z. and the Z.C.T.U. responded by prohibiting their officials from participating in those elections, and then by suspending the small number who subsequently did so.[105] The result was an acrimonious exchange between party and union leaders, and strong criticism by the National Council of M.U.Z. and Z.C.T.U. leaders for their alleged 'indiscipline'.[106] In December individual members of the Central Committee made biting public attacks on the labour leaders, including a threat that the party would crush its enemies as it had done in the past,[107] while the President himself made a powerful personal attack upon the chairman of the Z.C.T.U.[108] In the meantime, the government had backed down in the face of miners' opposition, and the legislation, when passed in December, included substantial amendments that effectively removed the threat to the miners of the loss of their own services.[109] Nevertheless, and despite Z.C.T.U.'s reinstatement of its suspended officials, in January the Central Committee first suspended and then expelled from the party seventeen M.U.Z. and Z.C.T.U. leaders.[110]

On 20 January, five thousand miners at Konkola mine in Chililabombwe stopped work in protest, and the rest of the mine labour force across the Copperbelt quickly followed in a strike that undoubtedly constituted the most serious industrial action that had faced the country since 1966.[111] It took place at a time not only of acute economic difficulty but also great political uncertainty, in the wake of the alleged coup attempt the previous October and with a treason trial pending.[112] It lasted eight days and resulted in considerable violence, culminating in police action on the 25th in Kitwe in which a fourteen-year-old schoolboy was shot dead, and in Mufulira on the 27th when three miners were seriously injured.[113]

The strike, which was undoubtedly spontaneous, reflected not only the miners' protest at the expulsion of their union leaders but their concern also for their livelihood at a time of great difficulty within the mining industry.[114] Politically, its significance went beyond the miners' determination to maintain their independence from the party, for it demonstrated a new cohesiveness in the labour movement in its confrontation with the party. In contrast to earlier years, on this occasion the Z.C.T.U. and M.U.Z. were firmly united in their mutual defence. The threat of a general strike seemed to become a reality when, first postal workers stopped work in support of the miners,[115] and then bank employees struck after their union chairman had been assaulted by local U.N.I.P. officials in an incident at the Lusaka party office.[116] The party was unable to handle the conflict, which was ultimately resolved by the combined efforts of Ministry of Labour officials and the union leaders themselves.[117] In the process, the labour leaders showed themselves demonstrably concerned to effect a reconciliation, and their readmission to the party at a special meeting of the National Council in April finally defused much of the remaining tension.[118] Nevertheless, they had demonstrated not only the power of the labour movement in the one-party state, but also the weakness of the party at the local level. The growth of dissent must also, therefore, be placed within the context of the party itself, and its own reaction to the one-party state.

The party and dissent

The restoration of the party was recognised by U.N.I.P.'s national leadership in 1973 as their first task in the one-party state.[119] The first step was the creation of a new party headquarters and an enlarged party machine. The Central Committee moved into an imposing eight-storey office block which they took over from two government departments, and the party was granted an annual K4m subsidy from Parliament, to be used primarily for party salaries.[120] A number of civil servants were seconded to the party, and party officials (to regional level) became members of a party service of permanent and pensionable officers with the same conditions as government servants.[121] Central Committee members toured the countryside to discuss organisation with regional officials.

The enlargement of the party at the centre was not followed, however, by mobilisation in the locality. The poor turn-out in local government elections in 1975, the low primary poll in 1978 and the limited participation in the party's own branch elections in 1977 and 1980, all demonstrated U.N.I.P.'s weakness at the grass-roots level.[122] Furthermore, although the higher polls in the 1978 general elections suggested some improvement in the party's capacity to mobilise the voters, they also registered a higher vote against the party.[123]

While U.N.I.P.'s decline at the local level had begun, as we have seen, in the earlier intra-party conflict in the multi-party state, in the one-party state it was compounded by the need to absorb the former opposition parties. Constitutionally, the party was now open to any Zambian who accepted the party's principles and programmes, and the Choma Declaration had assured former A.N.C. members a place in the one-party state. In both Southern and Western provinces, however, former A.N.C. supporters continually complained at the difficulties they faced in gaining admission to the party.[124] The problems that had begun in the course of the 1973 elections continued, so that both provinces, which had traditionally been 'weak' U.N.I.P. regions, remained so, in so far as the party failed to build a new mass organisation. On the Copperbelt, U.N.I.P.'s paid-up membership was no more than 9 per cent of the population, and the legacy of the U.P.P. could be detected in the continuing allegations of the presence of 'opposition' and 'dissident elements' within the party, and the suspicion and intense in-fighting that accompanied branch and constituency elections.[125] The continuing divisions within Bemba society exacerbated such rivalry, which was affected also by the continued ambivalence of the national leadership towards the return of the former U.P.P. leaders, and especially Kapwepwe, to the party.[126] The Copperbelt failed to retrieve its old pre-eminence in the party, and at the national level the result was the serious under-representation of urban Zambian society in the party and government, at a time of continuing urban population growth.

While the national leadership controlled recruitment to national office, the A.N.C.'s experience demonstrated the extent to which the absorption of former opposition followers at the grass roots was inhibited by local party control. Although in 1978 Nkumbula was also, like Kapwepwe, refused the right to contest the presidency, both he and other A.N.C. national leaders had found a place in Parliament and the party in 1973, and two of them by 1977 in the Cabinet itself.[127] At the local level, however, their followers encountered greater difficulties when U.N.I.P. officials resisted Central Committee instructions to open up branch and constituency membership to all comers.[128] The reasons related to the nature of U.N.I.P. itself. Party office at branch and constituency level continued, as in the past, to carry with it status, privilege and access to resources, even where those resources were no more than the use of party bicycles for business purposes.[129] It carried with it access to patronage, in a party where control had always been directly related to the distribution of such patronage. U.N.I.P. 'loyalists' were bound, therefore, to resist any challenge to that position, particularly in a region like Southern Province where former A.N.C. local level leaders were likely to have a greater support than they themselves enjoyed.[130] The problem went beyond the former A.N.C. and U.P.P. however, for it reflected the generally defensive reaction of U.N.I.P.'s 'old guard' at the local level to competition for office, and their efforts to manipulate recruitment in their own interest.

The result was a vacuum in the party structure below the district level with the resulting loss in communication and control. In the Northern Province in 1975 it could be said that 'party organisation at sub-branch and village level was for all practical purposes non-existent'.[131] Elections for party office between 1975 and 1980 made it clear that this was a more widespread situation. In 1977, many local level posts across the country were left unfilled for want of candidates, and many of those that were filled were unopposed.[132] In 1980, in the section, branch and constituency elections required under the new U.N.I.P. constitution adopted at the party's general conference in September 1978, the experience was similarly of very small polls, a large number of candidates elected unopposed, and a significant number of posts unfilled.[133] U.N.I.P. at the local level, therefore, had become a party with more leaders than followers.[134] In many areas branches consisted only of officials, while in others they existed only on paper.

The image of U.N.I.P. at the local level therefore became increasingly that of a small clique of political activists who were frequently, but by no means always, long-standing party loyalists whose experience stretched back to the nationalist struggle. They constituted an 'old guard' who continued to interpret the role of the party as in the past, when the emphasis had been on the control of distribution on the basis of party loyalty and the coercion, if necessary by force, of 'dissidents' and 'disloyal elements'.[135] Local party officials were also, however, still the marketeers and small traders who expected party protection and who were willing to assert their independence of the centre in their own interests, creating what the national leadership termed a 'crisis of discipline'.[136] U.N.I.P., moreover, be-

came increasingly vulnerable to criticism as a result of the appropria-
tion of party funds by local officials,[137] and of the actions of local
militants. What finally produced the danger of a general strike in
January 1981 was the assault of a trade-union leader by local party
officials in the local Lusaka party headquarters.[138]

The local government changes made with the decentralisation measures of 1980 and which amalgamated party and government institutions up to district level, are best understood as an attempt to overcome this structural weakness, since the party to all intents and
purposes took over local government. Existing local government
bodies (both rural and urban) and the district administration were now
merged into a new local administration, responsible to a District
Council consisting predominantly of party officials and chaired by the
District Governor. Central control was provided by the Central Committee's continued power of veto over candidates for party office, and
through the District Governor whose responsibility was directly to
the President. In this respect, the changes contributed to the further
centralism of control in the executive. At the local level, however, the
party made significant advances which gave it access to new resources. The party ward chairmen, elected by party members, now
became the District Councillors. Other council members included
the M.P.s and representatives of mass organizations and trade unions
operating in the district, and a Chief.[139] The council was, however, to
all intents and purposes, a party institution, with the potential for
control of government resources, and councillors received a monthly
stipend. The new councillors elected in the local party elections in
1980 were for the most part local political activists.[140]

At the national level, although this same fusion of party and government did not generally take place, after 1973 party supremacy was
also increasingly asserted *vis-à-vis* government. In this respect, the
most important structural change in the one-party state was the
creation of a full-time Central Committee, whose members would
not be members of Parliament or the Cabinet. Under the 1973 constitution, Central Committee and Cabinet became separate and distinct bodies, the only overlapping membership being the President,
who remained chairman of both, the Secretary General of the party
and the Prime Minister. Apart from these three offices dual membership was excluded. The party constitution made the Central Committee supreme on matters of policy, providing that in the event of
disagreement with the Cabinet the decision of the former should
prevail.[141] The Zambian constitution was, however, silent in this
issue, as it was on the question of party supremacy, so that the role of
the Central Committee immediately became a subject of debate
which led to the second assertion of party supremacy.

The controversy surrounding the Central Committee and its relationship to the Cabinet was central to the growth of dissent, so it is important to consider briefly the underlying issues. In the multi-party state, the dominant party had formed the government, and ministers, most of whom were also members of the Central Committee, had been chosen because of their position within the party. Their authority and their power had derived from their party support. In the one-party state, this was no longer to be so, and the composition of the two bodies in 1973 emphasised their different constituencies. In his choice of ministers, Kaunda now put the emphasis upon administrative and managerial experience. Eight of the ministers were former civil servants, one was the former General Secretary of the Z.C.T.U., and two were former university lecturers.[142] While he had carefully balanced provincial representation, he therefore also set up a Cabinet of younger men whose experience had been in administration rather than politics, and subsequent changes did not alter that image.[143] The first Cabinet thus included a strong managerial element.

The Central Committee, on the other hand, epitomised the political tradition. The senior members of that body all had lengthy parliamentary and ministerial experience behind them. They were also long-established nationalist politicians. Still comparatively young, they had been at the centre of politics for twenty years. The 'second rank' members were also, with one or two exceptions, long-serving party politicians. Subsequent changes in the membership removed some of U.N.I.P.'s oldest and most experienced leaders, but they did not alter its essential character.[144] The Central Committee thus represented the nationalist leaders of the independence struggle, shorn of the Bemba-speaking leaders who had withdrawn to the U.P.P. The press labelled them the 'so-called old guard'.[145] Nevertheless, it was that body which represented the party tradition and whose prime function was the protection of the party and party policy.

Initially, the Central Committee was at a disadvantage, since as a new body it lacked many of the resources required for policy-making. The apparent duplication of positions and the costs of a full-time party executive appeared unnecessary to many people. The Cabinet was a known and tried institution with which everyone was familiar, and in government circles as well as among the public there was an implicit assumption that it was the new Central Committee that was on trial.[146] The separation of the two bodies had, furthermore, taken the latter out of the process of government; its members did not now, as they had as ministers, receive Cabinet papers, and there was no formal mechanism for ensuring party association with government except through the offices of President, Secretary General and Prime Minister. It was against this background that, in the course of the first

Parliament, the Central Committee steadily asserted itself in both party and government, and in the process extended party supremacy and control.

In the party the Central Committee's power was not in doubt. The general conference, the supreme policy-making organ, met only once in five years, the National Council only twice (and after 1979 once) a year.[147] While the Central Committee's role was in the first place to supervise the implementation of policy laid down by these bodies, it was also expected to provide party leadership and thus to initiate policy, as well as being responsible for party organisation.[148] Its power within the party derived, however, from its control over party discipline at all levels (including ministers and Central Committee members themselves), its control over regional party officials, and above all its control over recruitment, exercised through its power of veto of all candidates for all elections, save those for the presidency and the Central Committee itself. The constitution provided, moreover, that the Central Committee should put forward the names of candidates for that body at the time of election, thus going a long way, as one commentator pointed out 'towards making the Central Committee a closed system free of outside influences'.[149]

The party constitution provided that in the President's absence the Secretary General should assume the functions of the office, and questions of status were all decided in favour of the Central Committee. The party headquarters rapidly reproduced the structure and arrangements of central government, particularly in the office of the Secretary General.[150] Status and bureaucratisation alone could not, however, ensure the authority of the Central Committee within the governmental system. Cabinet Ministers had the resources of the entire civil service behind them and the support of established institutions.[151] There was a potential for friction between the two bodies that was not dispelled by the creation of joint committees, which brought Cabinet Ministers into the party's policy-making process. At an early stage, therefore, the party turned its attention to the formalisation of part supremacy, and in 1975 a constitutional amendment made the supremacy of the Central Committee over the Cabinet explicit.[152]

At the same time, a succession of institutional changes gave practical effect to party dominance. First, the Central Committee increased its presence at provincial level with the appointment in 1974 of provincial political secretaries, and in 1976 by the transfer of eight members of the Central Committee itself to the provinces to work with the Cabinet Minister over whom they took precedence.[153] In 1979, when the latter post was abolished, the former assumed full charge of the province in what was now known as the office of the

Member of the Central Committee (M.C.C.).[154] By that date, most regional party officials were housed in the District Governor's office complex, and so identified more closely, if still unofficially, with the government administration.[155] Second, the members of the Central Committee extended their presence into the central government machine. In 1975, Kaunda appointed Elijah Mudenda, then a member of the Central Committee, as Prime Minister, and from that date membership of the two bodies became to all intents and purposes interchangeable.[156] In 1979, when Grey Zulu, senior politician and the party's first Secretary General, was appointed to the new post of Secretary of State for Defence and Security, created in the face of the country's worsening confrontation with Rhodesia, he remained a member of the Central Committee.[157] Finally, with the formation of the new government after the second general election, he placed all ministries, formally at least, under the supervision of the Central Committee, and nominated five of its senior sub-committee chairmen, who now assumed a position similar to that of a ministerial overlord, to Parliament as well.[158] In this way, he announced, he had achieved the 'fusion of party and government' and party supremacy.[159] Increasingly, however, it appeared that these changes had concentrated control in the hands of a small group of key senior members around the President.

The stature of the Cabinet appeared correspondingly to decline. In part, this was a consequence of the expansion of the new Prime Minister's Office, which reduced the weight of other ministries, whether that was intended or not. It was also in part a consequence of Kaunda's decision in 1979 to abolish the post of Provincial Cabinet Minister and so reduce the Cabinet's size. The changed position of the Cabinet, however, also reflected changes in its composition, as it progressively lost its most educated and experienced members.[160] New Cabinet Ministers in January 1979, in general had a good deal less experience at the national level than their predecessors, and were constituency rather than national figures when they took office. In addition, there was on the one hand an increase of 'political' over 'technocrat' appointments, and on the other the continued under-representation in ministerial ranks of urban constituencies.

The concentration of power in the hands of a Central Committee perceived to be unrepresentative of key regions in the country was a major element in the criticism of the party that accompanied the rise of dissent.[161] Hence, one of U.N.I.P.'s oldest and most respected nationalist leaders could, in 1980, doubt whether U.N.I.P. was a party of reconciliation in the one-party state.[162] Moreover, the confrontation between labour and the party in January 1981 revealed not only the weakness of local party structures, but also the growing ineffectiveness of the Central Committee, despite its increased power. The Central Committee was shown to be out of touch with the grass roots, apparently dependent upon local militants whom it could not control.[163] Tacit recognition of that weakness was reflected in Kaunda's changes in both Cabinet and Central Committee leadership in the wake of the crisis. His direct intervention in the dispute also highlighted the dominance of the presidential executive, and the extent to which party supremacy was sustained, not by the party, but the presidency.

The executive and the assertion of authority

The dominant institution in the one-party state was not the party but the presidency, in which resided enormous power. The Zambian constitution provided that supreme executive power was vested in the President, and in its exercise he must act in his own judgement.[164] He enjoyed wide powers of appointment, including both the Secretary General and the Prime Minister both of whom were responsible to him. As chairman of Z.I.M.C.O., (Zambia Industrial and Mining Corporation) he selected a large number of senior management and board members of the parastatal sector, over which he ultimately exercised control. Under the Preservation of Public Security Act, he enjoyed extensive powers to meet an emergency, including the right to detain without trial.[165]

Kaunda also derived great power from his position as president of the party. While ultimately dependent on the party for nomination and election, his position as the only leader with a national constituency meant that he occupied an essential unifying role which gave him a powerful leverage over the National Council. His position as Chairman of the Central Committee ensured him the dominant role in that body. As the appointment of Cabinet Ministers was his constitutional prerogative, so in practice the elected members of the Central Committee were essentially his choice; in addition, he had the constitutional right to appoint three additional members.[166] The appointment of the District Governor, the key party office at district level, was also a presidential prerogative, assuring him of an important channel of independent communication with, if not always control over, the party hierarchy at district level.

In the one-party state there also developed an increased ritual identification of leader and party, reflected, for example, in the official welcomes accorded the President on his return from abroad. Whereas in the past, Kaunda went to the party headquarters, the Central Committee now came to State House. State House rather than Freedom House had become the symbolic centre of the party, and demonstrations of party support for the President now took place there.[167] Moreover, the combined crises of foreign affairs and economic decline throughout the 'seventies further emphasised the presidency as the *locus* of power in the state. The successive stages of the southern African conflict highlighted the role of the President in foreign affairs, and the power derived from Kaunda's constitutional responsibility for defence and security was made explicit by his declaration of a full state of emergency at the height of the Angolan crisis in January 1976.[168] The growth of state capitalism enhanced executive control of the economy, and the economic crisis was met by increased presidential intervention in economic affairs.[169] In addition, increasing problems of management and administrative inefficiency on occasion provoked presidential intervention in day-to-day administration, most dramatically by his decision in November 1974, announced without prior warning, to transfer responsibility for the Mechanical Services Branch of the Public Works Department to the Zambian army.[170] The growth of corruption in turn led to the increased exercise of presidential power of dismissal, and to amendments to the Penal Code which further increased executive authority.[171]

Kaunda's style demonstrated not only the pre-eminence but also the autonomy of the Zambian President, not least by his customary announcements of major and minor policy decisions from State House, to be implemented by the ministry concerned 'in response to President Kaunda's directives'.[172] Presidential style, however, also associated the party with each policy pronouncement, thus ensuring formal party support and, in due course, each became party policy.[173] The most important policy proposals that emerged in this manner were those contained in what came to be known as Kaunda's 'Watershed Speech' to the National Council in June 1975. Those proposals included the abolition of freehold land tenure and private hospital services, and foreshadowed the end of private enterprise within the following five years; and although they did not provide any clear picture of the nature of the post-capitalist state, they subsequently remained the key official statement of U.N.I.P.'s strategy for a socialist and ultimately Humanist society.[174] Kaunda thus used his presidential role to introduce major policy initiatives in the name of the party, acknowledging also the extent to which they were his decisions alone.[175] The Watershed Speech also included significant and difficult economic decisions taken in response to the growing economic crisis, and especially the reduction of government subsidies and the consequent increase in the prices of basic foodstuffs. Presidential style thus also suggested a strategy of legitimising unpleasant but essential governmental decisions by party ratification, and this was borne out by the subsequent budget speech in 1976 when the Minister of Finance pointed out to the National Assembly that, 'During the sixth National Council meeting . . . Government was directed to reduce subsidies . . .'.[176]

At the same time, Kaunda appeared increasingly to gather control into his own hands. It was not only his style that emphasised the centrality of State House in the decision-making process, but also the exercise of executive power in grappling with the country's continuing economic crisis. Major economic decisions were made outside the departmental structure, most notably in relation to rural development. Thus the Rural Reconstruction programme in 1975 and the Operation Food programme in 1980 both emanated from State House.[177] In 1979, prior to the introduction of the new decentralised administration, provincial and district administration was transferred from the Ministry of Local Government, which at that stage was abolished, first to the office of the President and then to the Prime Minister.[178] And in 1980 the National Commission for Development Planning was placed directly under presidential charge 'because economics must have top priority'.[179] At the same time, ministerial reorganisations concentrated governmental as well as political control increasingly in the hands of his three senior advisers, the Prime Minister, the Secretary General and (from 1978) the Secretary of State for Defence. The result was the steady concentration of power over decision-making in the central organs of the executive.

The costs, in institutional terms, were considerable. The concentration of decision-making in the top echelons of the executive contributed directly to the decline in administrative capacity, to which parliamentary debate increasingly drew attention. Presidential dominance inhibited collective and ministerial responsibility and effective inter-departmental co-ordination, which was further reduced by frequent movement of senior personnel. Government lost, or could not efficiently use, a number of the small pool of experienced administrators previously available to it. Bureaucratic inefficiency, not least because of the failure of communication, and the withdrawal of important policy areas from public scrutiny were the consequences.[180] The emphasis on political control equally inhibited bureaucratic performance at a time when morale was already sapped by the economic recession, and a growing tendency emerged for officials to wait for instructions from above, as Kaunda himself acknowledged in 1977.[181] The increased incidence of corruption in the public service was also in part a consequence of the decline in bureaucratic controls. Hence, at a time when the concentration of power in the executive ultimately increased its dependence on the bureaucracy, the resulting inefficiency frustrated and demoralised a growing number of civil servants.[182] Finally, presidential policy did not resolve Zambia's economic difficulties, which were more acute in 1980 than at any previous time, although the end of the Zimbabwe war had removed what had hitherto been accepted as the major constraint upon re-covery.[183] The increase of executive dominance meant, therefore, that the failure of policy now focused criticism on the presidency itself. Thus a succession of policy failures and the continuing economic decline produced a crisis of confidence which Kaunda could diffuse only by concessions and control only by the greater assertion of executive power.

The presidential assertion of party supremacy paradoxically in-hibited reform of the party itself. Kaunda undoubtedly used his power and influence over these years to prevent any change in the party's official commitment to socialist objectives. Moreover, certain key reforms, especially those in land tenure, were effected in this period which could provide a basis for subsequent socialist reform.[184] But his insistence upon the party as the basis of his support at a time when the party had declined, made him ultimately dependent upon the petty bourgeois and business class elements who now occupied party office, and who were unlikely to act as agents of socialist reform. The continued failure of the local party organisation forced him back on his centrally appointed officials to secure his control in the districts; but this in turn made him subject to a party bureaucracy concerned with upward mobility and access to office.[185] Communication be-tween the centre and locality was weakened as a result. Party control thus depended, in the final resort, upon presidential power over appointments and patronage, which subjected him to the pressures and demands not only of individuals but also of provincial and re-gional interests. This was reflected in the renewed emphasis upon equal provincial representation in the national party institutions, and by the change in the method of election of the party president in 1979, when his nomination was made dependent on equal sponsorship from all provinces.[186]

Kaunda's position over these years was unenviable. The country faced its most acute crisis since independence, both at home and abroad. He was fully aware of the deficiencies of the party organisa-tion and of the weakness of the party machine.[187] His policies did not enjoy the full support of either his Cabinet or his Central Committee, as several reshuffles made apparent.[188] On successive occasions during the Zimbabwe war, there were rumours of army disaffection, and Kaunda indoubtedly felt it necessary to include army leaders in the central government.[189] The core group of Central Committee mem-bers who occupied the most influential positions around him acted essentially as individuals, and their influence tended to divide rather than unite the party.[190] While the one-party state had eliminated the threat of fragmentation, it had not removed the sectional interests that had hitherto fought for dominance and which still had to be accommodated within the party. Corruption, which increased as the country became more subject to shortages, and while most material advantage was still linked to political power, did not bypass Cabinet Ministers or Central Committee members, as successive parliamentary and other inquiries made plain.[191] From 1975 the party headquarters was increasingly subject to charges of inefficiency and corruption, and Kaunda's extraordinary outburst against some of those he subsequently suspended suggested the depth of his frustration and concern.[192] By 1978 he himself acknowledged the failure of the Leadership Code when he suggested the possibility of extending civil service general orders to cover politicians, acknowledging thereby the weakness of party and ideology as a basis for a code of conduct.[193]

Kaunda's assertion of presidential power was thus his response to the growth of dissent at a time of acute crisis, and which he saw as a threat to the party he insisted was the one national institution that could represent all Zambians.[194] The difficulty was, however, that in 1981 the one-party state had not yet found a way to absorb the many new social forces and achieve a consensus. Thus the assertion of party supremacy and the maintenance of party dominance required the use of presidential power, and the extension of control. At the same time, he defined the parameters of legitimate opposition in such a way as to exclude, effectively, a challenge to the executive.

Notes

1 This chapter is based on research carried out while the writer was resident in Zambia until the middle of 1975, and on subsequent return visits in 1976, 1980 and 1981.

2 For a brief résumé of the alleged coup, see *Africa Confidential*, 22, 22, 28 Oct. 1981. We do not discuss it here, because the trial was still in progress when this chapter was written. It came to an end in September 1982 when ten of the defendants were found guilty of treason. Seven were sentenced to death. At the time of going to press appeals were still pending.

3 For Zambia's foreign policy and the development of the southern African conflict, see also Douglas G. Anglin and Timothy C. Shaw, *Zambia's Foreign Policy: Studies in Diplomacy and Dependence*, Westview Special Studies in Africa (Boulder,Colorado, 1979). For the Angolan and Mozambique wars and their effect on Zambia, the best source is C. Legum (ed.), *Africa Contemporary Record 1969–70 to 1975.*

4 *Ibid.*, for an excellent source. For the earlier period see Richard L. Sklar, 'Zambia's Response to the Rhodesian Unilateral Declaration of Independence', Tordoff (ed.) (1974), *op.cit.*

5 See especially, Robin Hallett, 'The South African Intervention in Angola, 1975–76', *African Affairs*, 77, 308 (1978).

6 *Africa Contemporary Record* 1978–80. Also *Africa Research Bulletin* 1977–80, Political, Social and Cultural Series.

7 *Times of Zambia*, 29 Jan. 1976; Anglin and Shaw, *op.cit.*

8 From 1970 defence spending was included in Constitutional and Statutory Expenditure, and not therefore subject to public scrutiny. It is difficult, therefore, to give figures for this increase.

9 Sklar, *op.cit.*

10 Z.I.S. *Background* 19/1978, 17th Oct. 1978, Press Conference by President K. D. Kaunda on the Reopening of the Southern Route.

11 Bank of Zambia, Report, 1973–1980, *passim*.
    See also *Times of Zambia*, 21 Jan. 1974; *Financial Times*, 15 Dec. 1977; *Economist*, 18 Mar. 1978.

12 Bank of Zambia, Report, 1980, p. 31.

13 *Ibid*; *Financial Times*, 20 Feb. 1981; *Observer*, 18 Oct. 1981.

14 Bank of Zambia, Report, 1980, p. 52.

15 Robert Chambers and Hans Singer, *Poverty, Malnutrition and Food in Zambia*, Country Study for World Development Report IV, University of Sussex, 3 Nov. 1980.

16 *Ibid*; see also Rene Dumont and Marie France Mottin, *Towards Another Development in Rural Zambia* (Lusaka, 1979, mimeo).

17 *Africa Contemporary Record* 1978–79, B 944–.

18 See below p. 104.

19 See above, Chapter 1.

20 Fabian J.M. Maimbo and James Fry, 'An Investigation into the Change in the Terms of Trade Between the Rural and Urban Sectors of Zambia', *African Social Research*, 12 (1971), University of Zambia, Institute for African Studies. See also the I.L.O., *Narrowing the Gaps*, 1977, *op.cit.*

21 Stephen Quick, 'Bureaucracy and Rural Socialism in Zambia', *Journal of Modern African Studies*, 15, 3 (1977).

22 See William Tordoff and Robert Molteno, 'Parliament' in Tordoff (ed.) (1974), *op.cit.* for a study of the National Assembly in the multi-party system.

23 See above, Chapter 3.

24 *Chona Report*, paras. 69–70.

25 *Daily Parliamentary Debates*, 22 Jan. 1974, col. 337.

26 See William Tordoff, 'Residual Legislatures in Tanzania and Zambia', *The Journal of Commonwealth and Comparative Politics*, XV, 3 (1977).

27 27 prospective candidates were vetoed in the second general election in December 1978, including 4 of the most articulate on the backbench. See Chapter 3 above. Maipose, *op.cit.*; also Elections Office, Press Release, 8 Nov. 1978.

28 U.N.I.P. *Constitution*, 1973, Article 46; *Daily Parliamentary Debates*, 14 Mar. 1974, col. 2923–6.

29 *Ibid*.

30 *Ibid*.

31   National Council Resolution 4, *Deliberations, Proceedings and Resolutions of the Fourth National Council*, Lusaka, 20–5 Apr. 1974. See also, address by H.E. Dr. K.D. Kaunda at the opening of the National Council, Lusaka, 20 Apr. 1974.

32   'The "Watershed" Speech', *op.cit. Progress Report*, December 1975. Presented to the National Council Meeting on 8 Dec. 1975, by the Secretary-General of the Party, Hon. A.G. Zulu, M.C.C., p. 7–8.

33   See *Africa Contemporary Record*, 1976–77; *African Research Bulletin*, 1–31 March 1979, 5191B; *Times of Zambia*, 12 Sept. 1979.

34   *Daily Parliamentary Debates*, 14 July and 2 Aug. 1974.

35   This criticism runs consistently through the debate. See, for example, *Daily Parliamentary Debates*, 17 Mar. 1978, col. 3315, when in response to the Minister of Finance's announcement of the I.M.F. Agreement backbenchers asked why government had not earlier taken the measures to which they had now agreed.

36   Nor, apparently, did all senior civil servants take this committee seriously. See, for example, *Daily Parliamentary Debates*, 2 Aug. 1978, cols. 35–7.

37   *Report of the Committee on Parastatal Bodies* for the Fifth Session of the Third National Assembly, appointed on 31 Jan. 1978. See also *Times of Zambia*, 9 Sept. 1978, and the *Africa Contemporary Record* 1979–80. Kaunda's reorganization of Z.I.M.C.O. in 1979 flowed from that report.

38   Again this became a consistent line of attack. See, for example, *Daily Parliamentary Debates*, 30 Jan. 1975, and 6 and 7 Feb. 1980.

39   For example, on education, some M.P.s demanded 'more socialism', others less. See *Daily Parliamentary Debates*, 22 Jan. and 13 Mar. 1975.

40   *Ibid.*, 20 Feb. 1975, col. 1576.

41   *Times of Zambia*, 6 Feb. 1976.

42   *The Report of the Special Parliamentary Select Committee* appointed on 14 Oct. 1977, (Lusaka, Government Printer, no date but published December 1977).

43   *Times of Zambia*, 28 Apr. 1981. It was above all the parliamentary debate which brought the charge of opposition on M.P.s at this stage.

44   *Daily Parliamentary Debates*, 14 Mar. 1974, cols. 293–6. Also 31 July 1974 and 22 Jan. 1975 col. 144. See also distribution of office in Central Committee and Cabinet.

45   *Ibid.*, 22 Jan. 1975, col. 144.

46   For example, *ibid.*, 16 Feb. 1979. And see above, Chapter 3.

47   Expressed more in private conversation than public debate until Parliament took up the issue.

48   Report of the Special Parliamentary Select Committee, *op.cit.*

49   See T. Southall, 'Zambia: Class Formation and Government Policy in the 1970s', *Journal of Southern African Studies*, 7, 1 (1980).

50   Report, 1977, *op. cit.*, p. 11 and 13.

51   *Ibid.*, p. 13.

52   *Ibid.*, appendix for list of those who gave oral or written evidence to the committee.

53 *Daily Parliamentary Debates*, 7 Feb. 1980. The same minister, while a minister of state, had earlier attacked lazy party officials. *Ibid.*, 2 Dec. 1974.

54 Regulation 5 of the Leadership Code provided that leaders might apply for exemption and continue in public office while retaining private business interests by not taking a salary. See Program Report of the Central Committee, 1973–78, no date but 1978, p. 29. Also above, Chapter 3.

55 Industrial Development Act, 1977 Act, No. 18. See Robert L. Curry Jnr., 'Zambia's Economic Crisis: A Challenge to Budgetary Politics', *Journal of African Studies* (UCLA), 6, 4 (1979–80), pp. 213–17.

56 Progress Report, 1973–78, Central Committee.

57 Put most powerfully by Elias Chipimo at a Law Society Dinner on the Copperbelt in April 1980, and reproduced in *The National Mirror*, 99, 25 April–8 May 1980. But see also Francis Nkhomo, M.P. for Matero, *Daily Parliamentary Debates*, 21 Aug. 1980, col. 1144–56. Neither in fact criticised the President.

58 *Marxism, Humanism and Christianity*, published by and signed by the Zambia Episcopal Conference, the Christian Council of Zambia and the Zambian Evangelical Fellowship, August 1979.

59 *Sunday Times of Zambia*, 1 Feb. 1981.

60 Hence the concern at the impact of Elias Chipimo's speech referred to above.

61 In the first Parliament David Mwila, President of M.U.Z., represented Nkana, and in the second Newstead Zimba, Secretary General of the Z.C.T.U., represented Chifubu, both Copperbelt constituencies. Other Copperbelt M.P.'s also raised labour and trade-union issues. See, for example, *Daily Parliamentary Debates*, 5 Feb. 1975, cols, 798–800, for Stephen Malama, M.P. for Wusakile, on miners' needs.

62 Bank of Zambia, Report, 1980, p. 52; Chambers and Singer, *op. cit.*, p. 28; Curry, *op. cit.*

63 Bank of Zambia, Report, 1980, Table 8.1.

64 *Guardian*, 31 Mar. 1976; *Financial Times*, 15 Dec. 1977; *Zambia Daily Mail*, 25 Dec. 1980; *Daily Parliamentary Debates*, 17 Mar. 1978, col. 3303.

65 Report of the Committee on Parastatal Bodies, 1978, p. 16.

66 *Daily Parliamentary Debates*, 8 Feb. 1978, col. 1132.

67 *Ibid.* The decision to reorganise N.A.M.B.O.A.R.D., for example, in an attempt to improve the marketing organisation, meant at the end of 1980, 8,000 employees faced the threat of being laid off between January and March 1981. See *Zambia Daily Mail*, 27 Dec. 1980.

. 68 See Kaunda's address to the emergency session of Parliament in October 1977. *Daily Parliamentary Debates*, 14 Oct. 1977.

69 *Monthly Digest of Statistics*, XVI, 4–9 (1980), p. 45. For price increases in selected commodities 1972–80, see *ibid.*, Table 64, p. 58.

70 *Daily Parliamentary Debates*, 17 Mar. 1978, cols. 3297–3326. Zambian experience with the I.M.F. over this period was not dissimilar from that of other third world states, on which see *Development Dialogue*, 1980 No. 2.

71 *The Year Ahead*, Zambia Information Services, (Lusaka, Government Printer, n.d. but 1976).
72 *Ibid.*
73 Bank of Zambia, Report, 1980, p7. *Economist*, 25 Mar. 1978.
74 *Times of Zambia*, 18–25 Nov. 1974; *Daily Parliamentary Debates*, 6 Dec. 1974, cols. 248–66.
75 *Times of Zambia*, 4 Apr. 1975.
76 See Chapter 3 above and Chapter 5 below.
77 *Presidential and Parliamentary General Elections Results, 1978*, Elections Office, Lusaka, May 1979.
78 Z.I.S. Background 40/75. Address by H.E. The President to a Meeting of the Supreme Council of the Z.C.T.U. at State House, Sunday 10 August 1975.
79 *Ibid.*
80 See, for example, *Times of Zambia*, 6 Aug. 1975 for a winding-drivers strike at Ndola Copper Refinery and a vote of no confidence in the M.U.Z. President, David Mwila.
81 *Africa Confidential*, 22, 22, (1981), using figures given by the Z.C.T.U., in the *Zambia Daily Mail*, 29 Dec. 1980.
82 Southall, *op.cit*; *Times of Zambia*, 8 Feb. 1980; *Zambia Daily Mail*, 30 Oct. 1980.
83 *Daily Parliamentary Debates*, 28 Jan. 1978, col. 644.
84 Progress Report, 1973–78 by the Central Committee.
85 Thus it was the Zambian Railways African Workers Union (Z.R.A.W.U.) that made the first call for an inquiry into the railways corporation which resulted in a commission that substantiated all the charges they had originally made. See Commission of Inquiry into the Affairs of the Zambian Railways, Report, March 1978 (The Munpanshya Report), Lusaka, Government Printer, 1978.
86 *New African*, No. 172, Jan. 1982.
87 *African Contemporary Record*, 1976–77, B410.
88 *Ibid.*
89 *Times of Zambia*, 18 Dec. 1980; see also *Times of Zambia*, 15 Sept. 1975, on a proposed compulsory savings scheme; *ibid.*, 11 May 1975 for criticism of the failure to implement the Leadership Code; also, *Africa Contemporary Record*, 1979–80, B451–2.
90 *Daily Parliamentary Debates*, 8 Feb. 1978, Col. 1131.
91 I.L.O., *Narrowing the Gaps, op.cit.*
92 He had carried out the first inquiry in 1969.
93 Southall, *op.cit.*
94 Report of the Commission of Inquiry into the Salaries, Salary Structures and Conditions of Service . . ., Vol. I, The Public Services and the Parastatal Sector, Lusaka, Government Printer, 1975.
95 I.L.O. *Report*, p. 38; Bank of Zambia, Report, 1976 and 1977.
96 *African Contemporary Record*, 1979–80, B946.
97 *Ibid.*; *Times of Zambia*, 9 Feb. 1980; *Zambia Daily Mail*, 29 Dec. 1980.

98 *The Local Administration Act 1980*, No. 15 of 1980. See *Daily Parliamentary Debates*, 14 Aug. 1980, and 19–21 Aug. 1980. We consider this further below with the discussion of party supremacy.

99 See *Daily Parliamentary Debates*, 14–21 Aug. 1980.

100 Elections for the ward chairman were indirect. They began at the section level at which all party members were entitled to vote for a member of the Branch Council, which formed an Electoral College for the ward council, which in turn elected the ward chairman. See U.N.I.P. *Constitution* (1979), s31–34, and U.N.I.P. Regulations.

101 *Times of Zambia*, 25 Aug. 1975.

102 *Zambia Daily Mail*, 22 Sept. 1980.

103 *Zambia Daily Mail*, 30 Sept. 1980. It was proposed to pay monthly salaries to Councillors. The Z.C.T.U. estimated that for 67 Councils with an average of 20 full-time Councillors paid at K400 a month, the bill would be K536,000 a month.

104 *Ibid.*

105 *Times of Zambia*, 18–22 Oct., 3 Nov. and 30 Dec. 1980.

106 *Ibid.*, 4 Nov. 1980.

107 *Times of Zambia*, *Ibid.*, 30 and 31 Dec. 1980, and 7 Jan. 1981.

108 *Ibid.*, 12 Jan. 1981.

109 *Daily Parliamentary Debates*, 2 Dec. 1980.

110 *Times of Zambia*, 10 and 17 Jan. 1981.

111 This summary account is based on a close reading of the Zambian press, and of the subsequent parliamentary debates, as well as on interviews with government and other officials after the event.

112 *Africa Confidential*, 22, 22, (1981).

113 *Sunday Times of Zambia*, 25 Jan. 1981 and *Times of Zambia*, 26 Jan. 1981. The extent of police action and the use of force against the miners was subsequently a matter of dispute. See *Daily Parliamentary Debates*, 6 Feb. 1981, Cols. 1002–28. But see also *Times of Zambia*, 2, 3 and 4 Feb. 1981, which suggested the Minister of Labour's own concern.

114 See *Times of Zambia*, 24 Jan. 1981 for a circular distributed at Roan. At the time of their expulsion, M.U.Z. was engaged in negotiations with the companies over incentive bonuses, and miners were obviously concerned at the implications of the expulsions for these negotiations. The mine township services were also of great importance to miners whose standard of living had been very adversely effected by the economic situation.

115 *Times of Zambia*, 24 Jan. 1981. One of the Z.C.T.U. officials expelled from U.N.I.P. was the postal union leader.

116 *Times of Zambia*, 24 Jan. 1981.

117 Interview, *Sunday Times of Zambia*, 1 Feb. 1981.

118 *Times of Zambia*, 16 Feb., 24 Apr. and 9 May 1981.

119 See, for example, Deliberations, Proceedings and Resolutions of the Fourth National Council . . ., 20–25 April 1974.

120 *Daily Parliamentary Debates*, 12 Feb. 1974, cols. 1316–22.

121 *U.N.I.P.* Paper No. 1 of 1978.

122   See, for the 1975 local government elections *Central Committee Report 1973–78*, p. 19, and *Times of Zambia*, 12 Sept. 1975; for the 1978 election, Chapter 2 above, and for the party elections, *Financial Times*, 15 Dec. 1977and *Times of Zambia*, February–March 1980.

123   See above, Chapter 2.

124   See, for example, *Times of Zambia*, 31 Aug. and 17 Sept. 1973, 20 Feb. and 5 Apr. 1974, 14 Mar. and 12 May 1975; *Daily Parliamentary Debates*, 6 Feb. 1980.

125   For example, *Times of Zambia*, August 1974.

126   *Ibid*, 3 Jan. 1973, 8 Sept. and 12 Oct. 1974; Zambia Information Services, Press Release 25/1977, 9 Sept. 1977.

127   6 of the 16 Southern Province M.P.s in 1973 were former A.N.C., including Nkumbula himself, as well as 2 from Western Province. Nalumino Mundia won a by-election following his release from detention in late 1974, was made a Cabinet Minister in 1977 (for North-Western Province) a member of Central Committee in 1978 and in 1981 Prime Minister. Mungoni Liso, Deputy President of A.N.C., was appointed to the Central Committee in December 1973, and Mr. Mufaya Mumbuna, Western Province A.N.C. veteran who won his seat in both 1973 and 1978, was made a minister in 1976.

128   For example, *Times of Zambia*, 12 Oct. 1974.

129   *Times of Zambia*, 10 Jan. 1981, reported that defeated party officials in Kabwe Rural had refused to surrender the party bicycles which they used to ferry charcoal and for other personal businesses.

130   See Harry Nkumbula's summing up of the situation in *Daily Parliamentary Debates*, 7 Feb. 1974, cols. 511–12.

131   Michael Bratton, *The Local Politics of Rural Development: Peasant and Party-State in Zambia* (Hanover, University of New England Press, 1980).

132   *Financial Times*, 15 Dec. 1977.

133   While the Elections Office conducted these elections, their primary concern was with the office of ward chairman, and it was this result that had to be forwarded to the office. Hence no complete results of these elections are available, and it is impossible to tell how many people voted. The Elections Office estimate was of 143,000. However, the newspaper reports indicated that in general the poll was very small. See, for example, *Zambia Daily Mail*, 10–16, 22 and 23 Oct. 1980.

134   Morris Szeftel, 'The Political Process in Post-Colonial Zambia: the Structural Basis of Factional Conflict', *The Evolving Structure of Zambian Society*, Proceedings of a Seminar held in the Centre of African Studies, University of Edinburgh, 1980, p. 237. *Times of Zambia*, 7 Jan. 1981, suggested that Lusaka region had 46,500 leaders for a population of 500,000, spread among 3,470 sections and 347 branches.

135   Ian Scott, 'Party Functions and Capabilities: The Local Level U.N.I.P. Organization during the First Zambian Republic (1964–1973)', *African Social Research*, 22, (1976). This remains relevant for the 'seventies. See Bratton, *op.cit*. For public comment, see *Times of Zambia*, 20 Feb., 5 Apr. and 16 May 1974.

136   As, for example, in 1974 when the urban opposition to increase con-
      sumer prices was led by local U.N.I.P. officials. See also, for example,
      Zambia Daily Mail, 22 Sept. 1980, for conflict between Central Com-
      mittee and the Choma (Southern Province) marketeers over prices.
137   For example, *Zambia Daily Mail*, 5 Sept. 1980, for corruption in Living-
      stone.
138   *Times of Zambia*, 24 Jan. 1981.
139   The Local Administration Act 1980, No. 15 of 1980.
140   Early admonitions by, *inter alia*, the Prime Minister, against party offic-
      ials abusing their official position, suggested moreover the importance of
      this increase in local patronage. *Zambia Daily Mail*, 2 May 1981; *Times
      of Zambia*, 28 Apr. 1981.
141   U.N.I.P. *Constitution*, (1973) 12/3.
142   For the membership of the Cabinet appointed in December 1973, see
      Zambian Information Services, Background 137/73, 10 December 1973,
      Statement by H.E. the President Dr. K.D. Kaunda . . . announcing the
      new government.
143   When Mr. Andrew Kashita, a former civil servant, appointed Minister of
      Mines in 1973, was dismissed from office in 1976, Mr. James Mapoma,
      also a former civil servant was brought into the Cabinet. *Times of
      Zambia*, 22 Jan. 1976.
144   Mungoni Liso, former A.N.L. Deputy President, became a member of the
      Central Committee in December 1973 to replace Mainza Chona, who
      became Prime Minister. In May 1975 Mr. Mudenda replaced Chona as
      P.M. and two Cabinet Ministers were moved to the Central Committee.
      Mr. Jethro Mutti resigned in May 1975 and Mr. Vernon Mwaanga in
      January 1976, when Mr. Sikota Wina was dismissed. See *Times of
      Zambia*, 14 Dec. 1973, 25 May 1975, Z.I.S. Press Release No. 11/1976, 2
      Jan. 1976.
145   *Sunday Times of Zambia*, 16 Dec. 1973.
146   This view, heard frequently in the years 1973–75, still prevailed in 1977.
      See Report of the Special Parliamentary Select Committee, 1977, *op.cit.*
147   U.N.I.P. *Constitution*, (1979) Art. 44, (1), (2) and Art. 46.
148   *Ibid*, Art. 54.
149   David Gwynn Morgan, 'Zambia's One Party State Constitution', *op.cit.*
150   How far there was a conscious attempt to replicate the government
      administration it is difficult to say. Certainly a visitor to the office of the
      Secretary General who was familiar with the Cabinet office would be
      struck by the similarity of office arrangements, including the guard and
      the barriers that had to be passed.
151   See, for example *Sunday Times of Zambia*, 19 Jan. 1975 and *Times of
      Zambia*, 20 Jan. 1975, for a clash between the Copperbelt Minister and a
      visiting member of the Central Committee who suggested publically
      that the provincial party machine required drastic reorganization.
152   Constitution of Zambia (Amendment) Act 1975. Act No. 22 of 1975,
      Sections 9–12. Gazette Supplement, 29 Dec. 1975.

153   *Times of Zambia*, 7 May 1974; Zambia Information Services Press Release 10/76, 28 Jan. 1976.

154   Zambia Information Services, *Background*, 1/79, 2 Jan. 1979.

155   Report of the Central Committee 1973–78, p. 29.

156   Thus when Fine Liboma was appointed to the Central Committee in 1975 he retained his parliamentary seat for Mulobezi. In 1978, before becoming Prime Minister, Daniel Lisulo was M.C.C. for Central Province, Deputy Chairman of the Constitutional, Political, Legal and Foreign Affairs Sub-Committee of the Central Committee and Minister for Legal Affairs and Attorney-General (*Africa Research Bulletin*, Political, Social and Cultural Series, June 1–30, 1978, **4880**). In 1981, when Mr. Maxwell Beyani, M.P. and minister of state, moved on to the Central Committee, he retained his parliamentary seat (*Times of Zambia*, 19 Feb. 1981).

157   Zambia Information Services, *Background* 1/79, 2 Jan. 1979. Act No. 10 of 1980, Constitution of Zambia (Amendment) Act 1980, *Gazette Supplement*, 29 Sept. 1980.

158   Zambia Information Services *Background* 1/79, 2 Jan. 1979.

159   *Ibid*. Also *Africa Research Bulletin*, Jan. 1–31 1979, 5121 C.

160   Thus, for example, in 1976 Andrew Kashita was dismissed, in 1978 John Mwanakatwe decided to retire, and in 1980 Alex Chikwanda also retired.

161   See above, page 91.

162   *Daily Parliamentary Debates*, 6 Feb. 1980, col. 1260. The leader was Dingiswayo Banda.

163   *Sunday Times of Zambia*, 2 Jan. 1981, carried a powerful condemnation of the Central Committee for its apparent tacit acquiescence in the beating up of the trade-union leader discussed above.

164   Morgan, *op.cit*.

165   Preservation of Public Security Act, cap. 106.

166   U.N.I.P. *Constitution*, Art. 49. He was also empowered to appoint up to 6 advisers to each sub-committee.

167   See, for example, *Times of Zambia*, 9 Mar., 9 July and 2 Dec. 1974; 30 Jan. and 9 May 1975.

168   *Times of Zambia*, 29 Jan. 1976. Although a State of Emergency had existed in Zambia since 1965, Kaunda had not used his emergency powers to the full. He indicated now that he was prepared to do so.

169   For example, the Rural Reconstruction Programme on which see *Daily Parliamentary Debates*, 17 Jan. 1975, col. 11 *et seq*; on the Operation Food Programme, see *Times of Zambia*, 28 Apr. 1981.

170   *Sunday Times of Zambia*, 4 and 10 Nov. 1974.

171   On dismissals see, for example, *Times of Zambia*, 20 Feb. 1979. On the penal code, see especially *Daily Parliamentary Debates*, 22 Aug. 1980, col. 1181–321, for debate on Corrupt Practices Bill 1980.

172   For example, *Times of Zambia*, 1 Sept. 1973, 6 July 1974 and 24 Jan. 1979.

173   See, for example, the Resolutions of the National Council, June 1975 (printed in Progress Report, December 1975), presented to the National Council Meeting on 8 Dec. 1974) and compare with 'The "Watershed"

Speech', *op.cit.* See also *Orientation to Consumption versus Production*, speech by H.E. the President, Dr. K.D. Kaunda, at the opening of the 10th National Council, 27–30 June 1977.

174 'The "Watershed" Speech', *op.cit.*

175 See *ibid*, p. 33, for his comment that he had not discussed his proposals for changes to the media with either the member of the Central Committee or the minister concerned.

176 *Daily Parliamentary Debates*, 30 Jan. 1976. In this respect it is noteworthy that the reduction of government subsidies in 1975 and, in 1980, the merger of mine township services with the local authorities — two steps necessary for a more equal access for urban and rural society — were both originally announced in this way.

177 See above, footnote 169.

178 Zambia Information Services, Background 1/1979; Gazette Notice No. 186 of 1981, *Government Gazette*, XVII, 21, (1981).

179 *Blueprint for Economic Development*, 1979, p. 45.

180 As in the case of the Rural Reconstruction Programme, which came under the Zambia National Service and so the Ministry of Defence. See *Financial Times*, 15 Dec. 1977.

181 *A New Economic Take-Off*, *op.cit.*, pp. 14–5.

182 See, for example, *Daily Parliamentary Debates*, 21 Aug. 1980, col. 1144–56. See also *Sunday Times of Zambia*, 8 Feb. 1981.

183 See *Financial Times*, 21 Feb. 1981.

184 *Times of Zambia*, 15 July 1975; The Land (Conversion of Titles) Act, 1975.

185 See Roy Lewis, 'Kenneth Kaunda', *Round Table*, July 1976, for an interesting comment on the relationship between Kaunda and the party.

186 U.N.I.P. *Constitution*, February 1979.

187 As successive speeches to the National Council made clear. See, for example, 'The "Watershed" Speech', 1975, or his address to the National Council, April 1974.

188 See, for example, *Times of Zambia*, 22 Jan. 1975 and 26 Apr. 1977.

189 *Economist*, 4 Mar. and 18 Nov. 1978.

190 *Times of Zambia*, 24 Jan. 1975.

191 For example, Report on Parastatals, 1978, *op.cit.*; *Mumpanshya Report*, *op. cit.*

192 *Times of Zambia*, 25 Dec. 1979.

193 *Ibid.*, 9 Sept. 1978.

194 'The "Watershed" Speech', *op. cit.*, p. 50; *The National Mirror*, 22 Apr.–14 May 1980. Also Z.I.S. 52/80 and *Times of Zambia*, 22 Apr. 1980; see *A New Economic Take-Off* in which, in reply to parliamentary criticism of U.N.I.P., he insisted: 'We cannot destroy the Party and survive . . . Remove U.N.I.P., there is going to be no peace in Zambia' (p. 18). Z.I.S., Background 40/75, *op.cit.*

Part two

Responses to political change: centre and locality and the transition to the one-party state

Politics in an African urban setting: the role of the Copperbelt in the transition to the one-party state 1964–73

Introduction

In this essay we look at political conflict in the urban industrial society of the Copperbelt and its influence upon the transition to the one-party state.[1] Zambia is today one of Africa's most urbanised societies, with an estimated 40 per cent of its population living in urban areas. The influence of this level of urbanisation has been central to political development, and in no region has it been more significant than on the Copperbelt, one of the most important concentrations of industrial labour on the Continent. The dominance of the Copperbelt in Zambian politics has derived from the continued and overwhelming dependence of the economy on the copper industry. Historically, the forces of economic and social change generated by mineral development on the Copperbelt provided the major stimulus to African nationalism. The copper-mining industry created a small but organised industrial labour force which pioneered the techniques of mass confrontation.[2] Indeed, the issues of race and African advancement which were central to the independence struggle had their sharpest focus in the urban industrial situation, where they provoked a particular style of militant mass politics, which persisted into independence. Notwithstanding the essential contribution of the rural areas to the growth of a broadly-based, anti-colonial protest, urban-based politics on the Copperbelt was thus fundamental to the outcome of the nationalist movement and to the distribution of power at independence.[3]

The high expectations of urban labour, borne out of the nationalist struggle, combined with the tensions of economic and social change, made the Copperbelt after 1964 a significant *locus* of potential challenge to the authority of the independent state. A highly politicised urban electorate, while loyal to U.N.I.P. as the nationalist party, was nevertheless prepared to make demands which were frequently in conflict with party and government perceptions of 'the national interest'.[4] Hence the Copperbelt constituted the major problem of control for a central government which derived much of its core support from the region.

The centrality of the Copperbelt in Zambian politics was manifest during the political crisis between 1967 and 1971, which split and weakened U.N.I.P. in the very area where its local organisation had been most committed and efficient. Kapwepwe took with him into his new party an important group of leaders who had close links with the Copperbelt, and who had been prominent in the independence struggle and in successive U.N.I.P. governments. His victory in the Mufulira by-election in December 1971, as argued earlier, was the catalyst for the decision, announced in February 1972, to introduce the one-party state. The full consequence for U.N.I.P. of the U.P.P. crisis did not, however, become evident until the general elections in 1973. Those elections revealed profound weaknesses and divisions in U.N.I.P. and called into question its organisational capacity. Many voters on the Copperbelt did not vote and the poll, while the third highest in the country, was the province's lowest on record, raising serious doubts concerning urban support for the new system. It is with that urban reaction, in the context of recent social and economic change, that we are concerned.

Background: the growth of an African urban industrial society — The Copperbelt to 1964

In the thirty years before independence, the growth of the mining industry transformed a sparsely-populated Central African plateau country into a major industrial region.[5] The demand for labour by the mines and their derived economic activities attracted an increasing number of Africans, and lively towns quickly grew up. By 1945, the four Copperbelt towns of Nkana-Kitwe, Roan-Luanshya, Mufulira, and Nchanga-Chingola formed the largest European and African concentrations of population in Northern Rhodesia, with 8,000 Europeans and 90,–100,000 Africans. A further 43,000 lived in Ndola, the provincial administrative centre.[6]

The end of the war saw a new period of expansion which continued into the 'fifties. Both mining companies opened new mines, and total ore mined and treated increased from 8.1 million short tons in 1945 to 27.4 million in 1964.[7] Economic activity outside the mines also expanded, although the inclusion of Northern Rhodesia in 1953 in the Central African Federation adversely affected that growth for the following ten years.[8] Economic needs drew an increasing number of Africans to the towns, and the Copperbelt African population increased from 175,747 in 1951 to 252,764 in 1956 and 485,654 in 1963.[9] Over the same years the European population had also grown, from 21,907 in 1946 to 73,000 in 1959. By independence, therefore, the Copperbelt was a cluster of fast-expanding, closely-linked towns.

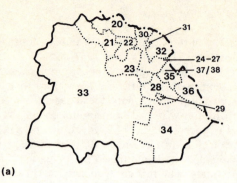

(a)

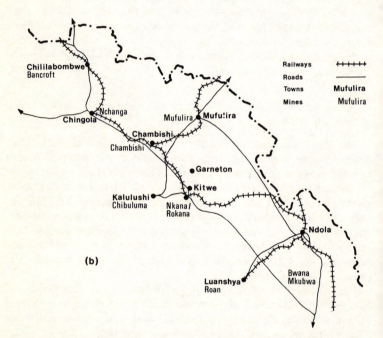

Railways	+++++
Roads	——
Towns	**Mufulira**
Mines	Mufulira

(b)

Copperbelt Province: (a) *electoral constituencies, 1973 and 1978* (numbered as on the map of all constituencies, p. xiv). 20. Chililabombwe, 21. Chingola, 22. Nchanga, 23. Kalulushi, 24. Chimwemwe, 25. Kwacha, 26. Nkana, 27. Wusakile, 28. Luanshya, 29. Roan, 30. Kankoyo, 31. Kantanshi, 32. Mufulira, 33. Luswishi, 34. Masaiti, 35. Chifubu, 36. Chiwala, 37. Masala, 38. Ndola. *Source.* Adapted from D. Hywel Davies, ed., *Zambia in Maps* (London: University of London Press, 1971), p. 53. Constituency boundaries approximated. (b) *Urban and mining centres. Source.* Adapted from D. Hywel Davies, *op. cit.*, pp. 83 and 93.

Kitwe, with a population of 109,300 and by virtue of its relative industrial and commercial importance as well as its central position, was the major centre; although Ndola, the administrative headquarters, with a population of 76,799, was growing fast. So also were the mining towns, Kalalushi (12,124), Chililabombwe (27,771), Chingola (50,387), Luanshya (64,609), and Mufulira (69,460).[10]

Patterns of urban living had been dictated by the nature of the mining industry. Race was the dominant line of social cleavage in colonial society, demonstrated most visibly in the arrangements of residential living, with the clear distinction in both mine townships and the municipalities between high-cost, low-density European housing and low-cost, high-density housing locations for African labour.[11] Africans were drawn to the Copperbelt from all over the country and beyond, so that it was an ethnically as well as racially heterogeneous society. At the same time, migration patterns determined from an early stage that the predominant element were the Bemba-speaking people of Northern and Luapula provinces. By 1959–63 they constituted 44 per cent of the mine labour force, and while they were not an absolute majority they were undoubtedly the most significant single group. More proletarianised and urbanised than any other group, Bemba-speakers played a key role in the development of urban society. Many languages were spoken on the Copperbelt, but the *lingua franca* was a town form of *Cibemba*.[12]

Urbanisation increasingly stabilised the migrant labour force recruited from the rural areas. Whereas in 1934, only 48 per cent of the African men on one mine, for example, had their families with them, by 1954 the figure was 75 per cent.[13] Government and company policies on labour stabilisation and urbanisation, as well as the steady rise in wages in the 'fifties, all contributed to a continuing decline in labour turnover, which by 1959 had been reduced on the mines to an annual 27.9 per cent.[14] By that date there was at the centre of Copperbelt society a stable, African urban wage-earning working class, two elements of which need to be borne in mind. First, while the great majority of African workers were unskilled labourers, that class was not an undifferentiated mass. There had always been a small group of more educated Africans in clerical and other junior administrative posts. In the 'fifties, their numbers began to expand as a result of economic development and the beginnings of African advancement. The new élite, which now also included businessmen, top African personnel in local government, teachers and trade unionists, constituted a very small proportion of urban African society; their standard of living was modest and the gap between richer and poorer was narrow. Nevertheless, many of them perceived themselves, and were perceived by, the majority of Africans to be such an

élite, whose interests, potentially at least, were different from those of
the mass of society.[15]

Second, the miners were the most influential element in the working class. On the one hand they were the best-paid workers, and in the
'fifties and early 'sixties the wage leaders for African labour.[16] Between
1946 and 1956 average earnings of all employees on the mines increased by 291 per cent, and miners also benefitted from bonuses. On
the other hand, the majority of African miners were still an unskilled
labouring class, working under harsh conditions; many were among
the worst housed on the Copperbelt. They were, however, by far the
most homogeneous and best-organised section of labour, with a powerful union that had a record of successful industrial action.[17]

The years after 1953 were for Africans a period of rising wages, but
also rising unemployment. Despite racial discrimination, conditions
generally improved for Africans in employment in central government, on the mines and elsewhere. Higher wages allowed for
increased spending and an improved standard of living, so that the
Copperbelt towns became known for their fine clothes, their large
shops (in African as well as European trading areas) and their con-
sumer-orientation.[18] It was, however, only a small proportion of
African society on the Copperbelt that benefitted substantially from
the improvements of the 'fifties, which, in any case, proved short-
lived. The slow-down of the economy, as well as stabilisation of
labour, contributed to a decline in the expansion of employment, and
from the mid-'fifties unemployment became a characteristic feature
of urban life.[19] From 1955 onwards, the economic system was therefore unable to meet the needs of a rapidly-expanding labour force. By
1963, when an estimated 93,000 were employed on the Copperbelt,
there were believed to be between 30,000 and 50,000 unemployed,
many of them youths.[20] At the same time, the continuing growth of
urban population meant increasing pressures upon urban services,
especially housing. By the late 'fifties, a rising sense of grievance and
frustration among Africans gave urban politics its greatest
momentum.

*The origins and growth of organised African politics on the
Copperbelt*

Colonialism created three centres of authority in each Copperbelt
town: the central government in the person of the District Commissioner; local government in the form of the municipal and township
authorities; and the mines. All three were dominated by Europeans,
and organised African politics on the Copperbelt grew out of the
African rejection of that racial domination. The result was the crea-

tion of two alternative centres of power, the unions and the party, and of a powerful tradition of urban protest.

The roots of that tradition lay in the 'thirties, when strike action by African miners in 1935 and 1940 had been followed in each case by serious disturbances in which Africans were killed. Those strikes initiated mass confrontation, and laid the foundations of a tradition and popular history of protest among African wage earners which has had a major influence upon urban African politics.[21] While the African Mineworkers Union (A.M.W.U.), formed in 1947, was not the first to be set up, it quickly became the most powerful, and its successful record of industrial action had a direct bearing on the growth of trade-union activity on the Copperbelt in the 'fifties.[22] In addition, the A.M.W.U. rejection in 1953 of Tribal Representatives in the urban industrial situation established the principle of a non-tribal working-class leadership.[23]

The Copperbelt responded gradually to the creation of the A.N.C. in 1948, and the early 'fifties saw branches formed and increasing political activity.[24] Although the attempts at a boycott of European shops in 1954 were largely unsuccessful, from 1955 there was an increasing urban militancy. The A.N.C. split between the party's more militant elements and the more moderate elements loyal to Nkumbula began on the Copperbelt, which became the scene of a bitter struggle before Z.A.N.C. emerged. It was therefore on the Copperbelt, in the final analysis, that nationalist politics were born.

The advance of constitutional change after 1960 in turn made the Copperbelt electorate essential to U.N.I.P.'s struggle for power at the centre. Whereas in 1958, on a restricted franchise, there were 17,295 voters along the line of rail, and only 7,253 in the rural areas, in 1962 three of the four urban constituencies and some 45 per cent of the territory's lower roll voters were on the Copperbelt.[25] To mobilise the population behind its demand for independence, U.N.I.P. constructed a tightly articulated party organisation which was a phenomenon of the high-density housing areas in both council estates and mine townships. The basis of the structure was a system of cells, or sections, in groupings of twenty houses, through which the party politicised existing social relations, and in the process created networks of social as well as political control.[26] There was a hard core of dedicated party workers, and party office at the local level carried with it acknowledged status.[27] Regional party officials, who lived among the people, were in a real sense popular leaders, since recruitment to regional office started with the local level organisation. Officials were, for the most part, representative of the less educated, the unskilled and semi-skilled, and the urban party developed a powerful anti-élitist ethic. Party officials also assumed an important societal role: the local as well as the national leadership saw themselves as the guardians of the norms and values of the nationalist movement for which they claimed total support, and regarded any who rejected their claim as the enemy. In due course they expected to receive their reward, so that U.N.I.P. also emerged as a party of patronage in an upwardly mobile society.

In this way, in a brief four-year period to 1964, U.N.I.P.'s Copperbelt leaders at regional and local level built a powerful, mass-party organisation, which acted as an important agent of integration among Africans. In this respect, the party benefited greatly from the fact that urban life and wage employment had eroded the bases of 'tribal' attachment. The prominence of the Bemba was not in doubt, nor their key role in the development of urban politics, as of the labour movement. Nevertheless, the party on the Copperbelt owed a great deal to non-Bemba as well as Bemba skills, and its leadership in its formative period included the party's most powerful Lozi politicians whose appeal to the urban populace was not in doubt. Nor was that of Dingiswayo Banda, an Easterner, who turned the Youth Wing into an effective militant urban institution. Lozi, Nyanja and others mobilised urban support for U.N.I.P. by deeds as well as oratorical skill without reference to ethnic loyalty. Both the 1962 and the 1964 elections demonstrated U.N.I.P.'s ability to win on the Copperbelt, regardless of the ethnic background of its candidates.[28] There were undoubtedly different groupings which constituted potential bases for rival power centres within the party. They related, however, at that stage to generational differences, and to different ideas about party and politics, rather than to ethnicity.

Nevertheless, U.N.I.P.'s support was never complete and its authority did not go unchallenged. The continued presence of the A.N.C. on the Copperbelt, and its ability to sustain a degree of support, meant a competitive inter-party competition, which was in part responsible for the intensity of the region's politics. A more serious limitation upon U.N.I.P.'s authority in those years derived from its ambiguous relations with the trade unions. Militant trade-union leaders, who provided the stimulus for the early trade-union developments during the 1950s, were themselves deeply involved in the political struggle, and by 1955 most of them held posts in the A.N.C. on the Copperbelt. When Z.A.N.C. was formed, a majority went over to the new body, and then in due course to U.N.I.P., believing workers should be engaged directly as labour in the political struggle. U.N.I.P. therefore enjoyed close links with the unions and with the Trade Union Congress through its Copperbelt leadership. The links were, however, personal. No trade-union body had an official association either with the A.N.C. or subsequently with U.N.I.P., and the trade-union movement as a whole was deeply divided over the issue of a formal relationship between unions and party. In particular, and of greatest significance, the A.M.W.U., as the most powerful union on the Copperbelt, steadily resisted the subordination of union to party. While there was no doubt of the miners' support of the nationalist struggle and of U.N.I.P., there was equally no doubt of their determination to resist political direction. The authority of U.N.I.P. stopped at the union doors.[29] Hence the nationalist struggle engendered conflict within African urban society as well as with the colonial power.[30] That conflict, although it was subordinated to the nationalist objectives, had important consequences for the style of urban politics, characterised as they were by intense popular participation and by frequent violence.[31]

There was no doubt, however, that at independence U.N.I.P. enjoyed the support of the great majority of the electorate on the Copperbelt. In the 1962 elections, 85–88 per cent of the voters, and in 1964 well over 90 per cent, went to the polls, in which U.N.I.P. won every seat.[32] Nor was there any doubt of the dominant position of the Copperbelt in the national political system. The region sent the largest number of delegates to the U.N.I.P. general conference. Cabinet and Central Committee included many nationalist leaders recognised as having a Copperbelt base, regardless of whether or not they represented Copperbelt constituencies. A majority of the eleven M.P.s elected from the province in 1964 had strong urban party records; one of them was Sikota Wina, a central party and government leader. In 1968, when parliamentary representation was increased to eighteen seats, Reuben Kamanga, Wesley Nyirenda and Kapwepwe himself, all key national leaders, moved to Copperbelt seats.

Relations between the Copperbelt and the centre, 1964 – 69

The Copperbelt benefitted enormously from the rapid growth that accompanied the first five years of independence, when high copper prices kept the economy buoyant, notwithstanding a slower growth of production than planned. Although the Rhodesian UDI in 1965 created serious economic difficulties for the country, the imposition of sanctions meant a considerable increase in protection for Zambian manufacturing, and consequent employment opportunities, the advantages of which went largely to the Copperbelt. Of the 532 manufacturing establishments set up between 1964 and 1969, 317 were on the Copperbelt, compared with 166 in Central and 41 in Southern provinces.[33] When the economic reforms in 1968 and 1969 increased Zambian participation in business and commercial activity, much of that development took place in Kitwe and Ndola, both of which were more economically diversified than the smaller mining towns.

Economic expansion was accompanied by a massive increase in population to 816,309 in 1969 and in 1971 to just over 1 million, 90 per cent of whom now lived in five large closely related urban, industrial centres. The greatest number of migrants continued to be drawn from Northern and Luapula provinces, both of which suffered a net decline of population in this period, so that the predominance of Bemba-speakers in urban society was unchanged. Similarly, the population remained a very youthful one, with 48 per cent of the population under the age of twenty. A good many of those young people, moreover, had been born in the town, so that they were more rooted in urban life and urban values. In some cases, there was now a third generation of workers on the mines.[34]

In the first five years after independence there was a significant improvement in the material standard of urban living.[35] This urban progress was bought largely at the expense of rural Zambia, and on more than one occasion Kaunda felt it necessary to warn urban Zambians of the growing cleavages between rural and urban society.[36] Nevertheless, Copperbelt residents perceived themselves as subject also to relative deprivation. Zambianisation and rapid promotion at a time of acute shortage of skilled Zambian manpower undoubtedly increased rapid upward mobility. Job fragmentation in the course of Zambianisation, however, while it contributed to increased bureaucracy, also slowed down the growth of average earnings. Wages on the Copperbelt were higher than the national average, but the gap with other provinces was narrowed.[37] Central government employment expanded more rapidly in Central Province and especially in Lusaka.[38]

Hence relations between the Copperbelt and the centre were characterised by persistent claims from the former that they were denied their fair share of development. Lusaka was described as *Bambazonke* ('grab everything'). The local authorities, themselves under attack from Copperbelt residents for inadequate services, criticised the central government for inadequate support for city expansion.[39] Workers consistently demanded higher wages. The specific grievances varied from one centre to another, but generally there was an insistent demand for employment, education, housing and higher wages.

The immediate causes of such discontent were not in doubt. Neither central nor local government had the resources to meet the demands of a rapidly-expanding urban population. By 1971 there were Copperbelt children seeking places in rural schools because of the urban shortage.[40] There was an acute shortage of housing. In Kitwe alone in 1973, the waiting list for council housing was 22,000, and the squatter population of 60,000 indicated the magnitude of the problems.[41] More fundamental, from 1969 the cost of living began to rise significantly, and the real value of wages was falling.[42] The most serious urban problem was, however, undoubtedly that of unemployment. Unemployment estimates must be treated with care. One cautious estimate based on provincial employment enumeration in 1969 suggests the size of the problem: formal employment was 129,750, just 53.8 per cent of the total labour force; 53,486 were in informal sector employment; and an estimated 50,244 were unemployed, 23.01 per cent of the work-force.[43] A social survey of Kitwe in 1972 found that unemployment was higher in the mine townships than in other residential areas, implying that the miners bore the heaviest burden of support for unemployed kinsmen, at a time when employment on the mines was no longer expanding.[44] If so, it would be unlikely that wage increases on the mines, after the dramatic 22 per cent increase in 1966, could have kept pace with the cost of living, and the miners were no longer necessarily the wage leaders for workers in other sectors.[45]

Economic development and Zambianisation, in a situation of great scarcity of skilled manpower, had also produced, by the end of the 'sixties, greater differentiation within the work-force, and with it a greater inequality. While the average African wage in Kitwe was K945 in 1969, compared with K361 in 1962, the great majority of households on the Copperbelt still had an income of less than K80 a month.[46] While the charcoal burner might expect to earn K30 a month, those in the higher echelons of the bureaucracy and management might have salaries up to K7,000 a year. Social stratification was, moreover, physically emphasised by the inherited urban residential patterns.

Beneath this increased stratification, more fundamental changes were also taking place in the structure of the labour force itself, within which the separation between labour and management had become more distinct. These changes, which had begun in the 1950's, had proceeded farthest in the mines, where Zambianisation, modifications to the manning structure and job evaluation produced a more marked division between skilled and unskilled labour. As the opportunities for rapid promotion slowed down in the late 'sixties, and employers instituted wages on the basis of the rate for the job, so the earlier clear ladder of advancement available out of the unskilled labouring categories also began to disappear. Wage agreements after the Brown award in 1966 also generally favoured the more skilled workers, to the increasing disadvantage of unskilled labour. As a result, the mass of lowly paid unskilled workers were now more clearly differentiated as a distinctive category, movement out of which was becoming more difficult, and within which they were at a disadvantage in the wage-bargaining process.[47]

Industrial unrest, which constituted the most serious challenge to the authority of the government, reflected the interaction of these complex changes. In the immediate post-independence years, urban grievances were fuelled by the high expectations bred during the nationalist struggle, which in turn created a strong sense of frustration at the slowness of change.[48] When the miners went on strike in August 1966 after months of tension, the immediate cause was not in doubt. They believed they had been a major force in the nationalist struggle, and they now expected their reward. As one miner put it to the Brown Commission, set up to inquire into the miners' grievances, 'We are poor . . . We have waited a long time'.

In the face of such expectations, government faced an acute dilemma. On the one hand, the legacy of racial inequality and the inequities of the colonial wage structures demanded an increase in wages and recognition of the true value of labour. On the other hand, the government had been advised it could have higher wages or increased employment, but not both, and that economic development demanded wage restraint.[49] The then Minister for Labour summed up what was a crucial political issue when he justified the 22 per cent wage increase granted to the miners in 1966:

On wages I am told the Government is increasing wages unnecessarily. Now let us admit here that the Government has thrown £420,000,000 into the economy by way of the Four Year Development Plan. All this money is going into the hands of private companies — expatriate companies for that matter. All the companies in this Republic are branches of bigger companies overseas. All the £420,000,000 is going into the pockets of expatriate workers who have the technical know-how the technical show how. What is there left then for the African worker? Yet you say we should not increase that bit of it in wages . . . There must be a way in which the African worker, the ordinary worker, will share in this £420,000,000. They are not only going to look at massive structures of parliament or the new airport; they have to have something in cash just as you have cash for the expatriates from overseas . . .[50]

That comment summed up the crisis posed for government, not only by the miners but by urban labour as a whole. The working class on the Copperbelt had supported U.N.I.P. in the nationalist struggle. While development economists might demand wage restraint, unfulfilled expectations carried with them the potential for political opposition. In that situation the government employed two major strategies for control: on the one hand they agreed to wage increases, and on the other they used the power of the state to extend government control over the labour movement and its leaders. That strategy reduced, but did not end, industrial unrest. Although the number of strikes decreased, continuing industrial tension was demonstrated by the persistence of spontaneous work stoppages, or 'wildcat strikes'.[51]

While continued industrial tension could be explained partially by the rising cost of living, by the end of the decade urban grievances also reflected a growing disillusionment at the uneven distribution of resources. Government officials themselves discerned, beneath the continuing demands for higher wages, a greater awareness among lower paid workers at the way in which wage increases disproportionately benefited the higher income groups.[52] Thus industrial unrest reflected also the new inequalities in Zambian urban society. The fundamental cause of the 1966 mine workers' strike had indeed been an underlying resentment among the mass of ordinary miners that, notwithstanding the wage increase negotiated the year before by the union, the new wage structure had in the long run benefitted skilled rather than unskilled workers.[53] Four years later, unskilled lashers in Luanshya went out on unofficial strike against the new 1970 Wage Agreement because of the implications for low-paid workers, the downgrading of a number of jobs and the consequently diminished promotion prospects.[54] There was also by that time a widespread rank-and-file disillusionment with union leaders[55] and an increasing willingness to take action, even when it might lead them into confrontation with government.

The government, faced with such a situation, proved unable to use the party as agent of control, since the old tensions between U.N.I.P. and the unions persisted. Immediately after independence, the majority of unions remained organisationally weak, and U.N.I.P. was often involved in the settlement of labour disputes. The result, however, was continuing rivalry between party and union officials over their respective boundaries, which in turn brought the local party into conflict with the centre. Rivalry between A.M.W.U. and U.N.I.P. was demonstrated when the miners overwhelmingly rejected U.N.I.P. candidates in the 1966 union elections.[56] Party officials, especially District Governors after 1969, were warned increasingly to refrain from interference in labour affairs, while government steadily extended its control over labour through legislation rather than the party.[57] Thus the Labour Department reported, quite candidly, of the industrial unrest on the Copperbelt in 1971,

it was not until Government restricted [dissidents] that a dangerous trend towards widespread disorder was arrested. After this swift action by government the situation returned to normal.[58]

Despite its inability to control the industrial arena, U.N.I.P.'s sweeping electoral victories between 1965 and 1969 nevertheless demonstrated the party's continued urban support. In the second general election in 1968, when both parties contested every seat, U.N.I.P. won all eighteen in a poll that averaged 91.4 per cent, although the results indicated a small growth in A.N.C. support outside Mufulira. They won the 1969 referendum with a 76.0 per cent 'Yes' vote, and in the 1970 local government elections took all seats except one in Mufulira.

The political debate in the multi-party state was less about policy differences between the parties or about development, than about U.N.I.P.'s control of the distribution of resources. National leaders and the resident minister might rebuke Copperbelt local level officials who warned A.N.C. supporters that they would receive no assistance unless they joined the party; they could not prevent them from doing so.[59] Competition for resources was thus translated into inter-party conflict, conducted in the same militant style as in the past, and erupting as in the past on successive occasions into bitter, violent confrontation and intimidation at the local level.[60] The capacity of the centre to control such conflict reflected a new dilemma. U.N.I.P.'s critics blamed the Youth Wing for the violence.[61] In 1972 a number of witnesses to the Chona Commission, and the Commission itself, recommended that it be abolished.[62] In a more stratified and increasingly unequal urban society, however, the Youth Wing saw itself as the upholder of the party's populist, anti-élitist tradition, and defender of the less-educated and poor elements of society.[63] The extent to which U.N.I.P. was the distributive organisation for loans, trade licences and employment opportunities in the first expansionist period, when such distribution was manifestly unequal, had already, however, been called into question. What became increasingly at issue therefore, was who the party should now both represent and support.

At the same time, U.N.I.P.'s local organisation faced significant constraints upon its control over urban resources. First, the structures of urban administration made it difficult for the local level organisation to extend the control it had exercised in the high-density townships across the urban region as a whole. The transformation of the local authorities into African-elected councils, for example, opened up access to new offices and resources; but the local government system itself inhibited local party control over their distribution. It was significant that party officials continued to play their most important societal role in the expanding squatter townships, where local government authority was most ambiguous; but the party youth in Kitwe, for example, found themselves in conflict with the city council when they arrogated to themselves the authority to distribute land in the squatter townships.[64] Second, old and new functional groups began to challenge the claims of local party officials to control local affairs. In Kitwe, for example, battles occurred between the city council, the African Fisheries and Marketeers Union and party officials as to who should regulate the market and control prices.[65] There were similar conflicts with the charcoal-burners over the price of charcoal, with the Rent Payers Association over the control of rents in the townships, and with the Zambia African Traders Association, which in 1970 reformed itself into the Zambia National Council of Commerce and Industry (Z.N.C.C.I.).[66]

The issue of representation was complicated by the fact that many U.N.I.P. officials were themselves now marketeers, charcoal-burners and tavern-keepers who expected the protection and patronage of the party. The charcoal-burners were told that they could not raise prices because urban consumers could not pay; yet they were one of the poorest, most disadvantaged sections of urban society. In the middle of 1965, the then Minister of Local Government had closed down four hundred traders at Mufulira market because their prices were too high. But the marketeers were party men who expected the protection of the party, just as much as the businessmen whose aspirations were to assume control of the larger expatriate and Asian-owned concerns in the city centres.[67]

The popular response to these constraints took a number of forms, but for U.N.I.P. the most important was the increased emphasis upon party patronage, both as a means of advancement as well as the basis of an appeal for support. The result was a chain of patronage networks and small political machines which extended upwards through the political and governmental system. But, since not all aspirations could be satisfied, patronage was ultimately a fragile basis on which to build support. Further, such patronage networks tended to strengthen ethnic connections.

The rise and fall of the U.P.P. and the end of the multi-party state

The most serious threat to the internal cohesion of the local party was the struggle for power at the centre, which also became (after 1967) the dominant issue in Copperbelt politics.[68] The reasons were not difficult to discern. Control of the Copperbelt remained essential for the retention of power at the centre, and the protagonists of the factional struggle within U.N.I.P. all had strong links with the region. Hence each group appealed to the Copperbelt for support, at a time when the local party organisation had begun, as we have seen, to face the disintegrative influences of social and economic change. The resulting crisis affected the party on the Copperbelt in three ways. First, it set regional officials and leaders against the centre. The Copperbelt members of the National Council were highly critical of the changes in provincial representation introduced with the 1970 constitution, on the grounds that they departed from majority rule. What concerned them most, however, was the threat to Copperbelt dominance at the party's national, decision-making level. Second, the power struggle brought to the surface local rivalries which hitherto the party had been able to suppress, and set regional officials against each other. There was an increasing reference on the Copperbelt to 'tribalism', and allegations of Bemba domination from within the party. Third, the U.P.P., when it was formed, took with it an important section of U.N.I.P.'s Copperbelt leadership, which both weakened that party's urban organisation and opened up the possibility of the loss of popular support.

The factionalism out of which the U.P.P. was born thus had a considerable impact upon U.N.I.P.'s position on the Copperbelt, to understand which it is necessary to consider briefly the place of the U.P.P. in Copperbelt politics as the latter had developed over the years. U.N.I.P. depicted the new party as a Bemba-dominated faction, whose objective was to ensure Bemba dominance in government at the expense of the 'national interest'.[69] The U.P.P. reversed the charge, to accuse U.N.I.P. of discrimination against the Bemba, and rejected the claim that it was a tribal party. One issue for both parties therefore concerned the place in Zambian politics of Bemba-speaking people, that linguistic grouping of just over a million who live in Northern and Luapula provinces and who had since the 1930s constituted the dominant element of Copperbelt urban society. This had been the central issue in Zambia since the Bemba-Tonga alliance had put Kapwepwe into the vice-presidency at Mulungushi in 1967. It had a particular importance in the Copperbelt for two reasons. First, the central role the Bemba had played in the urban nationalist movement, and second their dominant position in the work-force and the occupational structure. If copper was Zambia's major resource, then the Bemba-speaking people stood in relation to that resource in much the same way that the Kikuyu have stood in relation to land in Kenya. As competition for employment increased, it drew attention to the dominant position of the Bemba in the work-force. 'The Bemba', it was said, 'appear to be everywhere.' They were 'rich because they are on the mines'. Their dominant position in the mine labour force was seen as a consequence, not of their long urban and labour experience, but because Bemba personnel officers 'preferred their own'.[70] Competition for a scarce resource acted to ensure that 'tribe' could be utilised as an element in the struggle for economic advantage, and the central place of the Bemba in U.N.I.P. ensured that this was translated into political terms. 'Tribalism' was thus effect rather than cause.

An early example of this process was demonstrated in a violent clash between U.N.I.P. officials and the residents of a squatter compound outside Chililabombwe in August 1968, in which two U.N.I.P. officials, as well as a woman and two children, were killed. The clash was precipitated by intense conflict between U.N.I.P. and the recently formed U.P., and led to the arrest of a number of that party's officials and the banning of the party.[71] The incident might have ended there had not the Copperbelt Minister of State, Peter Chanda, himself an urban Bemba, allegedly laid the responsibility for the murders on 'ex-WENELA Lozi'. In doing so, he drew attention to the increased number of Lozi seeking employment on the Copperbelt.

There had always been a Lozi presence on the Copperbelt, although in the past they had been employed as clerks and in other white-collar jobs rather than as unskilled labour. There had also been some rivalry between Lozi (and also Nyanja) and Bemba for white-collar employment; but this had not led to political conflict, and Lozi and Bemba had worked together in the nationalist struggle. By 1968, however, the situation had changed. First, the government's prohibition in 1966 of the recruitment of Zambian labour for the South African mines meant that Lozi who could no longer go south in search of work turned instead to the Copperbelt. The squatter compound where the clash took place belonged to a construction company which had taken on unskilled labour at a time when there was a shortage of such employment in the province, and when the Bemba urban community, as noted, bore the heaviest burden of unemployed kinsmen. Nor was it only at the level of unskilled labour that allegations of 'tribalism' were heard. At the white-collar and management level, there were vigorous complaints of 'tribal discrimination' which frequently involved Lozi employees.[72] Second, the U.P. had been characterised as a pre-eminently Lozi party, and the circumstances of Chanda's alleged charges necessarily translated the incident into a Lozi/Bemba confrontation. His statement, which he subsequently denied, drew a swift response from the five Lozi ministers then in government, and during a tense parliamentary debate they emphasised the dangers to nationhood of ethnic conflict.[73] While the debate may properly be placed in the context of the growing party conflict at the centre, its significance here lay in the extent to which it reflected a heightened consciousness on the Copperbelt of 'tribal', rather than racial, rivalry for resources.

At one level, the U.P.P. constituted a Bemba reaction to that challenge to their position within the work-force as well as in the party and government, and given the common Northern Province origins of its leaders, it was not surprising that the party acquired the popular image of a party of Northern Province Bemba. Nevertheless, the reduction of Copperbelt politics at that stage to a confrontation between Bemba-speakers and the rest of society ignored several important points. First, the Bemba had never been a politically homogeneous group, and in 1970 Northern and Luapula Bemba divided in their response to the U.P.P.[74] Second, the U.P.P. failed to win over Northern Province as a whole in 1971, losing both seats contested in that province. On the Copperbelt itself, moreover, Bemba from Northern Province were obviously divided. Most of the miners, for example, remained loyal to U.N.I.P., regardless of their region of origin.

A further point concerns the position of the U.P.P. leaders in Copperbelt politics. What made them a group, much more than their Bemba parentage, was their urban political record.[75] They were all town Bemba, who had grown up, gone to school and learned their politics on the Copperbelt. Most of them had started their political careers in the early trade unions, and all of them had strong links with urban labour; one of them, John Chisata, had indeed been president of A.M.W.U. They had all been founding members of U.N.I.P. who stood in the mainstream of militant nationalist politics, and they therefore constituted an important section of U.N.I.P.'s original Copperbelt leadership, which represented the party's populist and militant tradition. They sought in their new party to carry that tradition with them. The U.P.P. constitution announced that it would, 'pursue a socialist policy and safeguard the sovereignty and independence of Zambia based on socialist principles'.[76] Kapwepwe justified his appeal for support, moreover, with the charge that U.N.I.P. had failed to fulfil the nationalist objectives that he had helped to draw up. 'Independence is good', he argued, 'but it is meaningless and useless if it does not bring fruits to the masses . . .'[77]

In the months prior to the new party's public appearance, Kapwepwe's supporters had all made similar charges against the U.N.I.P. leadership.[78] The U.P.P. appeal was thus directed to those who felt deprived, in an attempt to exploit the sense of generalised discontent that pervaded the Copperbelt. Notwithstanding their profession of socialist objectives, this was a populist rather than a class appeal, and they made no clear attack upon the incipient class divisions emerging in urban society. Indeed, the U.P.P. made clear overtures to, and had strong links with, Zambian businessmen on the Copperbelt who were by 1970 aggrieved that the economic reforms of 1968–70 had not brought them as many benefits as they had expected. Populist politics were thus perceived to be challenging many aspects of government policy.

The structure of U.N.I.P., its recruitment system and its tradition of patronage meant that U.P.P. leaders were likely to have strong patron/client relations, reaching down to the local levels of the party. Nevertheless, there were U.N.I.P. leaders who did not leave the party who shared the same Bemba urban Copperbelt background as the U.P.P. leaders. Many factors may have influenced those who stayed: a desire to retain office, a greater loyalty to the party and a fear of victimisation among them. What was clear, however, was that U.N.I.P. members on the Copperbelt were as a result subject to divided loyalties, since the dispute with the U.P.P. was in many respects still a family affair.

The result was a period of intense inter-party violence. U.N.I.P.'s reaction to the new party was to tighten its ranks, replace those officials who joined the new party, and institute an intense card-checking campaign to assert its control. The party also reaffirmed its control over patronage and distribution, so that the appearance of U.P.P. was followed by threats to withdraw licences, evict council householders, and dismiss employees who were found not to support the ruling party. Those interest groups who had challenged U.N.I.P.'s control became the more suspect as a source of opposition. The by-elections in December 1971 were accompanied by further violence, highlighted by the stoning of Kapwepwe's car on nomination day. The U.P.P. contested two seats, Wusakile-Chamboli, which U.N.I.P. retained, and Mufulira, which Kapwepwe won. The high level of ministerial and central party official involvement and the resources which U.N.I.P. poured into the campaign, demonstrated the importance the party attached to the occasion. Kapwepwe's victory represented the defection of a sizeable number of U.N.I.P. voters and the failure of many U.N.I.P. supporters to vote at all.[79] The fundamental weakness of U.N.I.P.'s urban party organisation, in a situation where both parties were appealing to the same group for support, was suggested by the intensity of suspicion within its local organisation at this time. The full consequences for U.N.I.P. of this party split, however, became clear only with the first general elections held two years later under the one-party state.

The general election of 1973: social and economic change and electoral response on the Copperbelt

In the aftermath of the U.P.P. crisis, the 1973 general elections had a particular significance for the Copperbelt, since they provided the first opportunity to measure the extent to which U.N.I.P. had overcome the divisions that had led to that crisis. Hence it was important that the campaign was, for the most part, peaceful and orderly, and free of the serious violence that had marked previous electoral experience. The new electoral system opened up parliamentary office to a much larger section of Copperbelt society than had previously participated, and there was a significant increase in the number of candidates standing for election. Against this, however, had to be set a significant decline in public participation, measured in terms of attendance at

election meetings, general public interest, and above all by the polls:
only a minority of party officials voted in the primary election, and in
the general election the poll was the lowest recorded since independence.

Given the urban nature of the Copperbelt and its long tradition of
organised politics and party activism, that decline was more
significant than the general decline elsewhere in the country. Only
46.59 per cent of registered voters voted in Copperbelt Province. The
highest turn-out was in Luanshya (56 per cent) and the lowest in the
rural constituency of Masaiti (37.2 per cent). Five constituencies
polled over 50 per cent of the registered vote, ten between 40 and 50
per cent, and four under 40 per cent (including Luanshya's predominantly mining constituency of Roan). In the case of the presidential election, the poll was little better: 151,208 voted in the presidential election, a mere 385 (0.12 per cent) more than in the
parliamentary poll. Of those casting valid votes 88.6 per cent voted
'Yes' for President Kaunda.

Table 5.1   Percentage of registered voters casting votes in parliamentary elections in Copperbelt Province 1964–73

Year	Election	Poll (Copperbelt) (%)	Poll (Zambia) (%)
1964	General election	95.1	94.8
1968	General election	91.4	82.5
1970	Local government elections	61.0 (contested wards only)	43.8
1971	Parliamentary by-election Wusakili/Chamboli Mufulira	55.78 } 52.79 46.93 }	
1973	General election	46.59	39.8

*Source. U.N.I.P., Results of the First Presidential and General Elections under
the One Party Participatory Democracy Constitution in Zambia, December 5,
1973; and Elections Office, Parliamentary By-Elections, December 1971.*

The low poll suggested first of all that the party had lost its old ability
to turn out the voters for elections. In the 'sixties, electoral mobilisation had been the party's most effective political activity, when con-
trasted both with its other activities and with the electoral appeal of
other parties in Africa. In 1968, 90.8 per cent of voters in a 91.4 per
cent poll (83.33 per cent of all registered voters) had voted for U.N.I.P.;
in 1973, 88.6 per cent of those voting in the presidential election voted
for the President and party. But given that this was a 47 per cent poll,
in effect only some 41 per cent of registered voters actually voted
'Yes'. The outcome of the parliamentary election presented even more

serious considerations. In Luanshya, for example, the constituency with the highest electoral turn-out on the Copperbelt, the winning candidate, who polled 55.2 per cent of the poll, received in fact just 30.91 per cent of the registered vote. In Kwacha constituency, moreover, where the winner received 66.9 per cent of the poll, this was in fact only 28.35 per cent of the registered vote. Such low returns clearly did not represent strong legitimacy for a new system of government which had grown out of serious earlier conflicts.

The candidates and the campaign

There was a good deal more participation among aspiring candidates than had been possible in elections in the multi-party system. In comparison with thirty-six candidates who had stood from both parties in 1968 ninety-nine people lodged nominations for the primary election, and after the primaries fifty-two went on to contest the general election.[80] Of the eighteen M.P.s who had represented the Copperbelt in the 1968–72 Parliament, only six now stood (all of whom were re-elected), ensuring that thirteen constituencies would have new M.P.s, one additional seat having been allocated to the Copperbelt in 1973. This meant that there was a much greater turn-over of parliamentary representation than almost anywhere else in the country.

Candidates were drawn from a fairly wide spectrum of Copperbelt society. In addition to the six former M.P.s (two of them Cabinet Ministers, three ministers of state, and one a backbencher), they included: several full-time trade unionists, including the President of the Mineworkers' Union and the President of the Zambia Congress of Trade Unions (Z.C.T.U.); two District Governors; a dozen local councillors, three of whom were mayors; a number of professional men including two lawyers, a magistrate, several teachers, a diplomat and a former diplomat; a number of local party officials, local businessmen, and a small number of workers, some at supervisory levels. The occupational distribution of candidates was thus a good deal broader than in the past. At the same time, a majority of the candidates had stronger links with their local community than with the political centre in Lusaka. Perhaps more significant, however, was the extent to which the local party leaders now asserted themselves, in a system perceived by many as a means of ensuring that 'party people' were pre-eminent.[81] Both primary and general election demonstrated the importance for success of links with the political system, and especially of party office (see Tables 5.2 and 5.4). Further, voters tended to go along with the preferences expressed by the local party officials in the primaries, primary winners tending to win general,

Table 5.2   Copperbelt Province: linkages of candidates to
formal political system

Category	Provincial total[a]		
	P	E	W
Sitting M.P.	—	—	6
Local party official	3	8	5
Local councillor	4	1	1
Party official/local councillor	2	7	3
Party official/civil servant	1	1	—
Civil servant	3	2	—
Diplomat	—	1	—
Total	13	20	15
Not in formal political sector	19	5	2
	32	25	17
Unknown	15	8	2
Total	47	33	19

Total candidates:	99
Total known background:	74
No. of party links:	49
No. no-party:	25

Notes:
a.   P = Eliminated primaries, E = Lost general election, W = Won.

Table 5.3   Copperbelt Province: party choice in primaries compared with
electorate choice in election. (In 15 seats where a primary election was
necessary — excludes Chiwala, Luswishi, Masaiti [all rural], Wusakile.)

In the general election:	Provincial total	
	(%)	(No.)
1. Primary winner came		
First	60.00	9
Second	20.00	3
Third	6.66	1
Disqualified	13.34	2
2. Primary second came		
First	33.34	5
Second	40.00	6
Third	26.66	4
3. Third in primary came		
First	—	0
Second	40.00	6
Third	53.34	8
Disqualified	6.66	1
Promoted candidate came		
First	33.34	1
Did not run	66.66	2

Table 5.4   Degree of party control and/or measure of voter loyalty to party

Link to pol. system	Lost primary	(%)	Lost general election	(%)	Won	(%)	Total (= 100%)
Sitting M.P.s	—		—		6	100	6
Party official (regardless of other position)	6[a]	20	16	53.3	8	26.7	30
Local councillors (regardless of other position)	7[a]	35	9	45	4[b]	20	20
Civil servants and diplomat	4	50	4	50	—		8
Not in political system	18	72	5	20	2	8	25

Notes:
a.   Two disqualified
b.   Includes three party officials

electoral support (see Table 5.3). Only in Chimwemwe constituency in Kitwe was there a marked diversion from the norm, when a candidate who had been defeated in the primaries won the election after being promoted to replace a disqualified candidate. Only one other such case occurred in the whole country. Indeed, Kitwe was exceptional: only one of the other four constituencies where primaries were necessary returned the winner of the primary to Parliament.[82] There was, therefore, a strong congruence between party preference and electoral choice. This suggested a strong tendency among voters on the Copperbelt to remain loyal to the party and to follow party choice when voting (see Tables 5.2 and 5.4).

The new electoral system therefore undoubtedly enhanced the party's control over the outcome of the elections in favour of the party and party officials. The local party was able to screen aspirants through the primaries, so that people with no standing in the party often had difficulty in passing on to the next stage. After that, the Central Committee disqualified four of the candidates in the Copperbelt. An analysis of the successful candidates indicates that the system ensured a remarkable degree of party control, despite its necessary bias towards local issues and personalities, and despite the political and economic difficulties against which the election was held. What this meant, effectively, was that the Copperbelt party was able to prevent any suspected U.P.P. supporter from being elected.[83]

Despite the victories of all six M.P.s on the Copperbelt,[84] the elections ensured a greater turnover of parliamentarians than at any time since 1964. They also produced a very different group of M.P.s. The combination of the U.P.P. crisis, the introduction of the one-party state, and the first general election in 1973, removed virtually the whole generation of Copperbelt nationalist politicians from leadership. Until 1971–72, the Copperbelt parliamentarians had provided a significant proportion of the central leadership of both party and government, drawn from what we may now acknowledge as the dominant factions within the party, each with its own base of support in the Copperbelt region. In 1973, the new Copperbelt representatives did not, as a group, reflect the same degree of national political prominence. Of the nineteen elected candidates, apart from the former M.P.s, only a trade-union leader and a mayor could be said to be widely known outside their areas.

Table 5.5.   Copperbelt Province: performance of candidates by occupation

Category	Lost primary	Lost general Election	Winners
M.P.s	—	—	6
Civil servants	2	5	1
Teachers	2	3	1
Businessmen	12	6	5
Professional (law, medicine)	2	—	1
Employees			
Executives	—	2	—
Supervisory/personnel	2	6	1
Workers (manual)	2	—	—
Full-time trade unionists	—	3	1
Others	6	2	1
Total known	28	28	16
Unknown	14	10	3
Total	42	38	19

Equally important, however, was the extent to which the elections brought into political prominence the new Zambian business class which, we have noted, had been frustrated by their inability to benefit from the economic reforms to the extent hoped for by many. While some had looked to the U.P.P. in 1971, many more now took advantage of the absence of central candidate selection and a single party list to enter the political arena. Thus, twenty-three of the seventy-two candidates for whom data was available were businessmen. Only five of those businessmen were finally elected, (26.31 per cent of Copperbelt M.P.s), but this was still significant in comparison with one trade unionist, one supervisory level employee, one teacher and one civil servant, and when we bear in mind that no one was elected from the Copperbelt's urbanised, industrial working class. Moreover, those businessmen who won also held party office. The rapid emergence of a business class since 1968 had therefore produced an early impact on the composition of political leadership on the Copperbelt.

The campaign, both for the primary and the general election, followed the same general pattern across the Copperbelt. Election meetings were in general poorly attended, and this had much to do with organisational inadequacies. In the primary elections, there was some confusion in a number of constituencies as to who were and were not involved, and when the election turned to the general campaign, there was a general paucity of publicity, so that many Copperbelt residents might have been forgiven for not being aware that an election was in progress at all. There were, indeed, occasions when even candidates themselves were unclear as to arrangements for meetings. In Kitwe, the disqualification by the Central Committee of two highly popular candidates, which was strongly protested by local party officials, resulted in their temporary boycott of meetings in the two constituencies concerned, Kwacha and Chimwemwe. Election meetings became, in the event, generally something of a ritual, in which candidates discussed abstract notions of development, unity and Humanism, as well as local grievances and demands, before small unresponsive audiences.

All candidates dwelt upon the importance of the presidential election, urging voters to vote 'Yes' for President Kaunda, and discussion of national policy issues was far less direct and precise. Generally, local and national issues were telescoped together and turned into a list of local grievances which, while they varied from town to town, were dominated by housing and employment, reflecting the problems described above that had faced the urban areas since independence. Within each constituency, therefore, candidates clearly identified and espoused local needs and local demands. Seldom did they differ on the question of priorities. The common platform which they shared created pressures for conformity, and such differences as existed about party policy were seldom evident in public utterances. Finally, party officials, particularly in the latter days of the election, put a good deal of effort into the presidential campaign, for which they set up committees whose function was to educate voters on the mechanics of the presidential vote.[85]

Local party organisation and the informal campaign

The election was in fact conducted at two levels, of which the public campaign proved the less significant. Notwithstanding the prohibition on such activity, a second, informal and private campaign, which directly involved the local party organisation, proceeded along several different lines. First, door-to-door campaigning, or some variant of it, undoubtedly took place on a considerable scale. Second, there was undoubted pressure upon particular candidates to withdraw, although it was not always clear whether such pressure was directed from the centre or locally.[86] Hence, there were stories, for example, of Luapulan Copperbelt residents manœuvring to set up a 'slate' of candidates across Copperbelt constituencies to ensure what they saw as 'fair' Luapulan representation. Again, in Ndola, unsuccessful approaches were made to one of the candidates running against a minister of state to suggest she ought to withdraw.[87] Partisan support for a candidate also contributed to a certain degree of harassment of candidates at meetings, where party officials on occasion produced questions clearly designed to embarrass. Regional officials presiding at such meetings showed no impatience with this situation, and for the most part no desire to protect any particular candidate, even when on certain occasions such conduct threatened to disrupt the meeting.

The nature of the primary elections, in which party officials formed the electoral college, made such campaigning almost inevitable, since those elections politicised party officials in this particular context. Clearly, if party officials voted for a particular candidate in the primary election, they were bound to support him through the general election. Hence, they were likely to ignore the prohibition upon canvassing.

This informal campaign within the party was carried on in a highly democratic atmosphere, especially at meetings with district, regional and national leaders concerned to check their enthusiasm, when local party officials obviously felt free to speak openly on matters of concern to them, and to criticise the central leadership. Several such meetings were held, but the one which most dramatically demonstrated this populist and democratic character of U.N.I.P. on the Copperbelt, was that which took place in Kitwe's Buchi Hall, following the Central Committee's veto of the two Kitwe candidates, Harry Lupili and Francis Kapansa. Lupili and Kapansa were both extremely popular candidates, so their disqualification caused much surprise and anger in Kitwe, despite attempts by the District Governor and regional officials to calm the protests. The situation became sufficiently serious for three members of the Central Committee to call a meeting of all branch and constituency level officials in Kitwe at Buchi Hall.[88]

Although the Central Committee members continuously pointed out that the power of veto had been constitutionally granted to the Central Committee, they were unable to make the reasons for the disqualifications known, and this did not placate the feelings of those officials (including many among the Youth Wing) who felt aggrieved. The meeting was extremely animated, and in the course of a wide-ranging discussion the Central Committee members were not always treated with respect.

The meeting in Buchi Hall demonstrated two important characteristics of U.N.I.P. on the Copperbelt at that time. On the one hand, these local leaders insisted without exception that 'we are all members of one house'. On the other hand, the strains that had contributed to the earlier conflict and the emergence of the U.P.P. could be detected underlying the bitter reaction to the Central Committee veto. Kitwe's Buchi Hall, symbolically, had been the scene of those earlier intra-party debates, and this meeting suggested that the removal of the U.P.P. had not brought them to an end.

While no such admission was at any time made, there could be little doubt that the underlying objective of the unofficial campaign (as indeed of the primary election itself) was to 'flush out' suspected U.P.P. supporters. It also, however, had the effect of exacerbating other local rivalries within Copperbelt constituencies, and emphasising parochial interests. Thus, in Ndola Rural, for example, the Lamba chiefs fought successfully to retain Lamba and therefore rural representatives in those two seats, notwithstanding the significant proportion of urban dwellers within the boundaries of at least one of the constituencies. In general, across the Copperbelt there was an increased emphasis upon parochial interests and upon having a 'local man'.

The diminished capacity of the party to manage the electoral system revealed a number of organisational problems that the U.N.I.P. electoral guidelines had failed to anticipate. The party failed, for example, to foresee the difficulties that candidates would encounter in campaigning effectively within the formalised, controlled system of organised meetings, and the frustrations likely to emerge because candidates were unable to discuss local and personal grievances effectively on a shared platform. This was bound to provoke the unofficial campaigning to which reference has been made. Second, while the regulations clearly defined the role of District Governor and regional officials in the election campaign, they did not take sufficient account of the possibility of partiality on the part of those officials.

For the most part, District Governors remained neutral, although some more so than others, and one governor had to be transferred in the course of the elections. Some regional officials were similarly involved and as a result were less effective in organising a campaign that depended on their own impartial administration. Where the regulations were weakest, however, was in their failure to anticipate the partisan behaviour of constituency officials, who were in theory responsible for running an impartial campaign.[89] It was local level engagement on behalf of a particular candidate that created the most serious weakness, for this divided branch and constituency officials and inhibited a united party campaign. As one youth official at branch level put it: 'The one-party system is destroying the party. We are no longer united and are campaigning tribally against each other'.[90] Officials became alienated from each other, in several cases to such a degree that the local organisation was unable to hold meetings. Yet the underlying cause of the problem was not in doubt. The fact that Wusakile constituency, also in Kitwe, had not succumbed to the same problems that affected the others, was attributed by all concerned to the fact that its branches had not divided in support of particular candidates.[91] The division of branches thus promoted a serious deterioration in the affected local organisations. This undoubtedly impaired the ability of the party to mobilise support for the one issue on which it was united and for which it was permissible to mobilise — the presidential election.

Divisions within the party in support of different candidates also promoted, or were translated into, the factional cleavages that had characterised Copperbelt politics in the past. The difference in 1973 was that such cleavages were now articulated at the local level in a situation where the unity formerly derived from the need to fight an opposition party was lacking. Cleavage at the local level contributed to a greater fragmentation, which made it more difficult for the local party to act as an agent of mobilisation or of integration, and this contributed to electoral apathy.

Faced with such pervasive divisions within the local party organisations, district and regional officials sought to use the presidential election as a mechanism to promote unity among lower level activists, with the Minister for the Province insisting upon the need to focus on the presidential election rather than local divisions. A good deal of emphasis was placed, for example, upon the need to counter the alleged underground campaign to persuade voters to vote 'No' against the President. Whether or not such a campaign existed, it was undoubtedly used to dramatise the need for party unity in the face of an external enemy. While that strategy may well have prevented any more serious divisions at the local level, it did not, however, overcome them.

The party and the electorate: ethnicity, inequality and electoral response

The organisational problems presented by the new system, and the divisions exacerbated by parochial interests, did not, however, constitute a sufficient explanation of the failure in popular participation. There were many party officials and supporters who worked hard for the party, not least among the candidates themselves. There were a large number of candidates who had genuine appeal within their locality and were well known in the constituency for their honesty and hard work. And there were a number of exciting contests in which at least two powerful, able and appealing candidates ran against each other. Nevertheless, such constituencies showed no greater degree of electoral participation than those where the quality of the candidates was lower. And even where there were boycotts by some party officials, as in Kwacha and Chimwemwe, their final polls were no lower than those in more trouble-free constituencies. Thus, the organisational problems described do not permit us to distinguish between constituencies. Nor do they account for the fact that the low poll was, as Table 5.1 shows, part of a trend of declining electoral support since 1964.

Furthermore, organisational problems, while important in themselves, seem to us to be manifestations of deeper difficulties rather than causal variables in their own right. Divisions within the local party help us to understand why the party performed poorly, but they do not explain why the divisions should have existed in the first place. Moreover, such divisions focus largely on the leadership; organisational capability is also a function of the links between leaders and followers. Even in constituencies where the leadership was not divided, voters exhibited a great deal of apathy. It is therefore necessary to probe further to understand the relationship between voters and party.

This takes us back to the intra-party conflict that had reached its climax with the formation of the U.P.P. The U.P.P. crisis had created serious divisions within U.N.I.P. on the Copperbelt which, coupled with the acknowledged survival of pockets of unreconciled U.P.P. militants, meant that the party entered the election in serious disarray, with its organisation and its channels of communication with the people unrepaired. U.N.I.P. officials now recognised — as they had denied during the inter-party battle — that there had been a good deal of support for the U.P.P., especially among people living in the poorest areas of the towns, such as Twapia and Masala in Ndola, or the older, more derelict compounds in Kitwe. They also acknowledged that U.P.P. had received tacit support (at least) from many local party officials and others.[92] Furthermore, they accepted the fact that the period prior to the banning of the U.P.P. had been one of great violence, in which some of them had themselves suffered serious attack. The U.P.P. had cost U.N.I.P. a degree of public support, for reasons that we have considered above, and it was conceded that there had been insufficient time to heal the wounds and overcome the divisions. At the same time, the U.P.P. crisis had cost the party much of its provincial leadership of national politicians, who were also the Copperbelt's populist leaders. The Copperbelt populace, traditionally responsive to the militant style of Copperbelt protest and agitational politics, was therefore left to a significant extent without recognisable leadership. At the local level, many branches had been purged during the struggle between the two parties, and so they too suffered from a lack of leadership. It is instructive that in Kitwe Central, one of the oldest and the most powerful of U.N.I.P. constituency organisations, the chairman at the time of the election was an older man who, though clearly able, had little popular support, and prior to 1972 had held no party office. Although as a candidate he topped the primary poll, he came a very poor third in the general election. The implication was a breakdown in the links between the local party leadership and the populace in one of U.N.I.P.'s traditional strongholds.

The Buchi Hall meeting at which Kitwe party officials had confronted the Central Committee demonstrated the legacy of suspicion that the internecine party conflict of the late 'sixties had left behind. Suspicions that U.P.P. sympathisers remained within the U.N.I.P. fold were frequently voiced.[93] Whatever the truth or falsity of such allegations, they highlighted the nature of the problem that faced U.N.I.P. on the Copperbelt as a result of its confrontation with the U.P.P. In spite of the secession of some of those leaders who best expressed the Copperbelt style of militancy, as well as some of U.N.I.P.'s old Bemba-speaking leaders, many of its militants had remained loyal to the party. But the inability of the party to determine conclusively who had been U.P.P. meant that suspicion of loyal Bemba politicians aggravated relationships within the party and made co-operation difficult.

Clearly, for many Copperbelt Bemba, the choice between U.N.I.P. and U.P.P., and between Kapwepwe and Kaunda, was one they had not relished being forced to make. Many regarded those two leaders as epitomising the type and style of the U.N.I.P. which they supported, and both men were deeply respected as the leaders of militant defiance campaigns during the days of the nationalist struggle against the colonial government. Among the more experienced party officials, many of whom recalled the struggle with deep nostalgia, and especially among those who could be called populists, many would

have preferred the two to remain united and other leaders to have
been removed instead from the party. The problem, therefore, was
that populist style, or being a Bemba, or being a militant, did not in
the final analysis demarcate a member of U.P.P. The difficulty of
identifying U.P.P. sympathisers ensured that U.P.P. support could not
be fully 'flushed out' of U.N.I.P., and that U.N.I.P. officials could
never be certain that they had succeeded in expelling such dissidents.
In consequence, suspicions remained strong during the elections and
became increasingly totalistic in their embrace. Thus family, patronage or friendship ties were enough to condemn someone in the opinion of many others. And being under suspicion ensured that one's
friends might be suspected. Moreover, the situation was undoubtedly
used by some to settle other scores, since the condemnation of
someone as U.P.P. was an effective method of attacking an opponent.

The persistence of suspicions that the U.P.P. remained as a force
within the local party organisation strengthened the tendency to
exploit ethnicity as a device for mobilising support. Having been
identified as a Bemba party, the U.P.P. could then be equated with all
Bemba and all Bemba identified with the U.P.P. It was thus possible to
attack the most numerous group on the Copperbelt under the guise of
proclaiming loyalty to the party and President.[94]

Underlying this recourse to 'tribalism' and allegations of Bemba
dominance was, we suggest, the same fear that had been prominent
earlier: of unfair access to resources and especially employment in a
situation of scarcity and increasing economic difficulty. People making such allegations were apt to point out that the fact that there were
more Bemba-speaking people in an industry showed that they
operated tribally and promoted their own. One candidate, in fact,
produced a large list of companies, organisations and a mine and
claimed that they were totally dominated by Bemba. In other words,
ethnicity, having once been employed as a device in the competition
for position, tended to be self-sustaining: the fact that Bemba-speaking people were numerically the largest group did not seem to be
important to those who saw a majority of jobs going to them. In the
event, however, we need also to bear in mind that a majority of the
successful candidates, representing, as we have suggested, on the one
hand proven party supporters, but on the other a significant number of
the new Copperbelt bourgeoisie, were also Bemba-speaking towns-
men.

While ethnicity was without any doubt exploited by a number of
candidates and their followers, as a method of organising patronage
and manipulating support, it was by no means the only appeal used in
this election. Moreover, it is also essential to bear in mind the extent
to which the appeal to ethnic loyalty was interwoven with other

loyalties. The very nature of Zambia's fluid, rapidly-changing society, permitted a remarkable flexibility of choice in the line of cleavages used in a conflict situation. Given the nature of patronage and its links with the extended family structure, combatants often had a number of strategic options open to them.[95] In seeking political or economic power, individuals tended to find ethnic appeals valuable as a rapid and simple way of aggregating support and preserving patronage networks (the District Governor's Office was frequently called upon to mediate in labour disputes, for instance in parastatal branches, as factions defined in ethnic terms sought to keep outsiders out). Such an appeal was, of course, of value only if it gave a candidate an opportunity to win by aggregating a large measure of support. Where an ethnic appeal meant certain loss of a contest, disadvantaged candidates tended to abhor 'tribalism' and to call for national unity. Ethnicity proved to be a manipulative division utilised in the struggle for power and economic reward, rather than a very deep, ingrained form of social grouping, and frequently on the Copperbelt 'us' by contrast, was defined more by the militant style we have discussed earlier than by language, region or tribe. Nevertheless, during the election, ethnic association promoted and intensified cleavages within the party and provided a thread around which competition for power and rewards, political divisions, and élite manipulation of voters could operate. In such a situation, it was not surprising that district and regional officials were, for the most part, unable to re-direct the energies of the party towards the presidential election and away from internecine struggles.

Across the Copperbelt as a whole, it was difficult to identify any clear, overt demonstration of class consciousness. Nevertheless, the Nkana constituency suggested an underlying sense of grievance, among miners at least, against the growing inequality that had now emerged, and that was increasingly a feature of the party leadership. We have already identified the emergence of a new business class on the Copperbelt, and their place in the party leadership. A significant number of the new professionals and managers had also now gravitated to the party. At the same time, it must be borne in mind that many other party officials, at the local and lower levels of the party, had since independence become small traders or businessmen, or obtained positions in parastatal organisations. Local councillors, for example, many of whom were also constituency officials, had become traders, some of them large ones. At the same time, there had also been a discernible tendency for the general status or affluence of U.N.I.P. local officials to rise, and U.N.I.P. officials had since independence been drawn increasingly from more highly paid occupations.[96]

To some extent, this indicated promotions attained after independence and even a 'glamourisation' of the nomenclature of jobs after 1964. In addition, some new branches had been formed by people in higher paid employment, particularly in the aftermath of defections to the U.P.P. The result was a change, in some areas at least, first in the image of the party at the local level, as it became more characteristically shaped around a local élite, and second in the way in which it operated. In not a few cases it became a 'part-time, after-five party'. In the course of the 1973 elections, at not a few meetings, officials arrived from office or business, discussed business with colleagues, and generally gave the impression that party work was a spare-time occupation. In addition, many of the newer branch and constituency officials tended to have somewhat tenuous links with the independence struggle, in marked contrast with earlier officials who had often endured prison. Finally, party officials, recent recruits as well as old, tended to be of the same generation, and there was a singular absence of young people in their ranks. Not only had the party at the local level become more affluent and less committed, but it had also become a generational party.

This changed image of the party was not true of all Copperbelt constituencies. A notable exception was Chifubu, where the successful candidate, Credo Kaunda Banda, was a youth constituency official in his early twenties. Moreover, the party tended to have a stronger presence in the squatter settlements that ringed the towns, where it often still performed societal functions similar to those it had done in the past. Nevertheless, in many places the party branch had undoubtedly lost its old dynamism, and the distance between party and people had increased.

If the local level party officials had by 1973 become relatively more privileged than the communities in which they lived, this was even more true of many of the candidates, and one significant influence upon the vote was the attitudes that many candidates held and expressed, for they could not fail to affect public response. Many candidates spoke disparagingly of their less-educated and lower status rivals. Among some wealthier candidates, there was a relationship between the privileged position they enjoyed and a cluster of negative attitudes towards local party officials and government policies. A businessman who was eliminated in the primary election, considered the entire proceedings were dominated by party record rather than ability, and by 'tribalism' rather than fitness for representation of the constituency. He regarded government as compromised by the lavish standard of living of many leaders, the one-party state as a form of 'communism' in which government was reduced to a rubber stamp for a few party leaders, Humanism as a set of ideas which were preached rather than practised, and the Leadership Code as a blunder which would discourage initiative while enabling a few to acquire wealth.[97] Another candidate of wealth and high education who was also eliminated in the primary election felt that he had chosen the wrong constituency, since the one in which he had registered his nomination was 'full of slums' and the people treated him with suspicion when he arrived in a suit to address them. In both these cases, privileged candidates had failed to survive the primaries and clearly were not inclined to be charitable about the mechanism which had produced such a result. Nevertheless, their attitudes indicated the gap which now existed between those of high status and/or income and the bulk of the population. Although views such as these two were exceptional in their forcefulness, similar attitudes were expressed by a number of others in more moderate terms.

The Copperbelt remained, however, above all the heartland of Zambia's working class, so that we need to consider further, to the extent that is possible, the reaction of the workers on the Copperbelt to this changed situation. We can say little about the urban work-force as a whole, but we can look more closely at the mine labour force, whose position on the Copperbelt remained of crucial political importance. When we examine the size of the 'No' vote in the pres-idential election, it emerges clearly that in predominantly mining constituencies or constituencies in which mine employees formed a significant proportion of the voters, the 'No' vote was significantly greater than in predominantly non-mining constituencies. As Table 5.6 shows, the proportion of 'No' voters in mining constituencies was twice the proportion in non-mining constituencies, expressed either as a percentage of voters actually casting valid ballots or as a propor-tion of registered voters. In aggregate terms, too, more people voted 'No' in the former than in the latter, despite the fact that fewer voters were represented by the mining constituencies. And when we exclude the two Mufulira constituencies of Kankoyo and Kantanshi from the mining constituencies, the proportion is still greater.[98] The table shows that a proportionately greater number of voters went to the polls in non- mining than in mining constituencies, and also that even in towns where both types of constituencies were found, the experi-ence in most cases tended to be that of a higher negative vote among miners.[99]

Although the pattern is clear, it is more difficult to draw firm conclusions about the underlying implications. Certainly it is inter-esting that greater 'No' votes should have been recorded in Nkana and Wusakile than in Kwacha and Chimwemwe where there was so much controversy over the disqualifications. But since few constituencies are purely mining or purely non-mining, we should treat the correla-

Table 5.6   Comparison of presidential 'no' vote in mining and non-mining constituencies, 1973 elections

(a) All Copperbelt constituencies	*Non-mining*	*Mining*
Registered voters	173,169	127,225
Poll (%)	54.62	44.5
Number voting	94,588	56,620
Valid votes in presidential election	89,399	53,458
'No' votes	6,617	9,614
'No' poll (%)	7.4	18.0
'No' of registered voters (%)	3.82	7.56

(b) Individual constituencies

Non-mining constituency	*'No' as % of poll*	*Mining constituency*	*'No' as % of poll*
Chingola	6.9	Chililabombwe	12.5
		Nchanga	19.2
Chimwemwe	7.6	Kalulushi	6.9
Kwacha	5.9	Nkana	11.7
Luanshya	6.2	Wusakile	18.2
Mufulira	17.0	Roan	5.1
		Kankoyo	46.1
Luswishi	1.9	Kantanshi	37.4
Masaiti	4.8		
Chiwala	4.3		
Chifubu	6.4		
Ndola	7.7		
Masala	10.9		

(c) Excluding Mufulira constituences of Mufulira, Kankoyo and Kantanshi		
	Non-mining	*Mining*
Registered voters	160,368	101,543
Poll (%)	55.34	45.79
Number voting	88,754	46,492
Valid votes in presidential election	83,830	43,776
'No' votes	5,670	5,559
'No' poll (%)	6.8	12.7
'No' of registered voters (%)	3.54	5.47

tion with some care, and our conclusions are therefore advanced somewhat tentatively. Although the evidence was somewhat impressionistic, we did not find widespread animosity or opposition towards President Kaunda. Indeed, no matter how much candidates, officials and voters may have differed on other matters, they were largely united in their desire to return the President to power and were generally approving of him. We can therefore only conclude that the 'No' vote constituted less a comment on the President than on the party and government. In the one-party state, elections provided a mechanism for commenting on local issues, but did not really provide any way in which voters could comment on events and policy at the national level. We would therefore suggest that to a large extent the 'No' vote represented a method by which people expressed their grievances over issues such as employment, social amenities, inflation and the performance of the party and government. Thus, the higher proportion of 'No' votes in mining constituencies would reflect less a vote against the President than a protest against such problems.

There was some evidence that miners felt a stronger sense of grievance than other workers over several issues. For example, nine years after independence, many miners felt that race was still a factor on the mines and that it worked to their disadvantage.[100] One regional party official, for example, remarked that there had been less change in patterns of racialism on the mines than he would have expected at independence when he was still a miner. And the mine shift boss who stood in Nkana complained angrily that he spent weeks familiarising new expatriate personnel with the mine and showing them around, only then to have them placed in positions of authority over him.

The Nkana election, where the President of the Mineworkers Union was pitted against a shift boss, permits an understanding of alienation from the union and anger over what was perceived as an unsatisfactory rate of progress. Indeed, a strong dissatisfaction with the Union leadership was clearly manifest and seemed to grow the poorer the worker.[101] Edwin Simwanza, the shift boss, was constantly referred to in a scornful manner by his opponents and their agents, who made much of his poor education and somewhat crude manner of expression. Yet he self-consciously represented a protest against older, more experienced officials whom he argued had done nothing. In the poor parts of the constituency, he clearly evoked a most favourable response against opponents who represented élite levels in the union and in the local party. It was in the wealthier mine areas of Nkana, where many shift bosses, supervisors and personnel officers lived, that he seemed to draw little support — an impression confirmed for us by several election agents. Thus, despite having won a 22 per cent pay rise for the miners immediately before the elections, Mwila, the union president, scored a surprisingly narrow victory. Simwanza's performance, therefore, indicated that problems within the union were expressed politically in the election.

Similarly, in Chililabombwe, the election was contested by the local union chairman who had a history of attacking the union head office and who came within 300 votes of defeating a minister, Dr. Sefelino Mulenga. The policy of curbing trade-union action against the mining companies, which government had pursued since 1966, and the practice of moving powerful unionists into government, had clearly weakened the union, and angered workers who felt frustrated with the lack of militancy in articulating their demands. This carried over into the election and hampered party efforts at mobilisation. The unions, as we have noted earlier, had jealously guarded their independence, but were now seen by many to have been compromised by their leaders. In that context, the larger negative vote may have been an expression, not of antipathy to the system, but of a desire actively to express grievances within it, although the low poll implied that many saw little purpose in participating.

The first elections under the one-party constitution took place in the aftermath of serious political cleavages within U.N.I.P. The elections — both campaign and outcome — indicated that certain positive results were achieved for the government. The recruitment of new leadership to the National Assembly attracted a large number of candidates and ensured a large number of prominent local leaders being returned for the first time. As an exercise in control, the elections were also a success, with local party officials being returned in significant numbers and no outspoken opponent of government policy winning a seat. In addition, the nature of the electoral system ensured an airing of local issues and grievances, linking candidates more closely with matters relevant to their constituents. The overwhelming proportion of voters who voted affirmatively for the President indicated a high degree of loyalty to him.

However, the low poll continued a pattern of diminishing electorate participation since independence and constituted a serious setback to government hopes of legitimising the new system through the ballot. An examination of the causes of the low level of participation indicated that, to some extent, the one-party system itself lessened the capacity of the party to mobilise the vote. However, the serious divisions within the party as a result of the formation of the U.P.P. in 1971 had also weakened the local levels of U.N.I.P. and reduced its ability to function free of internal suspicion and recrimination. In addition, government policies and what was perceived as ineffective trade-union leadership alienated many workers, particularly the mineworkers, and this alienation was carried into the elections. Further, the pattern of patronage which characterised the search for advancement after independence, and which contributed significantly to popular disaffection and cleavages within the party, also helped to promote divisions among local officials during the campaign. And finally, and most significant, growing social inequality lessened the commitment of many leaders to the party organisation, distanced them from the mass of voters, and induced among some of them a new cynicism about the aims and activities of the party.

Government economic policies had induced fundamental changes in the social structure which were manifest in a growing degree of social inequality. Within U.N.I.P., too, a perceptible degree of social differentiation weakened the party's links with the people and lessened its effectiveness as an organisation. Patronage, while ensuring advancement for some, had not satisfied all demands for consumption and so competitive forces within the party intensified, often taking the form of ethnic appeals for support. These further weakened the party as a unified organisation. By 1971, inequality, the failure to meet mass demands for services and other forms of consumption, and the internal competition for scarce rewards had resulted in the division between 'populists', articulating the militant Copperbelt political style, and 'modernists', being expressed in the formation of the U.P.P. That further divided and weakened the party through the defection of some of its members and through the mutual suspicion that remained between members of U.N.I.P. In this context, the one-party system, by removing the internally-unifying device of a political opposition, in 1973 encouraged party members to compete against each other along lines of cleavage already determined by the strains and crises mentioned. In the event, it seems unreal to speak about 'the party'. The centre was linked to the district by the district and regional offices; but below that little central control could be exerted on large numbers of fragmented constituencies and branches.

The problem of the U.P.P. might be regarded as a short-term problem which would diminish in importance over time, and from which the party could recover by improving its organisational capacity. Similarly, the use of ethnic symbols to win support might be regarded as a longer term transitional problem, capable of diminishing in time as other forms of cleavage and differentiation become more strongly rooted. Equally, the alienation of many workers might be seen as a problem capable of amelioration through improved contact between party and workers and through the creation of workers' participation in industry (as was the government's declared intention). But the fourth source of problems which afflicted the party had led to a decreasing capacity to mobilise mass support. Hence, the growing social stratification of society in Zambia posed a more difficult problem for the party, and in many ways underlay the other difficulties. In particular, because there was little consciousness of class or status in any coherent form, stratification was seldom perceived by leaders or followers as acting upon the political system. Nevertheless, the 1973 election on the Copperbelt provided some evidence that growing class and status differences had increased between party and people, and within the party.[162]

Notes

1   This chapter is based on research carried out by both authors over the period 1970 to 1973, including field work on the Copperbelt over those years. While we have written the chapter together, the analysis of the election itself is based primarily on Morris Szeftel's work on the Copperbelt during the campaign, while the earlier sections draw on Cherry Gertzel's work, both then and earlier, on labour and politics as well as the party.

2   Ian Henderson, 'The Copperbelt Disturbances of 1935 and 1940', *Journal of Southern African Studies*, 2, 1 (1975); A.L. Epstein, *Politics in an Urban African Community* (Manchester, Manchester University Press, 1957).

3   David Mulford (1967) *op.cit., passim.*

4   Robert Bates, *Unions, Parties and Political Development: A Study of Mineworkers in Zambia* (New Haven and London, Yale University Press, 1971).

5   There is an excellent literature on the growth of the mining industry. See, *inter alia*, R.E. Baldwin, *Economic Development and Export Growth* (Los Angeles, University of California Press, 1961); Charles Perrings, *Black Mineworkers in Central Africa* (London, Heinemann, 1979); Elena L. Berger, *Labour, Race and Colonial Rule* (Oxford, Clarendon Press, 1974).

6   All population figures for these years must be taken as estimates, since the first African census was not carried out until 1963. See, for example, R.R. Kuczynski, *Demographic Survey of the British Colonial Empire*, Vol. II, (London, Oxford University Press, 1949). From 1951, estimates of Africans in employment were included in non-native censuses. The figures here are from W.V. Brelsford, *Copperbelt Markets : A Social and Economic Study* (Lusaka, Government Printer, 1947); and Lord Hailey, *Native Administration in the British African Territories*, Part II (London, H.M.S.O. 1054), p. 104.

7   Baldwin, *op.cit.*, is the best general account. See also Francis L. Coleman, *The Northern Rhodesian Copperbelt, 1899–1962*, (Manchester, Manchester University Press, 1971); Berger, *op.cit.*

8   Baldwin, *op.cit.*

9   Helmuth Heisler, 'The Creation of a Stabilised Urban Society: A Turning Point in the Development of Northern Rhodesia/Zambia', *African Affairs*, 70 (1971).

10 Patrick O. Ohadike, *Development of and Factors in the Employment of African Migrants in the Copper Mines of Zambia, 1940–1966*, University of Zambia, Institute for Social Research, Zambian Papers, No. 4, 1969.

11 The most sensitive description of Copperbelt society in this period is still undoubtedly A.L. Epstein, *op.cit.* See also his *Ethos and Identity* (London, Tavistock Publications, 1978).

12 Ohadike, *op.cit.* P. Harries-Jones, 'The Tribes in the Town', in W.V. Brelsford, *The Tribes of Zambia*, (Lusaka, Government Printer, 1965).

See also Merran McCulloch, *A Social Survey of the African Population in Livingstone*, Rhodes-Livingstone Papers, No. 26 (Manchester University Press, 1956).

13   J.C. Mitchell, *African Urbanisation in Ndola and Luanshya*, Rhodes-Livingstone Communication, No. 6, 1954. See also Hailey, *op.cit.*; Epstein, (1958) *op.cit.*

14   Information from Philip Daniel. See his *Africanisation, Nationalisation and Inequality: Mining Labour and the Copperbelt in Zambian Development*, (Cambridge, Cambridge University Press, 1979), Ch. 3.

15   Peter Harries-Jones, *Freedom and Labour* (Oxford, Basil Blackwell, 1975), Ch. 6.

16   Philip Daniel, *op.cit.*, pp. 146–7.

17   Epstein (1958), *op.cit.*

18   See Clyde Mitchell, *Manchester Guardian*, 19 Sept. 1957; Godfrey Wilson, *An Essay on the Economics of Detribalisation*, Parts 1 and 2, Rhodes-Livingstone Papers Nos. 5 and 6 (Livingstone, Rhodes-Livingstone Institute, 1941, 1942).

19   Daniel, *op.cit.* For Zambia as a whole, employment actually fell from 271,000 in 1957 to 221,000 in 1963. See *Manpower Report*. A Report and Statistical Handbook on Manpower, Education, Training and Zambianisation 1965–66. Issued by the Cabinet office (Lusaka, Government Printer, 1966).

20   *Report of the Commission of Inquiry into unrest on the Copperbelt in the months of July and August 1963*, p. 5 (Lusaka, Government Printer, 1963).

21   Henderson, *op.cit.*

22   Berg, E.J. and Butler, J., 'Trade Unions' in James Coleman and Carl Rosberg, *op.cit.*

23   Epstein (1958), *op.cit.*, pp. 98–101.

24   See *Ibid.* Ch. 5. The best general account of these years is in Mulford, 1967, *op.cit.* See also Robert Rotberg, *The Rise of Nationalism in Central Africa: The Making of Malawi and Zambia 1873–1964* (Cambridge, Mass., Harvard University Press, 1966).

25   Mulford (1967), *op.cit.*, pp. 232–6.

26   Ian Scott (1976), *op.cit.*, pp. 107–29.

27   See Harries-Jones (1975), *op.cit.*, Ch. 1, for a fascinating autobiographical account of the experience of one U.N.I.P. woman party official in Luanshya.

28   In 1962 U.N.I.P.'s three successful candidates were Sikota Wina (party official and Lozi), Grey Zulu (party official and Nyanja), and John Chisata (President of A.M.W.U. and Bemba). In 1964, of the 11 U.N.I.P. Copperbelt M.P.s, only 3 were Bemba-speakers. All, however, had an urban background and 6 were 'party' men.

29   The best introduction to trade-union relations with A.N.C., is W. Richard Jacobs, *The Relationship between African Trade Unions and Political Organisations in Northern Rhodesia/Zambia, 1949–61*. (Geneva, International Institute for Labour Studies, 1971); Berg and Butler, *op.cit.* and Bates (1971), *op.cit.*, are also very helpful.

30 Mulford (1967), *op.cit.*

31 *Report of the Commission of Inquiry into Unrest on the Copperbelt*, *op.cit.* Aristide Zolberg, *op.cit.*, pp. 19–27, notes that most African mass parties won independence through 'marginal increments of organisation', rather than through any ability to mobilise the overwhelming majority of potential voters. He notes that in countries such as Ghana and Ivory Coast, dominant parties received huge majorities of the registered vote, but that this represented a minority of the potential electorate. It is of interest that U.N.I.P. constitutes an exception to Zolberg's argument. In 1964 U.N.I.P. managed to register most of the adult population of the country and received, in 1968, some 68 per cent of those registered votes.

32 Mulford (1964), *op.cit.* and (1967), *op.cit.*

33 The details of economic expansion in the immediate post-independence years are best followed in Charles Elliott (ed.), *Constraints on the Economic Development of Zambia* (Nairobi, Oxford University Press, 1971). See also *Second National Development Plan, January 1972–December 1976*, Ministry of Development Planning and Guidance, December 1971, Part I and p. 167.

34 Republic of Zambia, Central Statistical Office, Lusaka, *Monthly Digest of Statistics*, XI, I (1975), Table 2. See also *Preliminary Report, Sample Census of Population 1974* (February 1975). Between 1963 and 1969, 37,442 people moved from Northern and Luapula provinces to the Copperbelt, compared with 12,361 from Eastern, 10,361 from North-Western, 5,457 from the Mkushi side of Central Province, and 3,787 from Western (Barotseland).

35 Turner Report, *op.cit.*

36 See, for example, *Towards Complete Independence*. Speech by H.E. the President, Dr. K.D. Kaunda, to the U.N.I.P. National Council held at Matero Hall, 11 Aug. 1969.

37 Daniel, *op.cit.*, Table 2.15, p. 55. See also Central Statistical Office, *Report on Employment and Earnings 1963–1968*, and *Report on Employment and Earnings 1969–74*, Lusaka, 1969 and 1974.

38 *Ibid.*

39 *Northern News*, 8 Mar. 1965. See also Harries-Jones (1975), *op.cit.*, p. 80.

40 *Zambia Mail*, 21 Dec. 1971. 'Education: Free but it's still a struggle', *National Assembly Debates*, 9 Feb. 1971.

41 Kitwe City Council Development Plan, 1973.

42 Daniel, *op.cit.*

43 *Ibid*, pp. 36–7 has an excellent analysis of Copperbelt employment and unemployment over this period. On Copperbelt squatter settlements, see A.G. Tipple, *Squatters and Housing*, University of Zambia Seminar Paper, September 1974 (mimeo). Also *The People of 'Zambia City'*, The Research Unit of Community Development, Ministry of Mines and Co-operatives, 1966 (mimeo).

44 *Kitwe Social Survey* (1972), *op.cit*; Daniel, *op.cit.*, also analyses the data in that survey.

45 *Ibid*; *Statistical Digest*, VI, 1 (1975), pp. 48–9.

46 *Kitwe Social Survey* (1972), *op.cit.*

47   Charles Perrings, 'A Moment in the Proletarianisation of the New Middle Class: Race, Value and Division of Labour in the Copperbelt 1946–1966', *Journal of Southern African Studies*, 6, 2 (1980); Daniel, *op.cit.*, p. 138, argues that the miners' strike in 1966 was the 'last time when concerted action by the mass of unskilled mineworkers, acting with the backing, however tardy and feeble, of their union, secured a substantial general wage increase in the Zambian copper mines'. See also *Sunday Times of Zambia*, 16 Sept. 1973.

48   *Annual Report*, Ministry of Labour 1965, commented, 'most workers have showed commendable patience at waiting for the dramatic upturn in wage levels which all expect . . . The patience could turn into frustration and increased industrial unrest through which this could find expression should not be ruled out.'

49   Seers Report, *op.cit.*

50   *Livingstone Labour Conference*, 1967, p. 9. See also Bates (1971), *op.cit.*, and C. Gertzel, 'Labour and the State', *Journal of Commonwealth Political Studies*, XIII, 3 (1975).

51   *Annual Report*, Labour Department, 1972, p.4.

52   *Ibid*, 1970, p.11

53   Bates (1971), *op.cit*; Brown Report, *op.cit.*

54   Daniel, *op.cit*; Michael Burawoy, *The Colour of Class on the Mines: From African Advancement to Zambianisation* (Manchester).

55   *Ibid*; Bates (1971), *op.cit.*; Gertzel (1975), *op.cit.*

56   Compare Bates, Burawoy and Daniel on this point.

57   Cherry Gertzel, 'Industrial Relations in Zambia to 1975', Ukandi G. Damachi, H. Dieter Seibel and Lester Trachtman (eds.), *Industrial Relations in Africa* (London, MacMillan, 1979). See the Trade Unions and Trade Disputes (Amendment) Ordinance No. 3 of 1965, and the debate thereon, *Daily Parliamentary Debates*, 14 Dec. 1965. Also the Industrial Relations Act 1971, No 36. of 1971, and the debate thereon, *Daily Parliamentary Debates*, 30 Nov. and 1 Dec. 1971.

58   *Annual Report*, Labour Department 1972, p. 14.

59   For example, *Northern News*, 17 May 1965.

60   See, for example, *Northern News*, Jan. 1965, for reports of severe assaults upon A.N.C. supporters in Ndola; *Times of Zambia*, 24 Aug. 1970, for violence during local government election campaign; and *Times of Zambia*, 14 Aug. 1968, for Chililabombwe disturbance discussed below.

61   *Times of Zambia*, 31 Oct. 1968.

62   *Chona Report*, p. 50.

63   For example, *Daily Mail*, 4 Apr. and 20 July 1972; *Daily Parliamentary Debates*, 24 Nov. 1971.

64   Information from Kitwe City Council.

65   *Times of Zambia*, 14 Feb. and 25 May 1972; *Sunday Times of Zambia*, 16 Sept. 1973.

66   For example, *Times of Zambia*, 5 Nov. 1969 and 11 Apr. 1973; *Zambia Mail*, 24 Jan. 1970; *Sunday Times of Zambia*, 8 Aug. 1971.

67   Ian Scott (1978), *op.cit.*

68   The events of these months are best followed in the local press. See also
     C. Gertzel, *et al, op.cit.*

69   *Times of Zambia*, 21 Aug. 1971.

70   In the words of a senior civil servant on the Copperbelt in an interview in
     November 1973.

71   *Times of Zambia*, 14 Aug. 1968.

72   For example, *Times of Zambia*, 15 Jan. 1972.

73   *Daily Parliamentary Debates*, 16 Aug. 1968, cols 160–203.

74   *Times of Zambia*, 9 Feb., 20 Mar. 1970.

75   Based on detailed biographical data drawn from both documentary
     sources and from interviews with most of those involved.

76   U.P.P. Constitution, 1971 (mimeo).

77   *Times of Zambia*, 21 Aug. 1971.

78   For example, *Daily Parliamentary Debates*, 21 Jan. 1971, cols 155–158.

79   Gertzel *et al, op.cit.*

80   97 prospective candidates initially lodged nominations before the
     primaries. In the constituency of Luswishi, the sole nominee was sub-
     sequently disqualified by the Central Committee and new nominations
     were invited. Two new aspirants were successfully nominated and con-
     tested the general election, thus bringing the number to 99. Primaries
     were not required in four constituencies (there being fewer than four
     nominations in each): these were the two rural seats in the Copperbelt,
     Luswishi and Masaiti, the heavily urban Wusakile, and Chiwala which
     was predominantly urban in terms of registered voters, largely rural in
     area, and where the candidates were rural dwellers promoted by the
     chiefs. Four candidates who qualified for the general election (either by
     primary victories or because no primary was necessary) were disqual-
     ified. In three cases, the leading primary loser was promoted to candidacy
     in the general election, but two of these did not run in the election. The
     fourth case, Luswishi, has already been noted above.

81   Interview, 7 Nov. 1973 with a lawyer defeated in the primary in Ndola.
     He felt strongly that the new system was biased against non-party people
     and that the primaries ensured that the elections were for 'the Party boys
     and girls'. In a subsequent interview, on 8 Nov. 1973, another candidate
     stressed the need for candidates to have a full understanding of local
     problems and experience in dealing with those problems. A lack of those
     qualities would result in 'bad' candidates, he felt. Most of those inter-
     viewed felt local experience to be necessary in an M.P., and several saw
     this as a means of distinguishing 'idealistic' from 'opportunistic' candi-
     dates. It is frequently difficult to determine the primary role or occupa-
     tion of a candidate. Many party officials were also local councillors and/
     or businessmen. We have presented data (see below) on both formal
     political positions and on occupations from which candidates earned
     their living.

82   Kitwe, with Ndola, was generally regarded as the heartland of U.N.I.P.
     The effects of the U.P.P. on the party were most clearly seen here. In the
     four Kitwe constituencies (leaving Kalulushi aside), only one was con-
     tested by a sitting M.P. (and he had been returned in the 1972 by-election

rather than in 1968). Only one other candidate was nationally well known.

83 The point can perhaps be illustrated by the example of Masala constituency in Ndola, which had had strong U.P.P. support in 1971. One of the candidates who entered the primary there was a former Deputy Mayor of Ndola, Mishek Kabungo, who had been detained along with the leaders of the U.P.P. but subsequently released. Kabungo was eliminated in the primaries, before it became necessary for the Central Committee to veto him. In fact, only four candidates were disqualified in the Copperbelt, compared with seven in Northern Province and eight in Eastern Province, neither of which areas had experienced anywhere near the same level of political ferment in 1971 and 1972.

84 The Minister of Defence, A.M. Milner, the Minister of Health, A.B. Chikwanda, three ministers of state, M.J. Banda, N.S. Mulenga and J.C. Mutale (all of whom subsequently became Cabinet Ministers), and a backbencher, S.M. Malama.

85 A presidential visit to the Copperbelt on the eve of polling day was, however, arranged from State House.

86 In some provinces, observers noted that some candidates could be regarded as officially favoured by the centre, and many candidates often felt that there were such 'official candidates'. In the Copperbelt, this was far more difficult to discern, probably because most of the leading figures of Copperbelt politics had been removed into the Central Committee or into opposition during the U.P.P. troubles. In Ndola, it was clear that candidates were pressured to withdraw in favour of the Minister of State, Misheck Banda, and in Kalulushi, there was some evidence of pressure exerted in favour of the then Minister of Health, A.B. Chikwanda. But if there were pressures to advance the campaigns of sitting M.P.s (for instance, in Chingola, Chililabombwe or Wusakile), these were not easily observed. In any event, as stated, such pressures were resisted. In two cases where disqualifications led to primary losers being promoted, the promoted candidates did not come forward for the general election. This abstention favoured the campaigns of other candidates from the same ethnic groups as the promoted candidates, rather than reflecting any pressure.

87 Interview, 9 Nov. 1973. Although the candidate was subsequently defeated, it did not diminish her loyalty to the party, although it soured some of her supporters.

88 One of the authors and one other researcher were present at this meeting held on 14 Nov. 1973. Indeed, one significant point concerns the fact that they were included in the meeting without any opposition. The four disqualifications on the Copperbelt were H. Lupili in Kwacha, F.T. Kapansa in Chimwemwe (both Kitwe), P.M. Shibuchinga in Luswishi (rural), and P.N. Chelelwa in Mufulira. At least one other candidate, in Masala, would probably have been disqualified had he survived the primary, and a fifth, P.S. Katongo, was detained in Kalulushi on the eve of the primary poll — a fate which doubtless contributed to his defeat in the primary. One speaker at the meeting constantly reminded the audi-

ence that the new constitution had been created by them through consultation with the Chona Commission. This claim was not well received by local party officials whose comments clearly indicated that many of them had not anticipated any such disqualifications. It is noteworthy that during the subsequent 1975 local government elections, applicants were first vetted by the Central Committee and then went forward to the primary elections. In the 1978 general elections, however, the Central Committee returned to the 1973 practice in this regard.

89 Further, not only did supporters unofficially canvass for candidates, but, as noted below, these tended to be largely drawn from the ranks of local party officials, often resulting in branches becoming divided and ineffective when called upon to promote the presidential election.

90 Meeting in the offices of the District Governor, Kitwe, on 13 Nov. 1973, the Governor appealed to candidates not to 'divide the people when we are trying to unite them'. He clearly regarded the attitudes of many candidates as being counter-productive to the major aims of the one-party system.

91 Interview, 16 Nov. 1973. This was reaffirmed in a later interview with Nkana candidate, the Constituency Chairman for Kitwe Central, who noted that his Constituency Secretary was actively campaigning for one of his opponents, and expressed concern about whether or not they would be able to work together after the election.

92 U.P.P. was able to attract a number of small businessmen who were active members of Z.N.C.C.I., and a number of local party officials, middle-rank civil servants and so on. The Z.N.C.C.I. constantly articulated the demands of its members for more credit and for less competition from the parastatal trading sector.

93 Interviews, 7 Nov. 1973, 8 Nov. 1973 and 15 Nov. 1973. Candidates and party officials felt that Twapia and Masala in Ndola, and Kwacha and Chimwemwe in Kitwe, as well as several squatter areas, all still retained much sympathy for the U.P.P.

94 One candidate was quite explicit in making this equation; 'birds of a feather . . .', he stated when asked whether it could really be possible that all Bemba were U.P.P. He also alleged that U.P.P. members continued to pose as U.N.I.P. loyalists and to promote their own kind in the mines, parastatals and private companies. Interview, 17 Nov. 1973.

95 Thus, in Chifubu Constituency in Ndola, the Bemba candidate was also a party constituency official and the Eastern Province candidate was a national trade-union leader. In Nkana, the three candidates were a union leader, and two party constituency officials, one of whom was also a shift boss, but all three were Bemba-speakers.

96 See above, Chapter 1 and footnote 53.

97 This candidate did not discriminate between labelling a policy 'communist' in one sentence and 'capitalist' in the next. Once again, the lack of any coherent picture of either social system was clearly manifest, for instance in the definition of exploiting class as 'big shots' (we were unable to obtain any further definition of the latter term). One 'by-product' of our interviews was the clear demonstration of the fact that

political education within the party was needed to ensure that party officials and local leaders were provided with much clearer definitions of the problems they confronted in undertaking their party responsibilities.

98 Mufulira constituted a special case in Copperbelt politics and would weight any figures in favour of opposition to the government. It is therefore significant that the same trend obtains even without Mufulira. The 'special' character of Mufulira derives from its peculiar history as a *locus* of opposition to U.N.I.P. on the Copperbelt. The A.N.C. was traditionally strong in the town and mine and, when the Copperbelt led the move of African political organisation to Z.A.N.C. and then U.N.I.P., Mufulira was the one centre to resist conversion for a time. In the 1964 elections, it went to U.N.I.P. but A.N.C. still polled 40.9 per cent (its next best in the province was 18.6 per cent). In 1968, A.N.C. lost all three Mufulira seats but still did far better there than anywhere else on the Copperbelt, including 35 per cent in Mufulira West. When the creation of U.P.P. forced a number of by-elections in 1971, U.N.I.P. was able to defend four seats successfully against the new party, but Mufulira West returned Simon Kapwepwe for the U.P.P. It has never been a town — still less a mining community — on which the government could automatically count for support.

99 The one exception to this last-mentioned fact was in Luanshya, where the mining constituency polled a lower 'No' vote than the town. In this case, the year before the elections had been dominated by a serious division within the local party, and this may have affected the 'No' vote among non-miners.

100 See Michael Burawoy, *op.cit.*, for an analysis of grievances expressed by miners, in the late 'sixties, including racism and the slow pace of Zambianisation.

101 At an election meeting at Mindolo, there was clear hostility towards the President of the Mineworkers' Union from an audience of party officials, many of whom came from what is the poorest mine compound in Kitwe; he was asked how he, as an educated man, could represent poor people and was also told that his work for the people was not visible to them. In contrast, the second candidate, who was a shift boss on the mine, was well received.

102 See below, pp. 238–240, for a discussion of the Copperbelt in the 1978 elections.

Luapula Province: economic decline and political alienation in a rural U.N.I.P. stronghold

Introduction

This essay considers the reaction of the electorate of Luapula Province to the one-party state, as demonstrated in particular by the experience of the 1973 elections and as analysed in the context of past economic and political experience. The structure of elections under the single-party system served to ensure that the issues raised emphasised local expectations of central government, thereby highlighting tensions between centre and locality. Though not necessarily typical of the nation's rural provinces, the electoral response in Luapula provided a general illustration of such tensions, while permitting an investigation of the manner in which local/central relations reflected, and were a consequence of, the specific pattern of development in a particular region.

It is that impact, of perceptions of deprivation upon political attitudes, with which we are primarily concerned. The next essay in this volume considers the manner in which underdevelopment affected the response of Western Province to the one-party state. Luapula was also a relatively disadvantaged rural area, and relations between that province and the centre at both party and government levels had been characterised since independence by periodic complaints of neglect, as regards both political representation and economic development. Luapula differed from Western Province, however, in two significant ways. First, although certainly one of the most underdeveloped of the rural provinces, Luapula had seen a period of economic development and of relative prosperity in the 1940s and 1950s, primarily as a result of its fishing industry. That development had, however, come to a halt in the late 'fifties, when a period of economic decline began from which the province had still not recovered by 1973; and it was that economic reversal which had contributed most to the prevalent notion that the area was disadvantaged and neglected by the central government. Second, Luapula had been in the forefront of the struggle for independence. A U.N.I.P. stronghold since that party's formation, the province's party organisation had probably been the most effective and extensive in the rural areas during the nationalist struggle. The Luapula people had certainly been among the most militant in the nation. In independent Zambia, however, the province, for the most part, had disproportionately fewer of its leaders in the central decision-making bodies than other provinces. This, in turn, encouraged the feeling that the province was disadvantaged, because under-represented at the centre.

In 1973, the electorate of Luapula gave President Kaunda the highest percentage endorsement of any of the eight provinces. At the same time, however, the poll was the lowest it had recorded, and the electorate rejected a number of candidates who were generally believed to have had the backing of the centre. These circumstances suggest several conclusions. First the high 'Yes' vote for the President indicated strong loyalty to U.N.I.P., which had persisted since the formation of the party in the province. Second, the failure of a significant proportion of the electorate to vote suggested a growing disenchantment with the ability of the individual to effect any substantial change through the ballot box. And third, the composition of elected M.P.s indicated the tenacity of the electorate in its opposition to those felt to have been imposed on it from outside.

In 1978 the Luapula poll increased, but the rise was considerably less than in other provinces. And while 82 per cent of the electorate still cast their vote in favour of President Kaunda, registering overall a continued loyalty to him and to U.N.I.P., the provincial average was only slightly higher than the national average. The drop in the proportion voting 'Yes' in the presidential contest over that in 1973, was greater in Luapula than in any other province. The voting figures for 1978 thus revealed an important increase in the political discontent of Luapulans, no doubt marking a protest against the action of the Central Committee in disqualifying a total of seven candidates in the province's constituencies, two of them sitting M.P.s. Figures for 1978 also showed a considerably smaller number of party officials voting per constituency in the primary elections as compared with 1973, suggesting a weakening of party strength in the area. Apparent in both elections, therefore, were tendencies toward both loyalty and independence of action which expressed the complexity of the relationship between province and centre.

The background: economic change in Luapula Province during the colonial period

Established as a separate administrative unit only in January 1958,[1] Luapula is Zambia's smallest but most densely-populated rural province. The people of the province, who today have a strong tendency

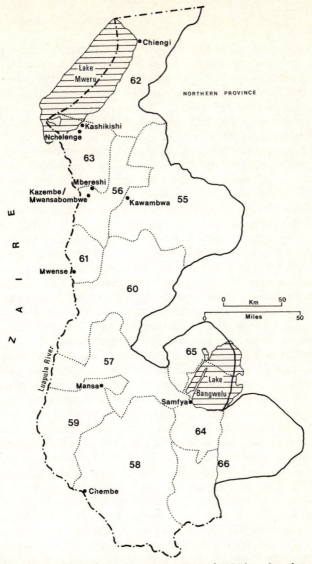

Luapula Province: electoral constituencies, 1973 and 1978 (numbered as on the map of all constituencies, p. xiv). 55. Kawambwa, 56. Mwansabombwe, 57. Bahati, 58. Chembe, 59. Mansa, 60. Chipili, 61. Mwense, 62. Chiengi, 63. Nchelenge, 64. Samfya Central, 65. Samfya North, 66. Samfya South. *Source.* Adapted from Robert H. Bates, *Rural Responses to Industrialization: a Study of Village Zambia* (New Haven, Conn.: Yale University Press, 1976). From Republic of Zambia, Ministry of Power, Transport and Works, road mileage map, Lusaka, January 1969. Approximations of the constituency boundaries have been added to illustrate the text.

to identify themselves as Luapulans,[2] are a mixture of ethnic groups, most of which migrated in a series of waves from Katanga. Although now predominantly Bemba-speakers, they are ethnically autonomous from the Northern Province group. The largest single ethnic category is the Lunda, who arrived in the area in the mid-eighteenth century and established a political empire incorporating many of the other inhabitants of the province.

The growing prosperity of the Lunda empire was disrupted in the nineteenth century by a succession of incursions of Arabs, Nyamwezi, Chishinga and Bemba, and finally at the end of the century by the extension of European political control over the region. The most fundamental change in economic activity occurred, however, when the Katanga mines were opened up early in the twentieth century, and the Luapula area was largely transformed into a labour reserve.[3] When the mines opened on the Northern Rhodesian Copperbelt in the late 'twenties, the colonial administration introduced measures to divert labour from Katanga to the Copperbelt.[4] Throughout the colonial period, 40–50 per cent of tax-paying males were characteristically employed outside the province, and although after independence the percentage declined, Luapula's ties to the Copperbelt by virtue of labour export remained strong.

The absence of labour from home did not initially disrupt the agricultural system, and although the colonial authorities gave little encouragement to crop production, the presence of a market in Katanga stimulated spontaneous increase.[5] Fish production was also boosted, fresh fish from the Mweru/Luapula area and dried fish from the Bangweulu swamps being transported to the Katanga mines.[6]

The supply of fish and labour for the mines have constituted the most important elements of the Luapulan economy since the mid-'twenties. Partly because fishing proved lucrative and partly because the British colonial authorities neglected the development of the agricultural infrastructure, giving the excuse that the area was remote,[7] agricultural production in the area diminished during the 1930s and 1940s. The province as a whole continued to export some of its surplus cassava and bananas to the Copperbelt throughout this period, but by 1954 the export market to the Copperbelt was virtually eliminated.[8] In 1958 the Provincial Commissioner remarked that 'reduced production by subsistence agriculturalists and increased importation from outside the Province has been the main feature of the year', and in that year, 12,730 bags of maize meal were imported into Fort Rosebery District.[9] The province has since that date remained an importer of a portion of its subsistence agricultural requirements.

Though production geared to local demand remained undeveloped, the province was far from impoverished. Indeed, as a result of the money flowing into Luapula, there was the appearance of relative prosperity. As early as 1936 a flourishing retail trade developed in the province as Luapulans put their earnings into hawking and village shops.[10] By the late 'forties, the inhabitants of the Luapula Valley were being praised for the relatively high standard of living they had achieved. As the Kawambwa District Commissioner noted:

The wealth of the inhabitants of this District is reflected in the excellence of their houses, and it is no longer exceptional to find houses of Kimberley brick, which are not infrequently fitted with glass windows. Chief Kasembe's village also provides an example of elementary town planning, and it is clear that, as in other matters, so also in housing there is an increased demand for improved standards.[11]

By 1949 some Luapulans had built up considerable transport/trading businesses based on the fish trade with the Copperbelt. The fishing industry itself continued to expand throughout the 'fifties, from both the Mweru/Luapula area and Bangweulu, contributing to the increase of local income and to the expansion of local commerce.[12] Moreover, a mining venture involved in the exploitation of manganese started operations in the 'fifties in the southern part of the province; the operation was small but must have provided the sense that the mines, which had formerly drawn so many out of the province, had now come to the people at home. Luapula's prosperity seemed assured. The Provincial Commissioner of Northern Province described the region as 'intensely interesting . . ., alive with potential development and already the possessor of a thriving and wealthy fishing industry and a young but promising mining venture'.[13]

Though outwardly thriving, the Luapulan economy was nevertheless highly vulnerable to dislocation, as two periods of depression demonstrated. The first occurred in the mid-'thirties. The completion in 1931 of the Benguela Railway linking Katanga with the Atlantic coast, the temporary closure of the Katanga mines a few years later, and the Congolese government's restrictions on the transport of foodstuffs across the Zaire pedicle which separates Luapula from the Zambian Copperbelt, all combined to push the Luapulan economy into serious decline. Small traders were pushed out of business, and such marketing of Luapula fish as continued was by European traders from Katanga and the Copperbelt.[14] Nevertheless, the Luapulan fishing industry revived, and in the following twenty years a renewed prosperity heightened Luapulan expectations that they were moving ahead. By the late 'forties, danger signs had already begun, however, to emerge, in the form of reports of a marked diminution in both size and quality of fish from Lake Mweru and the Luapula River in apparent consequence of overfishing. Conservation regulations were implemented but, even so, catches ultimately began to drop off.[15] Disruption also resulted from a change in Katangan demand from fresh to dried fish in 1958. A few years later, political unrest in the Congo cut off a large portion of what market remained, and in addition hindered transport of fish across the Zaire pedicle to the Copperbelt.[16]

Thus, by the early 'sixties, the fortunes of Luapulans connected with the fishing industry had declined. Though trade began to pick up in the mid-'sixties, the Mweru/Luapula fishery has never returned to the level of production of the late 'fifties.

The vulnerability of an economy based on exports of fish and labour and on small-scale internal commerce was also demonstrated by the fortunes of the small shopkeepers. In 1952, supplies of second-hand American clothing from the Congo were cut off as part of a series of restrictive steps associated with currency control. The colonial authorities reported that in consequence hawkers and traders received a 'severe setback'.[17] Another jolt occurred in 1960 when sterling and francs ceased to be interchangeable, and traders in the Luapula Valley were left with stores of unusable currency.[18]

In the late 'fifties, concern over the deterioration of the local economy and the continuing outmigration of the able-bodied men, prompted the colonial government to consider the developmental needs of the area. The mining companies were also concerned, given that the continuing migration to the towns, at a time when technological changes lessened the need for unskilled labour, was leading to a politically volatile situation as the volume of unemployed urban dwellers expanded. Aided by a substantial loan from the R.S.T. (Rhodesian Selection Trust) group of companies, therefore, the government launched the Northern Province Development Scheme, directed at that area from which the largest proportion of labour on the mines derived — the present Northern and Luapula provinces.[19] Though it undoubtedly contributed to the development of social and economic infrastructure within the provinces, the development scheme could be criticised for never having been seriously oriented towards transforming the rural economy. It gave little attention to either the establishment of small-scale rural industries or the improvement of agricultural production and marketing facilities, concentrating instead on the fishing industry and small-scale commerce on which the provincial economy was already specialised. And it failed to generate employment opportunities within the province to lure back those who had left for the line of rail.[20]

In addition the scheme had the effect of raising hopes that were subsequently disappointed. It made legitimate both the expectation that the central government had a responsibility to assist in the development of the rural areas and the complaint of neglect, themes that subsequently remained prevalent and continued to influence the relationship of the province to the central administration.

Given the ineffectiveness of the 'fifties' scheme, the picture in Luapula was, by the early 'sixties, one of economic stagnation. Agriculture was in a state of decline and maize meal was being imported from the line of rail. Due to overfishing and marketing problems, Luapula's major export industry had suffered dislocation. Though some shopkeepers had been aided by loans, political and economic upheavals in the Congo had led to the closure of many small commercial establishments. And following a slump in the world price for manganese, the local mining operations became unprofitable and were closed down. In sum, by the early 'sixties the fragility of a highly specialised provincial economy had been exposed to forces sufficient to undermine it. Feelings of general dissatisfaction were prevalent and no doubt reinforced by comparison of current economic fortunes, both with those which had prevailed within the area a decade previously and those in evidence on the Copperbelt, with which the Luapulan connection was strong through labour migration and trade.

Origin and emergence of organised political activity in Luapula

Luapulans engaged in political activity have been characterised as easily provoked, highly active and fiercely loyal. Colonial authorities spoke of the truculence of Luapulans during the Chachacha activities of.1961.[21] Mulford referred to residents of the province as 'easily the most volatile, militant and independent of A.N.C.'s cohorts during the fifties', and described Luapulan politicians in terms of their 'provincial pride and fearless militance'.[22] Provincial politicians have emphasised the sustained loyalty of the people of the province to the President and the party, noting that Luapula was, for all intents and purposes, a one-party province long before the Second Republic and the one-party participatory democracy were proclaimed.[23]

Luapula has also been characterised as a province with a tight level of party organisation and a multitude of party branches,[24] as well as an election record of consistently high percentage polls. In the Northern Rhodesian general elections of 1962, Bangweulu Constituency, which included most of Luapula (and for which Kaunda was candidate), had the highest percentage poll (91.6 per cent) of any of the lower franchise constituencies, and in 1964 the gross percentage poll was marginally higher in Luapula than in any other province. In 1968 the percentage poll in the only two contested constituencies remained relatively high, at 91.2 per cent in Luapula and 90.9 per cent in Samfya East. In the national referendum of 1969, Luapula had the highest percentage 'Yes' vote of any province (90.4 per cent as against the national average of 57.1 per cent) and the highest gross percentage poll at 92.7 per cent.[25] In the 1973 general elections, Luapula had a higher percentage 'Yes' vote for the President than any other province (98.7 per cent); and though the turn-out showed a decline, Luapula nevertheless had the highest gross percentage poll (54 per cent as against a national average of just under 40 per cent).

Enthusiasm for political activity and the seriousness with which it was approached may be indicated by such figures; but it remains to explain why Luapulans have displayed so high a level of political involvement and such sustained loyalty to U.N.I.P. While a comprehensive answer will not be attempted, contributing factors certainly include the economic depression of the 'fifties and early 'sixties, the influence of political events in Katanga, and the response of the colonial administration to local defiance. These helped to initiate a tradition of political activity whose themes persisted into the 'seventies. For an adequate analysis of the workings and outcome of elections under the single-party system, an understanding of the earlier political activity within the province is therefore essential.

Opposition to the colonial administration, focused specifically on the issue of Federation, became manifest in the early 'fifties. Though there were apparently no formally-registered party branches prior to the mid-'fifties, nationalist sentiment was already high among certain local groups, stimulated, in part, by communication with militants on the Copperbelt. Two events of importance occurred in 1953, leading the British administration to characterise both Fort Rosebery and Kawambwa districts as focal points of generalised political unrest.[26] The first was the participation of a number of Fort Rosebery civil servants in the two days of prayer called by the A.N.C. in April as a national expression of opposition to the Federation. The second, probably of more lasting significance, was the chiefs' uprising in the Fort Rosebery District, initiated by Senior Chief Milambo of the Aushi people, himself an A.N.C. sympathiser. In February several Aushi and Kabende chiefs determined to defy certain regulations relating to game, forestry, fisheries and agriculture.[27] Introduced by the administration largely as conservation measures, the regulations in question had generated antagonism from the people by imposing restrictions upon their means of livelihood. The chiefs' protest registered the fact that they, as Native Authorities, were reduced to mere agents of the British in being required to enforce extremely unpopular measures.

The provincial administration quickly suspended, deposed and then deported Senior Chief Milambo, Chief Kasoma Bangweulu and Chief Mulaka, the latter also being convicted for threatening violence. But local defiance continued with the refusal to pay licences for fish-nets, and further arrests followed what were termed unlawful assemblies.[28] The agitation only subsided in 1956 when the administration allowed the last of the chiefs to return home.[29]

During this period, the administration met resistance with a show of force, a policy continued throughout the nationalist struggle.[30] In the Fort Rosebery area, a blanket ban upon politics was imposed.[31] Political activists, however, were quickly able to exploit local opposition to government regulations, transforming it into a general political protest against colonial authority and the very system of colonial control.[32]

Open and successful party organisation for the A.N.C. began with a visit in April 1955 by A. Shapi and D. Banda from the Lusaka party headquarters. Although their visit was cut short by the authorities,[33] they made contact with a number of politically-active Luapulans and established several organisers in both the north and south of the province. In late 1956, when the ban on political activity was lifted, a public meeting established an official A.N.C. branch. Among the office bearers were a shopkeeper, a clerk in a European concern and an area representative of a European company.[34]

Thus began a period of intense political activity and party organisation. In 1957, the first district party organisation was established in Fort Rosebery with S. Chisembele, a former shopkeeper, elected district secretary, and, on instructions from A.N.C.'s Lusaka headquarters, which attempted to keep control over rural sectors of the party through appointment of key officials, Shapi appointed as district chairman. By the end of 1957, there were 200 branches in the Fort Rosebery area alone; and about the same time a provincial executive was set up with Chisembele as provincial secretary and Shapi as deputy president.[35]

When the split came within A.N.C. and Z.A.N.C. emerged in 1958 with Kaunda at its head, the Luapulans gave solid support to the new organisation, disenchanted, it seems, with Nkumbula's apparent moderation.[36] By 1959, the provincial administration acknowledged that political activities, and specifically the rise of Z.A.N.C., dominated the provincial scene; and in February they reported widespread 'intimidation', particularly directed against missionaries and the Native Authorities.[37] Although Z.A.N.C. was banned in March and most of its leaders in the province were arrested, popular militancy persisted. It was reported that 'arsons continued and there was a massing of several hundred armed men and attempts to continue Zambia [Z.A.N.C.] activity'.[38]

U.N.I.P. emerged in the province towards the end of 1959, when the Luapulan Z.A.N.C. leaders were released from prison. Among the party's first actions was a highly successful boycott of the Monckton

Commission, which toured the province in 1960 to assess African opinion of the proposed Federal Constitution revision. Political mobilisation proceeded rapidly, so that by the middle of 1961 Luapula Province constituted one of the most highly organised areas in the country, with 345 main branches as well as a large number of Women's and Youth leagues, all presided over by about 2,000 officials.[39] Popular defiance of the authorities also continued, with further burning of schools, churches and courts, with demonstrations and with attempts to undermine the Native Authorities. In Samfya District alone in 1960, there were five peaceful demonstrations each involving a thousand people. Tax collection was especially poor, and the government's mobile unit was active.

U.N.I.P.'s most effective and sustained campaign of defiance in Luapula occurred in 1961 during the period known as Chachacha. Although that period of planned defiance involved the whole country, in accordance with the Master Plan announced at U.N.I.P.'s Mulungushi Conference in June 1961, it was in Luapula and Northern provinces that the level of militancy among the people was highest, and where the most pronounced retaliatory police and military action on the part of the colonial authorities took place.

The height of the campaign occurred over July and August. In late July, a touring District Commissioner encountered 'non-cooperation and open disregard of authority' in Chief Matanda's area, and subsequently nine people were arrested for contravening customary law. Villagers remained defiant, and on 11 August a strong police patrol was required to subdue an armed attempt to rescue the prisoners through arresting the 'principal agitators'. A second incident occurred at Mwense when a scheduled meeting was disrupted by the mobile unit. Yet a third occurred in Samfya. And on 23 July, local residents blocked the road between Munkanta's village and the Kawambwa boma, occupied the plain on either side of it armed with spears and petrol bombs, and prepared for an all-out war with the authorities.[40]

The increase in militancy seems to have persuaded U.N.I.P.'s leadership at the centre to act on the party's Master Plan; in consequence, a widespread burning of identity and marriage certificates was simultaneously carried out in a number of centres across the province and the ashes delivered to the bomas. Although the administration, taken by surprise, arrested the provincial leaders and a large number of constituency and branch officials,[41] the opposition continued. Finally, after some initial reluctance on the part of the administration in the fear that ensuing underground activity might be more difficult to control, U.N.I.P. was banned in Luapula on 23 August.

Chachacha constituted a serious and widespread campaign of defiance that involved a great many people at the grass roots. In one instance, police attacked a group of 150 villagers said to be armed, leaving one killed and two wounded. In the latter part of August, schools were kept closed, houses were burned and bridges damaged. A good deal of the protest campaign was organised by party officials, and there was probably a higher degree of effective party organisation in Chachacha within the province than anywhere else in the territory. Yet there was also a great deal of spontaneous activity.

While to some extent a consequence of provocation on the part of the provincial administration, such militance was also influenced by political events in Katanga and local economic decline, which became particularly pronounced in 1960–61. The colonial authorities acknowledged that events in the Congo had a profound effect on residents of the province in 1960, especially those in Kawambwa District with close ties to the Katangese. While the Lunda Native Authority favoured the Conakat Party in Katanga, U.N.I.P.'s opposition to that political organisation undoubtedly caused tension in Kawambwa and increased division between the Native Authorities and nationalist sympathisers.[42] As indicated earlier, the crisis in the Congo also had economic repercussions for Luapula, with many African businessmen in the Luapula Valley being left with unacceptable currency, which further intensified the general depression of the local economy during a year that saw a decrease in fish production and agricultural output, and the liquidation of the Luapula Transport Cooperative Ltd.

The relationship between political militance and economic fortunes was not lost on the colonial administration; whereas in 1956, the Kawambwa District Commissioner had attributed limited A.N.C. membership to the flourishing fishing industry which 'encouraged some of the leading personalities to abandon politics for business which they have found far more rewarding', leaving politics mainly to 'the disgruntled and the unsuccessful',[43] in 1961 the Provincial Commissioner attributed the outbreaks of Chachacha in part to the lack of industry in the province, and suggested that 'people have no work and when they look around for something to do they find trouble'.[44] Such comments indicate a factor of considerable validity. The people of Luapula were clearly opposed to colonial rule, but the increased militancy of that opposition coincided with, and may be partially attributed to, a generalised economic decline on the one hand, and a gaining of political independence by their kinsmen in the Congo on the other.[45]

Relations between Luapula and the centre in the multi-party state, 1962–73

Along with parts of the Northern Province, Luapula was undoubtedly U.N.I.P.'s major rural stronghold in the nationalist period. Nevertheless, in contrast to the Northern Province, few of the Luapulan politicians were included among the top national leadership of the party.[46] Independence brought no immediate change, and the circumstance of a powerful party organisation at the provincial level lacking representatives in the national executive, generated much of the tension characterising Luapula's relations with the centre over this period.

An early expression of such tension was resistance to the system of central appointment of provincial party officials, brought into focus by the party's 1962 restructuring exercise. During the late 'fifties, the A.N.C. consisted of three levels in Luapula — branch, district and provincial. The provincial executive was appointed from Lusaka, but for the most part the party headquarters merely ratified those acclaimed by the people as leaders. All party offices below the provincial level were filled by election. With the formation of Z.A.N.C. in late 1958, incumbent officials continued to serve in a provincial body of approximately fifty-four members, renamed the divisional executive council, and ultimately responsible for all party activities in the province; its six top leaders formed a provincial cabinet.[47]

In 1962, however, U.N.I.P.'s National Executive proposed to substitute a system based on regions for one based on provincial party units, in order to facilitate organising activities throughout the territory and increase opportunities for communication between locality and centre. An additional objective was undoubtedly, as Mulford suggests, to achieve greater consolidation of the party and to bring its lower levels, including the Youth Wing, under greater control from the centre.[48] The proposed reorganisation divided Luapula into two regions, one for the northern and the other for the southern part of the province. At the outset, the Luapula leadership refused to accept the change. While potentially increasing the representation of some areas of the country where party organisation was weak, the move was bound to reduce the authority of leadership in Luapula, where local level organisation was so strong. No doubt that leadership had more to lose by the change than their counterparts elsewhere, and perhaps saw it as an unwarranted affront upon their past performance. But they also feared that, by disrupting the existing tight organisational structure in the province, the change might hinder unified action.

The general issue of reorganisation was significant because it concerned the structure of supreme power within the party; it centralised decision-making and limited it, to a large extent, to the party's innermost circles. Luapulans feared that the change had the potential, not merely for greater unity and co-ordination on a national scale, but also for the subtle advance of tyranny by whomever gained control in the centre. Many at the district and constituency levels opposed the restructuring of the provincial party organisation, alongside those provincial leaders who stood to suffer demotion; and Luapula's representatives on the National Council argued strongly though unsuccessfully against the proposed change.[49] While implemented in most parts of the country in March and April 1962, the new system was not imposed in Luapula until 1963 when it was accepted with perhaps a degree of resignation and only after several national leaders had toured the province.[50]

Appointments to the new regional positions drew largely upon those who had composed the provincial cabinet. Chisembele, for example, was appointed Regional Secretary for Mansa-Samfya, and Shapi Regional Secretary for Kawambwa. But there were fewer of the highest level positions under the new system, and it would appear that a number of the former provincial cabinet withdrew from active involvement in the party.[51] The restructuring was, moreover, never fully accepted or approved of by some Luapulan leaders, so that the change carried with it the increased possibility of conflict between elected officials from the province and the central executive, while guaranteeing that the balance of power would be with the centre. The issue of provincial versus central control over the local party continued, therefore, as a source of tension.

A related issue was the general operation of the system of appointments to high level position in both party and government, and the allocation of appointments to individuals of varying provincial origin. A number of appointees to administrative and party positions in Luapula during the period immediately following independence were of non-Luapulan origin. Several were from Northern Province, an area sharing a common vernacular with Luapula, and increasingly it came to be felt that Luapula was receiving more Northern Province officials than that province was receiving Luapulans. In the independent government's first Parliament, for example, only two of Luapula's six M.P.s were from the province by birth; and whereas three of the others were from Northern Province, only one Luapulan was an M.P. for a Northern Province constituency.

The system of political mobility through appointment was thus gradually perceived to be working to the disfavour of Luapulans, and the feeling grew among some that it was precisely because they had not made demands for equal representation in upper levels of the party on a provincial basis and precisely because of their staunch loyalty, that they were being overlooked in favour of those from other provinces.[52] Partly as a result of increasing Luapulan dissatisfaction with the appointments system, eight of the slate of ten U.N.I.P. candidates selected for Luapula constituencies in the 1968 parliamentary elections were of Luapulan origin with only two from Northern Province. In addition, one Luapulan stood on the Copperbelt and another in a Northern Province constituency. The increase in representation was, however, somewhat deceptive; for it was partly a consequence of the increased size of the National Assembly. The feeling of discrimination therefore persisted.

As the 'sixties drew to a close, the charge that Luapula was under-represented at the centre, and therefore politically neglected as a province, was presented with increasing vigour by Luapulan politicians. For some provincial leaders, the situation implied that their major claim to leadership and position — the support of lower level party officials and general party membership in the province — was in danger of disintegration; since they did not hold high level offices, they lacked the means to dispense rewards in the form of jobs to those below them. This point was made by a prominent Luapulan politician in 1974 who commented that the needs of local people could never be fully met unless there were someone from the area with a high level position in government, preferably a Cabinet appointment. There was need, he argued, not just for local development projects but also for employment opportunities outside the province. He noted that many ministries had parastatals attached to them, appointment to which was not covered by civil service regulations, thereby allowing considerable discretion to ministers and permanent secretaries in their choice of personnel. But in the case of Luapula, he lamented, 'freedom fighters' had not had the opportunity of receiving training or employment in such bodies, precisely because the province lacked leaders in the appropriate high level positions.[53]

Luapulan perceptions of discrimination in the operation of the appointments system were, on occasion, translated into an almost personal antagonism towards individual appointed officials working in the province. Symptomatic of the underlying grievances was the view voiced by some Mansa party members that everyone should work in his own locality.[54] Yet it was significant that some complaints were directed as well at Luapulan appointees, suggesting that what was at issue was not simply provincial origin, but the appointment of these officials from above rather than their selection by the people of the province themselves. At the local level there was on the one hand distrust of the delegation of powers and a desire for more direct participation in the choice of leaders, and on the other a misconceived tendency to attribute local problems to the presence of non-Luapulan appointed officials.

An expression of the general sense of frustration was a tendency to emphasise the distinction between Luapula and Northern provinces. U.N.I.P. representatives from the two provinces had, in fact, been allied at the party's 1967 Mulungushi Conference at which the Bemba/Tonga coalition unseated Kamanga and put Kapwepwe in his place as national Vice-President. Nevertheless, from 1968 Luapulan perceptions of Northern Province dominance solidified, leading to increasing tension between the two groups and a battle of verbal abuse in which the phrase *Tubulu* (mere fishermen) came to be addressed in a derogatory sense to Luapulans by Northern Province politicians.[55]

Luapulan M.P.s and politicians registered their discontent in two successive petitions to the President. In April 1969, seven M.P.s sent a note to the President complaining of the use of the phrase, 'Province of *Batubulu*', and of statements, apparently common on the Copperbelt at the time, that people of Northern Province were the ordained political leaders of Luapulans. They wrote as follows:

We bear no grudge against our brothers from the Northern Province for what they have said against us rather we thank them for making it possible for the people of the Luapula Province to discover themselves politically and to give themselves the important realisation that like other Provinces the Luapula Province should have her interests guarded by her proper sons. For the sake of communication with Your Excellency we shall choose one or some of us to make representations to Your Excellency and our traditional channels of communication are hereby disregarded as we have no confidence in them whatsoever.[56]

A second petition, in 1970, written by a group calling itself the Copperbelt Luapula Delegation, repeated the same general theme of underrepresentation and the overlooking of the province's leaders when appointments were under consideration. While expressing firm loyalty to the government and the party, the petition asserted that 'Zambian history can be positive only when Luapula is described as the most suffered but neglected province'.[57] Cataloguing the contributions of Luapulans to the independence struggle and their consistent return of U.N.I.P. candidates to national office, the petitioners noted that 'we have found that Luapula has been denied equal representation'.

The thrust of the petition was a request that Luapulans be considered when appointments of chairman of commercial firms, directors of government-owned enterprises and representatives of government boards might arise in the future, and that the number of representatives from provinces which had already 'monopolised' the country be reduced. The connection between central office and the opening up of employment opportunities was made explicit:

Because some of the Provinces have more and more Ministers, and most of their people in senior positions, most of their people are being sent out of the country to obtain more knowledge both educationally and professionally and just after a short time, the same people will come back fully equipped with the said knowledge. Admittedly, your Excellency, they will now be the people in senior positions and it will be very unwise for us to complain for we will be told if you want any doctor at Mansa then produce one, if you want any engineer at Samfya produce one, if you want any technician at Kawambwa or any lawyer at Mwense produce them. Luapula quite knowledgeably will not produce any for we are denied equal representation by the man we trust, the man we love the [man] we support in whom our undisputed confidence lies and that is you Dr. Kaunda.[58]

Perceived neglect of the province in terms of political representation at the centre was closely linked, via operation of the patronage system, to a perceived lack of opportunities for training and employment for Luapulans within the national arena. It was also linked to the perceived disadvantaged status of the province as regards development. It was the common complaint of local leadership that Luapula suffered from lack of infrastructural development, schools, health facilities, etc. While this complaint was perhaps characteristic of every rural province, Luapula's leaders argued that neglect in their case was relatively greater than elsewhere, because the province had been inadequately represented at the centre. Since some of its parliamentary representatives (prior to 1973) were non-Luapulan, went the argument, they had not been sufficiently responsive to the needs of the people of the area. Furthermore, because all M.P.s were selected as candidates by the party rather than by the local people, they were more beholden to the national executive of the party, than to their constituents. In sum, it was argued that the absence of Luapulan leaders from the central decision-making bodies of party and government prevented them from safeguarding the interests of the province.[59]

The cry of provincial neglect has been one of the most striking expressions of tension between the centre and the locality, not only in Luapula but in other rural provinces as well. It is anathema to the centre, being seen as a threat to national unity, and its advocates have been liable on occasion to rebuke. It seems partly in response to the manner of his championing of Luapula's provincial interests in 1971, for example, that Chisembele was suspended from his Cabinet position.[60] The charge of provincial neglect was an important feature of the 1973 elections and was subsequently articulated by newly-elected Luapula M.P.s in Parliament. Hence, it becomes important to look more closely at Luapula's actual situation, in terms of both political representation and of development.

So far as representation was concerned, Luapulans were no doubt justified in regarding the province as suffering some deficiency in the early years. No Luapulan was appointed a Cabinet Minister until 1969 and none was appointed to the Central Committee of U.N.I.P. until 1971.[61] Three M.P.s representing Luapulan constituencies in the first Parliament had, in fact, been members of the Cabinet, but two of these were from Northern Province and the other from Eastern. Two Luapulans were, however, appointed to the new Cabinet formed in January 1969, Shapi in January and Chisembele in November; and although the latter was subsequently suspended, Wilson Chakulya, a Luapulan and a Copperbelt M.P., was appointed as a Provincial Minister in April 1971 and Minister for Labour in June 1971. It was true, therefore, that few Luapulans had been appointed to ministerial office. But if clearly salient in the early years, the claim of underrepresentation had, perhaps, become somewhat less so in recent years. By 1978 Luapula still had a lesser number of 'its people' in high level positions than other provinces, but three of its M.P.s were Cabinet Ministers, two for provinces and one with portfolio; and two of Kaunda's appointees to the Cabinet were of Luapulan origin.

Luapula's development experience was also demonstrably less distinguished than other provinces in the early years. While a prime objective of the First National Development Plan (1966–70) was to redress the rural/urban imbalance, a breakdown of proposed expenditure indicates that the most disadvantaged rural areas received the smallest proportion of the funds, the bulk being allocated to the line of rail. Luapula Province was allocated only 4 per cent of the total expenditure; in contrast, approximately 40 per cent was allocated to Central Province. In terms of proposed per capita expenditure, Luapula and Western provinces ranked as the lowest with K66 and K65 respectively for the entire plan period.[62]

The projects envisaged for Luapula Province during the period of the first plan — new roads, schools, health facilities and assistance to fishing and forestry — followed the same pattern as the earlier Development Scheme for Northern and Luapula provinces. Indeed, the plan as a whole placed emphasis on the provision of social and economic infrastructure rather than direct productive activity, the latter being left to private enterprise.[63] Perhaps the most notable aspect of the First National Development Plan period for Luapula, however, was the low percentage of proposed expenditure which was actually made, and hence the high proportion of projects which were uncompleted or uninitiated. Actual expenditure during the period as a percentage of planned expenditure was only 60 per cent, yielding a per capita figure of K39, lowest of any of the eight provinces.[64]

Luapula was in some respects clearly not disadvantaged when compared with other provinces at the end of the first plan period. The percentage of its primary-school-aged population attending schools, for example, was about equivalent to the nationwide average. And Luapula had undoubtedly experienced an improvement in social amenities and infrastructure. By 1973 there were a teacher training college and seven secondary schools in the province, most of the latter being expanded under a nationwide scheme through a World Bank loan. One of the two hospitals in the province had been expanded and a number of new clinics and health centres set up. There was a nursing school at Mbereshi. An agricultural training centre, a tea scheme and a co-operative union were also in operation.

Yet in spite of these projects, the pace of development and rendering of developmental assistance were hampered by problems of insufficient personnel and inadequate infrastructure and transport facilities. Inadequate water supply was a chronic complaint. As regards the development of agricultural production, Luapula remained at a particularly low level, and as regards opportunities for wage employment, it appears to have suffered a relative decline. During the period 1963–69, both Luapula and Northern provinces experienced a net decline in population (which was slightly the greater in Luapula) indicating extensive outward migration in search of employment. For the period 1968–69, the value of agricultural production per farmer in the traditional sector was lower in Luapula than in any other province.[65]

The frustration voiced by some Luapulans concerning development was in many respects common to residents in all rural areas, which continued collectively to lag far behind the urban sector. A unique factor underlying the frustration of Luapulans in contrast to other rural residents, however, was the fairly recent decline in the level of economic activity. The struggle against foreign rule had been associated with an expectation that with independence, the state of the economy would once more improve. When this did not occur at as fast a rate or in the precise manner that people had expected, complaints arose that the contribution of the province to the struggle had not been matched by sufficient allocation from the central government to meet the development needs of the people.

In comparison, then, not to other rural provinces, but rather to the relative prosperity of Luapula some twenty or thirty years earlier, the province appeared to some to be stagnating or even moving backward; this was attributed by many not to factors relating to supply and demand so much as to the perceived inadequacy of inputs from the central government in the form of infrastructure and productive investment. And it was argued further that inadequate inputs from the central government were a consequence of the underrepresentation of

Luapulans on the higher decision-making bodies of the party and government at the centre of the system.[66]

The general election of 1973: expectations and electoral response in Luapula

The first general elections in the one-party state allowed a significant increase in popular participation at all levels of Luapula society. They provided the first occasion for local party officials to participate directly, not only in the choice between candidates but also in their recruitment. They enabled a much larger number of party members to make a bid for office; and they offered the electorate a wider choice between candidates than had formerly been the case, particularly in view of the number of U.N.I.P. candidates who had stood unopposed in previous elections. Moreover, given that in 1973 there were no unopposed candidates in Luapula constituencies and that the Central Committee refrained from vetoing primary winners, the majority vote of the electorate, on the whole, determined the results in both the primaries and the general elections. The outcome of the elections therefore provides a significant opportunity to examine the views of the electorate as reflected in their choice of candidate.

The issue that dominated the election at both provincial and constituency level was perceived neglect of the local area. For voters, the import of the election was the opportunity it promised to attempt to remedy this situation. In a number of constituencies, local leadership, either from the party or from the business community, actively attempted to recruit candidates whom they considered would be appropriate representatives; and several of those eventually elected claimed to have stood at the invitation of the local people. Those approached were invariably highly qualified and, while well-known in the area, had been away from it for sometime, working in Lusaka or on the Copperbelt. One, for example, was a senior civil servant in Lusaka who had formerly represented Zambia at the U.N., and another was a senior personnel officer on the mines.[67]

While by no means the only groups which had a particular interest in the outcome of the elections, party officials and local businessmen tended to comprise the most articulate and organised sections of the community. Before considering the election itself, it may therefore be useful to consider their roles and attitudes.

Lower level party officials and their orientation towards the election

While a great many Luapulans had participated in the nationalist struggle, party officials had necessarily been the most actively engaged; some had been imprisoned and others had gone into hiding to avoid arrest or had fled into exile in Tanzania. After independence, however, although the party rewarded some of its most active members, only a handful of local level officials achieved upward mobility by virtue of party connections; the majority were left unrewarded in position or employment. And while most 'left behind' retained their local level offices, their role in the independence situation became increasingly narrowed and ill-defined. Even though the number of party branches relative to the provincial population was still higher in Luapula than in the nation as a whole, the party appeared to have been unsuccessful after independence in recruiting new and younger men and women, so that the local leadership also assumed a generational concentration. Having been militants during the period of Chachacha, many local officials remembered the time when their role had been clearly specified, when they had had a purpose and a sense of optimism, and when the party structure had been open from bottom to top. In those days they had been leaders. Now it appeared there was nothing to lead, and they were frustrated by apparent inaction at the party's top and the loss of contact with the party hierarchy.[68] They held on to their offices because they believed that they were thereby accorded a measure of status, but at the same time they acknowledged that such status as had once been associated with the party had diminished.

A superficial survey of the occupations of lower level party officers indicated that the majority regarded themselves as 'villagers' without wage or self-employment, subsisting through fishing or the cultivation of cassava gardens.[69] In common with many others in the province, they had in recent years experienced a decline in economic situation, and there was a widespread feeling among them that one of the province's major problems was the lack of employment opportunities. Perceptions of provincial neglect among lower level party officials related therefore to their disappointment, both with the slow pace of development in the province at large and with their own lack of personal advancement.

While in Mwansabombwe parliamentary constituency, lower level party officials were most concerned that rewards to service be granted through the introduction of wages to branch and constituency party officials, elsewhere in the province, and especially in the Mansa area, it was alleged that party officials supported a particular candidate in the hope that he would, if elected, secure them jobs. That such expectations should prevail, particularly in Mansa, was perhaps partly due to the fact that one of the candidates there, Wilson Chakulya, was a former Cabinet Minister, who, if re-elected, might have been expected to wield weight in government. In addition, Mansa had a larger number of wage employees than other centres in the province, and the relative affluence of the area no doubt served to raise the expectations of its residents and make the situation of those seeking work seem more acute. The issue of employment was thus perhaps more prominent in people's minds, and characteristically the party was seen to be the proper mechanism for securing that employment.

The importance attached to employment by local level officials was reflected in tension generated by local party elections in April 1973, when the number of party constituencies in Mansa District was reduced from eleven to ten in accordance with the new constitution's specifications. The election saw the defeat of a set of former officials in Mansa Town and their replacement by a new group, the latter including a number who were either small businessmen or wage employees. While by no means the wealthiest members of the community, they were relatively affluent, whereas those they defeated were for the most part unemployed. On the basis of allegations that the District Governor had manipulated the elections to ensure support for himself, the defeated officials appealed, but were ultimately unsuccessful in having the results overturned.[70] In the general election campaign, the two groups of present and past officials ranged themselves separately behind opposing candidates.[71] The contention between the two factions did not end with the general elections, and in April 1974 a U.N.I.P. regional conference was set up to discuss what had become known as the 'Mansa problem'. At the meeting, the central issue of employment was openly acknowledged, the debate demonstrating the preoccupation on the part of constituency officials with jobs and their perceptions of the role of the party in providing them. This is well illustrated by resolutions passed at the end of the three-day conference:

1. The District Governor must find employment for the defeated constituency candidates.
2. There must be a rule that when there are development projects the DG and the RS should inform constituency officials who will then inform branch officials so that these will have a chance of getting employment.
3. Everything possible must be done to enable constituency officials to get a small allowance.
4. Constituency offices must be helped by the District Governor's office financially.
5. Watchtower members must be sacked from all employment so that jobs can be given to U.N.I.P. members. This must start tomorrow.[72]

This last resolution was removed as being in spirit and substance contrary to Humanism. But along with the others, it reflected the seriousness of the issue of employment in the minds of local leaders. For them to say that the province was neglected was, in part, to say that the party patronage system was not operating effectively so as to ensure sufficient appointments for Luapulans. It was a quick jump from that feeling to the position that those appointments which were most visible (regional officials and District Governors), should be confined to Luapulans and that indeed local party officials have a say in the selection of such individuals. In sum, while most of the residents of Luapula Province probably saw the problem of neglect in terms of their collective and immediate needs (for schools, water, clinics, etc.), for many lower level party officials the problem was compounded by the apparent inefficiency of the patronage system. They tended accordingly to support those candidates whom they felt could rectify that situation.

Businessmen – orientation toward the election

The perspective of the business community was in some respects broader than that of other residents of Luapula, given their ties with the national economy. As might be expected, businessmen perceived the problem of relative underdevelopment in Luapula primarily in economic terms and their main concern was with the slow pace of infrastructural development.[73]

There was a tendency among some businessmen to consider themselves a notch above the general population. Some felt that their very success in the field of business was evidence of their high capabilities. One Mansa businessman argued that those with money were often the most capable and most able to serve the community or the nation;[74] another, that money itself constituted a sign of good leadership.[75] Competence and success in business, in their opinion, qualified an individual to be considered a member of the local élite, which, at least in the minds of some, necessarily implied a political role. They considered that they *were* the community leaders, and therefore should be granted decision-making powers in local affairs. Hence, while not discounting the role of local party leaders, they implied that business success constituted an alternative route to power and to participation in decision-making at the local level.

Though not always currently active in the party, most businessmen in Luapula had had close ties with U.N.I.P. in the past and remained party members. Approximately 80 per cent of those interviewed in a survey early in 1974 were currently members of U.N.I.P. Approximately 60 per cent claimed to have been active in the struggle for independence or to have donated money or transport vehicles to activists. And 39 per cent had held party office in the past, mostly at branch or constituency level. Only 9 per cent were current holders of lower level party office. However, in accordance with the general practice in most parts of the country, a number of businessmen in the province were regional trustees.[76] Their appointment was probably mutually advantageous to both the party and the appointee. It allowed the businessman access to information concerning local party affairs and involved him directly in decisions being made by local party and government administration, while placing him at a higher level than locally-elected officials. At the same time, it allowed the party to co-opt local individuals who were gaining increasing prominence in the local community and whose influence might grow.

Although not entirely agreed on the matter, there was a tendency for businessmen in the province to see themselves as an increasingly cohesive community whose interests should be represented in Parliament. Hence, a Kawambwa businessman, also active in local government, argued that businessmen as sensible men could lead the country, and that it was important that they should be in Parliament to advise that body on commercial matters. In the 1974 survey referred to above, businessmen were asked what they considered the best way to deal with problems faced by all businessmen: to petition government through a business association, to elect a fellow business-man to Parliament, or to rely on some other method. Though 34 per cent said that the best method was working through an association, 31 per cent favoured the election of a businessman to Parliament. A further 8 per cent advocated the selection of a candidate by the business association. And 10 per cent said that both the business association and the election of a businessman to Parliament should be utilised together. When asked directly whether it was in general a good idea to elect businessmen to Parliament, 81 per cent said 'Yes'. In a majority of cases, their reasoning was that businessmen would know the problems of other businessmen and thus be able to repre-sent their interests. While perhaps not sufficiently organised to pur-sue their interests by collectively gaining access to political power, businessmen nevertheless constituted an active force in the 1973 election, underlined by the party's setting-up at least one campaign meeting exclusively for their number. Several were among the candi-dates, while others were intensely involved in unofficial campaigning.

Members of the business community preferred parliamentary candidates who were capable of interacting in government circles and who might be able to secure positions of real power. In Mansa, for example, many of the businessmen supported the former Cabinet Minister, whose record was, for them, a sufficient demonstration of his intellect and his capabilities in government. A contrasting case, however, was provided by Mwense Constituency where local busi-nessmen were pitted as opposing candidates against Dr. Henry Matipa (who eventually won the seat) even though Matipa, who had a Ph.D.

in economics and was a Senior Economist in the Ministry of Mines, might have seemed the type of candidate whom local, far-sighted members of the self-described élite would favour. The situation in Mwense was perhaps one involving a clash of personally-ambitious individuals whose very ambition tended to divide the business community and the larger 'élite' with which it identified itself.

The candidates and the campaigns in 1973

In the 1973 election, Luapula was apportioned twelve parliamentary constituencies, two more than in 1968. Former M.P.s stood for re-election in half of Luapula's constituences, though in some cases in other than those they had previously represented.[77] In addition, W. Chakulya, who had previously represented a Copperbelt constituency, returned to Luapula to contest Mansa Constituency, his birthplace, with the result that the contest in that constituency involved two incumbents.

Apart from the M.P.s, candidates included lower party officials aspiring to move up through the electoral process to positions of more national importance, civil servants working both within and outside the province, businessmen, farmers, teachers and a few local people who were either unemployed or working in some relatively low level occupation. Table 6.1 gives a breakdown by occupation and place of residence at the time of nomination of candidates in seven of Luapula's twelve constituencies.[78] Note should be taken that almost a third had business interests of some sort.

While many of the candidates had been active during the independence struggle and some had been imprisoned during that time, several had not since then held any official position within the party, and a few had never held any party office whatsoever. While for some, then, the election served as a means for retaining their current position and source of income, for others it served potentially as a means of moving into the ranks of paid politicians and toward possible sources of power. As might be expected, the candidates as a group had, as well as greater collective political experience, an average level of education which was much higher than that of the electorate. In terms of education, as well as income and occupation, they tended to be from the more privileged elements of Zambian society.

The issues raised in the campaigns may be identified as those which centred around criteria of choice for candidates. One of the most important was trustworthiness, which for some voters apparently required personal acquaintance with the candidate or with his or her relatives. It implied the difficulty that a candidate encountered who was not from the local area, or had been absent so long as to be

Table 6.1   Occupation and residence of nominees in seven Luapula constituencies, 1973

Occupation	Resident in Luapula	Resident outside Luapula	Total
Civil servants			
national level	—	3	3
provincial, district or local level	3	2	5
Constituency officials	2	—	2
M.P.s[a]	—	5	5
Businessmen	6	2	8
Teachers	3	—	3
Farmers	1	—	1
Clergymen	—	1	1
Professional	—	1	1
Self-employed	1	—	1
Other worker	—	1	1
Unemployed/unknown	2	1	3
Total	18	16	34

a. At least two of the M.P.s also had business interests at the time of the election.

unfamiliar with the electorate and their problems. Where all candidates were from the area, it tended to lead to a division of the vote along the lines of chiefs' areas or village groups, in accordance with the home areas of contenders. A second criterion involved the presumed capabilities of candidates for dealing with the problems of the constituency at the national level, and took account of their level of education and their past experience (or past performance in office in the case of former M.P.s). And perhaps a third criterion, interrelated with the previous two, had to do with whether candidates were sponsored or recruited by local groups, or appeared to have been sent or sponsored by those in national positions of power (or enjoyed no sponsorship whatsoever).

Though Luapula had the highest provincial poll, 46 per cent of the electorate still were unable to choose not to vote. It is probable that many had grown dubious of the impact which their vote had on the course of government policy. Local party officials interviewed during the campaigns stressed the importance of the 1973 elections as the first in which voters had a direct voice in choosing representatives who might rectify the situation of past neglect. Yet even among these stalwarts, some seemed uncertain in their conviction, giving the impression that, while they felt obliged to give the system a chance, they could merely hope that it would lead to an improvement of their personal and collective welfare.

Of those who went to the polls, 98.7 per cent voted in favour of President Kaunda, registering the highest proportionate 'Yes' vote of any province in the nation and demonstrating approval for the regime by a clear majority of the entire Luapulan electorate. In the parliamentary contests, three incumbent M.P.s, one a Cabinet Minister (Chakulya) and another a minister of state (Mambwe), were among the defeated; but four incumbents were re-elected. Other successful candidates in the province included two civil servants based in ministry headquarters in Lusaka, a Catholic priest, a businessman who had been resident on the Copperbelt, a rural council secretary, a teacher, a District Governor, and an individual who had once been a member of the African Representative Council and subsequently served as a local government official on the Copperbelt.

Though they had generally maintained close ties with their home areas, few of those elected were actually resident in the province during the several years prior to the election.[79] And apart from the former M.P.s, few had held party office subsequent to independence. In several of the contests it was the most highly educated candidate who was elected, but this was by no means always the case. In Mansa Constituency, for example, the successful candidate probably had had the lowest level of education of the three who stood for the final election. In general, however, the winners had had at least a secondary level education. They also tended both to have had considerable 'cosmopolitan' experience outside of the province or outside of the country and to have retained strong local ties — through frequent visits, through the mediation of locally prominent relatives or through patronage. Thus, even though the electorate seemed concerned to have representatives who knew local problems or spoke strongly for local needs, this did not always imply their support for local residents over those who had been 'absent' in government work or other external occupations. The desire to have a representative who *effectively* championed local needs ultimately seemed to be most crucial. This led to the re-election of several M.P.s who had been among U.N.I.P.'s early organisers and officers in the province, implying an endorsement by the electorate for a certain continuity of provincial leadership. Those M.P.s who were defeated tended to have been criticised for not having visited their constituencies frequently enough, thereby failing as effective representatives. The desire for effective representation also led to the election of a number of articulate non-residents relatively new to the national political scene, but apparently also able to demonstrate a satisfactory level of trustworthiness, on occasion by virtue of their ties with or sympathy for the orientation of the 'old guard' leadership.

Not one, but a number of factors, however, are important in explaining why certain candidates won, and the composition of victorious candidates for the province as a whole. Though similar, the
reasons were not the same across all constituencies, making
generalisation hazardous. In any given constituency, the specific
issues raised and the weight given to particular selection criteria
varied in accord with the composition of candidates and with the local
economic situation. This may be illustrated through examination in
greater detail of the campaigns and candidates in two constituencies
within the province: Mwansabombwe and Mansa. In both, the relative importance of education as opposed to local experience figured
as an important issue. But their contests differed as regards the extent
that they included candidates with extensive experience in national
level politics and government, and involved alleged intervention from
the centre. The contest in Mwansabombwe, for example, was
essentially a local affair, while that in Mansa involved two incumbent
M.P.s and, allegedly, national intervention in the campaign.

Mwansabombwe constituency Mwansabombwe was a new constituency marked off by the delimitation prior to the 1973 elections.
Its northern part had previously been in Kawambwa Constituency and
represented by J. Mwanakatwe, while its southern section had been a
part of Mununshi Constituency represented by J. Mambwe. The five
candidates for the primary election included the U.N.I.P. constituency chairman for Mbereshi who was a retired businessman, his
nephew, who was a former District Governor in the Ministry of
Planning and National Guidance and at the time of the election self-
employed with a small transport business, a rural council secretary, a
businessman resident on the Copperbelt and a secondary school
teacher. The incumbents who had represented its respective sections
stood elsewhere, while those nominated essentially lacked extensive
experience in national level politics and government. The three successful candidates in the primary were the Copperbelt businessman,
who received 29 per cent of the valid votes cast, the constituency
chairman and the ex-District Governor, each with 25 per cent. Of
these, the candidate with the highest level of education and training
was the businessman, P. Chanshi, while the candidate with the most
sustained level of local public and party service was L. Chisanga, the
constituency chairman.

Education emerged as a minor factor in the campaign, symbolised
by the tendency for the businessman to deliver his campaign speeches
in English in an apparent attempt to impress upon his audience his
level of sophistication and training. Of greater importance were two

other interrelated issues. One was the degree of personal familiarity of members of the electorate with the candidate or his family.[80] The second involved allegiance to, or strong sense of identification with, locality of residence. Some voters evidently wished to elect a candidate hailing from their immediate locality in order to rectify a perceived neglect of that locality, relative to others in the constituency. Hence, a strong sense of parochialism resulted in the electorate of Mwansabombwe Constituency being generally divided on a geographical basis in its support for particular candidates. The two most southern U.N.I.P. constituencies gave strong support to the businessman who came from that area. The two northern U.N.I.P. constituencies divided their support between the Mbereshi constituency chairman and the ex-District Governor. The division might be interpreted as partially tribal in nature, since the Lunda were concentrated in the southern two U.N.I.P. constituencies, while the Mbereshi area was ethnically mixed with substantial representation of Bemba, Tabwa and Lungu. The tribal factor, however, was probably more coincidental than real. One observer, knowledgeable of the area and its people, commented that the pattern of voter preferences was similar to that marking competition between sports teams, with each group pulling for its own area and for the candidate whom its residents associated with that area.[81] Members of the electorate seemed to be concerned not so much with tribe as such as with the immediate needs of their localities.

Thus, on one level, the contest was between the people of Mbereshi and its environs as against the people of the Kazembe (Mwansabombwe) area. But at the same time, it involved candidates' qualifications and was thus a contest between a reasonably well-educated businessman, who had been resident outside of the province since the 'fifties, and two long-term local residents. In the final election the businessman won with approximately 55 per cent of the valid votes cast; the ex-District Governor received 25 per cent and the constituency chairman 16 per cent. The fact that two of the candidates not only came from the same village but were also related, no doubt served to work against the possibility of either of them winning; but even so, the Copperbelt businessman received a clear majority in the poll.

Mansa constituency   The elections in Mansa District were of special interest for a number of reasons. First, they involved candidates of acknowledged national stature. Second, there were strong allegations that some of them had the support of national leaders and were 'official' candidates sent by the Lusaka leadership. The third, and perhaps most interesting, was that the three victorious candidates, all of whom won their contests with large majorities (Chisembele gaining approximately 76 per cent of the votes in Chembe Constituency, Kayope 68 per cent in Bahati Constituency, and Kaushi 62 per cent in Mansa Constituency) were openly associated in an informal alliance. Yet though clearly endorsed by the electorate as a whole, they had gained little favour either with the regional and district level officials or with many of the local businessmen. Mr. Kayope, in his subsequent interpretation of the campaign to Parliament, suggested that there had been three types of candidates in the elections: the history makers, the so-called government-sponsored candidates, and those who had been invited by the people to stand. Though the dividing lines between these groups may not always have been obvious, it is useful to explore this interpretation, given that it was put forward by one of the candidates and also because a number of party members in the Mansa area appear to have concurred with it.[82]

The history makers, according to Kayope, were individuals who had come forward independently and offered themselves to 'history' by standing for election. The second category of 'so-called government-sponsored' candidates, he alleged, had been selected or at least supported by members of the Central Committee.[83] All three were defeated. The three successful candidates in Mansa District's constituencies — Chisembele, Kaushi and himself — Kayope identified in contrast as those who had been invited by the people to stand.[84] A long-standing civil servant, Kayope had at one time been District Secretary in Mufulira, but more recently had been attached to the Ministry of Rural Development and resident in Lusaka. Chisembele and Kaushi were incumbent M.P.s, Chisembele representing the former Luapula Constituency and Kaushi the former Samfya Constituency. Both had been party officials at the provincial (or divisional) level during the early days of the independence struggle. During the early 'sixties, Kaushi had been a full-time U.N.I.P. official and had served as Divisional Treasurer for the whole of the province. When the party was reorganised and the regional system introduced in 1963, he had left active politics but had been called back to stand on the U.N.I.P. ticket in Samfya in 1968. Chisembele had been General Secretary for U.N.I.P. in Luapula prior to 1963 and subsequently Regional Secretary for Mansa-Samfya. He had served as an M.P. for Luapula since 1964 and a Cabinet Minister from 1969 until his suspension in 1971.

The three campaigns in Mansa District had a number of features in common, but that in Mansa Constituency was of particular interest, providing a good example of an alleged attempt by regional officials and the District Governor to promote the election of an official or preferred candidate. There were initially five candidates: a secondary school teacher, a local bar-owner who had formerly been a lower level party official, a civil servant (an Assistant District Secretary posted in Kabompo), a former M.P. (Kaushi), and a Cabinet Minister (W. Chakulya). The first two were eliminated during the primary and the real contest was always essentially between two candidates — Kaushi and Chakulya — with Kaushi maintaining a large edge in both the primary and the final election. In the primary, Kaushi received approximately 71 per cent of the votes cast as against 17 per cent for Chakulya. In the final poll, Kaushi's share was 62 per cent.

The contest centred around the fact that Chakulya was a national figure who, though born in Mansa District, had spent most of his life along the line of rail. He was criticised by his opponents for being a non-resident, and found it difficult from the outset to project a local image. Midway through the campaign, what national image he may have had was tarnished by an official reprimand from the Central Committee concerning a remark he had made that the Zambian newspapers were tribalistic and anti-Bemba.[85]

Kaushi, on the other hand, was criticised by his opponents as a backbencher who sat in Parliament but did little. A district level official remarked to the author, for example, that if Kaushi had had significant ability, this would have been recognised and he would have been appointed to the position of Cabinet Minister or to some other high post.[86] A Central Committee member who visited Mansa during the campaign advised the people that they should refrain from electing backbenchers 'who only said hear, hear'.[87] Though possibly a general comment rather than one specifically intended to discredit Kaushi, it was similar in tone to the general criticism.[88]

The Mansa campaigns were characterised by intense factional conflict which flowed over into the election and persisted afterward. Out of the welter of accusations and counter-accusations, it is possible to identify two distinct sets of supporters. On the one hand, Chakulya was allegedly supported by an alliance of District Governor, regional officials, a section of the party constituency officials, Mansa Town Councillors and businessmen.[89] Kaushi, on the other hand, was said to have had the support of a number of incumbents of the Mansa Rural Council and of party officials defeated in elections earlier in the year. He was also accused of campaigning on tribal and clan lines, exploiting his position as Chief Chimese's son.[90]

How far the Central Committee was associated with the provincial factions remained unclear. One visiting Central Committee member's remarks were interpreted by those who called themselves the people's candidates however as clearly directed against them, and that interpretation does not seem entirely unreasonable. It was equally unclear how extensive the alliance and co-ordinated effort was throughout the province of those said to be people's candidates. As noted earlier, a number of successful candidates claimed to have been invited by party branches or other groups from among the electorate. Yet evidence suggested that, in addition to this, there was a small group, referred to by one of its members as 'Luapula leaders',[91] which asked particular individuals to stand in some constituencies and which reviewed the list of those who had come forward independently in other contests, giving support to those whom they approved. That group was said to have included some former M.P.s and District Governors who hailed from Luapula, as well as some businessmen who operated both within the province and on the Copperbelt. In the same way that the efforts of those sending official candidates were said to have been concentrated in Mansa District, so too was the recruitment of individuals to stand by the 'Luapula leaders' focused here. According to one candidate, whoever wished to control the province, first went to Mansa to organise.[92] In other districts the people were left comparatively free to choose for themselves who should be their representative. The three successful candidates in Mansa District made little effort to hide their similar views concerning the political and economic neglect which they believed Luapula had suffered. They collectively and self-consciously posed themselves against those whom they claimed to have been sponsored by 'Lusaka'.

The dimensions of electoral competition

The effort to put through certain candidates, or certain blocs of candidates, seems to have been taken seriously by at least two leadership groupings, the boundaries of which were fuzzy but perhaps still distinguishable. Thus, the designation of candidates as official or people's candidates was not merely rhetorical, but a reflection of a real inter-factional competition for control. If not representing different class interests, or clearly distinguishable ideological positions, the separate identities and competition of the two groupings were apparent, and may be viewed as a consequence of the structure of power within the nation and the historical evolution of that structure.

Since independence, two factors important for determining political position had been, firstly, the approval of those in the inner circles with the authority to confer high level position and, secondly, the acclamation of the people though the ballot box. To some degree, these two operated concurrently, but in some cases they served as alternative means of access to power. One rested on the favour of those at the top, the other on the endorsement of those at the bottom, the dividing line between the two marking off the sphere of democratic procedure within the system. On either side the basis of approval was often fragile, underscoring the fluidity and instability of that group which owed its immediate income, status, and indeed privilege, to politics. It is partly for this reason that the competition was at times so intense. In the Luapula parliamentary elections of 1973, particularly in Mansa District, this competition was played out between groups differing precisely in terms of their source of, or claim to, power. On the one side were those whose positions were based on appointment, and whose interest was to seek a base of popular support, if not directly for themselves, then for those who were their allies. In Mansa Town, some from that group were allied with members of the local business community in support of their preferred candidate. On the other side were those out of favour with the centre and therefore with those having the authority to confer position. That second group included some who had come into conflict with the party's inner circles, and who had been suspended from the party or demoted from positions to which they had earlier been appointed.[93] They apparently wished to re-establish their legitimate positions among the ranks of power-holders by winning a strong popular mandate, or to demonstate that even if the centre had disapproved of them or their actions, the people clearly did not.

The distinction as regards means of access to power, alternatively by mandate of the people or by appointment from the centre, and indeed the related question of where the dividing line should be drawn between those elected and those appointed, have been seen as consistent points of contention for Luapulans. As noted previously, it was not that disaffected Luapulans wished to do away with the system of appointments or political patronage. Rather their complaint was that this system had not worked well for them, or to the favour of Luapulans. Their dissatisfaction led them repeatedly to stand up for the needs and interests of Luapulans. Feeling that they had been neglected and ignored as a group *because* they were Luapulans, these leaders had come to champion the interests of Luapulans as a group. To some extent, an appeal to the theme of neglect may have been chosen as a strategy for furthering one's own career. It is clearly conceivable that some Luapulans may have found playing on the general discontent over the pace of development the most reliable route to parliamentary office.[94] But the matter must rest without absolute conclusion; most of those interviewed during the campaign expressed genuine concern to represent their constituencies, quite apart from the possibility that their position as representative might afford them additional personal gains.

The category of Luapulan is, of course, an arbitrary one, the product of administrative structure established during the colonial period. It had become a salient category, capable of being called on by that group of politicians out of favour with the centre and their allies, for two reasons. First, within a structure whereby political organisation was based on the provincial unit, Luapula had had a particularly extensive party organisation. A number of present Luapulan leaders gained prominence during the period in which the provincial party organisation has been very strong; having not been absorbed into higher levels of leadership, they were often reluctant to relinquish their positions at the provincial level to a new group. Their original mandate having been from the people of the province, they tended first to consider themselves as provincial leaders and only subsequently as representatives of the province in the national arena. Thus they continued to see the province as a viable and real political entity. Second, the province maintained political salience precisely because administrative machinery was organised on the basis of this geographical unit. Development allocations were made to provinces, and in practice the distribution of those funds and of special development projects partly depended on the voice of provincial leaders within the party and government's inner circles.

Political and administrative organisation in the context of the one-party system, are clearly conducive to mobilisation on the basis of identification with the province. Such a system impedes a specific interest or class group (businessmen, workers, farmers, women, etc.) from campaigning on its own behalf and thereby gaining power through the electoral process, except where their predominance and organisation within an area is very great. But the one-party system does allow for an interest group whose boundaries are defined in regional terms (or which defines the boundaries in such terms so as to draw upon the support of a regional community) to gain representation for itself. This is particularly true when the selection process for representatives is decentralised; and it would therefore be expected that manifest cleavages in the parliamentary elections of the 'seventies would be on the basis of region, rather than explicitly of class.

This, of course, operated on a miniature scale within constituencies where, as seen in the case of Mwansabombwe, different sections of the constituency attempted to get one of 'their own' elected. But at the broader level of provincial politics, the cry of provincial neglect also became the basis on which 'people's' candidates differentiated themselves from those they labelled as official candidates. The administrative structure and provincial party tradition, then, set the context for mobilisation on the basis of identification with the province. But this only became feasible to the extent that real differences could be pointed to with respect to uneven development and unequal representation at levels of national decision-making among provinces.

As has been noted, evidence of disadvantage clearly did exist for the 'people's' candidates in Luapula in 1973.

The 1978 parliamentary elections

Subsequent to the 1973 elections, several of Luapula's M.P.s honoured their informal campaign promises, by speaking forthrightly for the developmental needs of the province. Early in 1974, V. Kayope articulated the case for the neglect of Luapula by the government in particularly evocative language:

We have become the exception in every respect. We have been underdogs and indeed Luapula has come to be treated as the political Cinderella of Zambia. We have been treated like spanners which once used are thrown away into the tool box. We have been like dairy cattle which once milked are thrown into open pasture. We have been discriminated against in every respect. We have been reduced to a position in which our leaders bow to this and that province to secure this and that little for our people.

Are we not educated? Are the degrees of our people inferior to those persons from other provinces? Are we an appendix of some other provinces and if so, can Government tell us which one? Why must we continue to regard Humanism as a sincere and genuine philosophy when it does not apply in our case.[95]

His bitterness towards the centre was taken up and expanded upon by others from the area. A Regional Secretary in Samfya issued a memo endorsing Kayope's remarks and also suggesting that the time was nigh for Luapula to secede from the nation. Perhaps not unsurprisingly, he was suspended from his office for this.[96]

Kayope and others continued to champion the requirements of the Luapulan people and of the provincial economy throughout the Parliamentary session. Their outspokenness at times appeared to consolidate into a general opposition to the centre on a number of points, though their critique was not in all cases internally consistent. In any case, by virtue of the image of its more active or vocal M.P.s, Luapula continued to be a 'troublesome' province.

In 1978 eleven of Luapula's twelve M.P.s stood for re-election. The exception was H. Matipa, who had been appointed to the Central Committee. Two of the incumbent candidates, Kayope and Chanshi, were disqualified by the Central Committee after the primary stage. Of the remaining nine, two lost in the primary election and three were defeated in the general elections. Only four were re-elected: Chisembele, C. Mwananshiku, M. Kainga and F. Kaya. This outcome presents a mixed picture. Since only a third were returned, it would appear at first glance that the Luapulan electorate was largely dissatisfied with its incumbent M.P.s. Clearly voters considered some incumbents to have represented them poorly or, having spent too little time in the constituency, to have become fundamentally 'Lusaka men'. But the apparent dissatisfaction with incumbents must be qualified and due consideration taken of the effects of the Central Committee's intervention. For had he been allowed to stand, it is probable that Kayope would have been successfully returned and Chanshi certainly so, since he was unopposed. Their elimination, along with that of five other candidates in Luapulan constituencies, created considerable bitterness in the province.[97] It was interpreted by many as punishment — a slap in the face — for Luapulans' 'independence of mind', particularly when seen against the 1973 situation when no disqualifications at all occurred in Luapula. In 1978, Luapula stood second only to Northern Province in respect of the number of disqualifications suffered. If not promoting official candidates, the Central Committee certainly made its influence felt in the Luapula contests. It must be assumed that the party perceived some threat from the province.

Given the evident bitterness, however, the electoral reaction of Luapulans was perhaps less than might have been expected. No boycott of proceedings occurred, and though the turn-out showed a proportionally smaller increase than in any other province, Luapula's poll of 70.4 per cent was still third highest in the nation. There was, moreover, no evidence of systematically lower polls in those constituencies where Central Committee eliminations occurred than elsewhere.

The drop in the percentage voting 'Yes' for President Kaunda was perhaps a more dramatic indicator of the incidence of disaffection among the electorate. In this case, the difference from the corresponding percentage in 1973 was greater than in any other province: 16.7 per cent down from the figure of 98.7 per cent, by which voters gave almost uniform acclaim in 1973. In the province's two most northern constituencies, respectively 39.8 per cent and 24.6 per cent voted 'No'. But again, the level of opposition was important only in relative terms, the 82 per cent voting 'Yes' overall indicating a continued, strong loyalty.

It is worthy of note that the number of party officials voting in primary contests was strikingly lower than in 1973. The average per constituency in that earlier election had been 730, higher than in any other province; but in 1978 the average was just 380. The change was in the opposite direction from that in all other provinces save Northern, and substantially greater than in the latter. The drop may have reflected a weakening of the party in the province, and if so, of marked degree. Alternatively, it might have reflected a more pronounced sense of alienation or frustration, evidence of which could already be detected just prior to the election in 1973, when some constituency officials professed that they would give the system just one more chance.

The 1978 contests featured many of the same names as in 1973, though often with different outcomes. In Kawambwa Constituency, two of the candidates, the incumbent and a local businessman, had contested in 1973. But the victor in 1978 was the third, Titus Mukupo, an official in the nationalist movement from the earliest days and latterly a businessman, having acquired shares in a Copperbelt firm in the mid-'seventies.

In Mansa Constituency the incumbent Kaushi found himself once again in confrontation with Chakulya. But either because Kaushi's local supporters, now lacking leadership positions in the local party, held little sway in 1978 or because the feeling had become much more prevalent that Kaushi was an ineffective champion of local interests, their positions in the final tally were now reversed. Chakulya won the seat with 47.6 per cent of the vote and Kaushi came third with only 13.9 per cent. It is probable that Chakulya's national status, most recently as Ambassador to Canada, served as a compelling attraction, marking for the voters the most effective means for securing alleviation of local grievances.

Relatively few national figures or even individuals of outstanding national experience or educational attainment contested Luapulan seats, though when such individuals stood, they did tend to win. Thus the two incumbents with ministerial positions were both successful, as was the Ambassador. In at least one case, however, the electorate's weighing of the merits of being well connected with those of retaining close touch with members of the constituency made victory far from certain. Indeed, as was the case in 1973, the electorate was almost obstinately concerned to elect an individual who 'knew' them and their problems firsthand, for only on this basis was a candidate assumed capable of effectively representing local interests. Nevertheless, as many as six of the eight new (non-incumbent) M.P.s were resident or mainly resident outside the province. Among these eight were two businessmen, the Ambassador, a parastatal employee, a District Governor and a teacher.[98] Luapulans were, of course, prevented in some measure from re-electing incumbents who had been particularly outspoken on their behalf. The victory of Chisembele, however, may point to a willingness to retain some continuity of 'old guard' leadership.

Conclusion

The economic and political experience of Luapula during the previous twenty-five years set the context for the issues raised during the parliamentary elections of the 'seventies, making possible the mobilisation of voters on the basis of presumed neglect of the province as well as of the immediate locality. The desire of the people for self-determination, and their conviction that only when they took an active role in the selection of their leaders would there be at least a chance of their complaints being heard and some remedial action taken, contributed to their cautious acceptance (and occasional rejection) of appointed officials and, to a certain extent, of the very system of delegation of powers through appointment. Particularly during the 1973 contests, that cautiousness served to tip the balance in favour of those previously chosen and acclaimed as leaders by the people of the province. There were, of course, some candidates elected who had not been active in the independence struggle locally, but even among these were several who strongly supported the view that Luapula had suffered neglect through previous underrepresentation. And they must therefore be regarded as potential or real allies of the 'old guard' leadership of the province which had consistently pushed this point.

This pattern of preference for 'old guard' leadership and the related rejection of so-called official candidates, however, did not signify a vote of protest against the regime (though the low poll may have indicated an increased apathy as regards the possibility for effective individual participation). For in the presidential poll, Luapulans gave overwhelming support to the President of the Republic, and thus to the party. Rather than a rejection of the system, the outcome of the 1973 elections in Luapula, then, reflected a complaint over the manner in which the fruits of the system had been allocated and the conviction that it was the prerogative of the people to choose their immediate leaders and representatives.

In 1978, the Central Committee's intervention through disqualifications generated substantial bitterness and was responsible for a reduced level of enthusiasm in support of the President, and probably a lower poll than might otherwise have occurred. Though the terms of the selection process and composition of candidates were altered by the Central Committee's action, the general tension between support on the one hand for the 'old guard', or apparently independent and outspoken champions of the needs of the locality, and on the other for well-connected and highly-experienced or educated candidates continued to operate. The outcome varied as between constituencies. Some 'old guard' leaders were returned. But the electorate also seemed willing to try out new possibilities, at least in so far as they promised faithfully to represent the interests of the people.

Notes

1 Prior to 1958, Luapula had been part of Copperbelt Province and then of Northern Province.

2 Kanta, Martin, 'General Study of Mwense District', Research Paper for PL 329, University of Zambia, February 1974. R. Molteno, *op.cit.*; Mulford (1967), *op.cit.*, pp.70–2.

3 Musambachime, M., 'Labour Migration from Mweru-Luapula 1900–24: A Study of African Response to Wage Labour', R. Palmer (ed.), *Zambian Land and Labour Studies*, Vol. II, National Archives Occasional Paper No. 2, pp. 40–3.

4 Native Affairs, *1931 Annual Report* (Livingstone, Government Printer, 1931) p. 30.

5 Musambachime, M., 'The Agricultural History of Mweru-Luapula Area to 1940', University of Zambia Library (mimeo), p. 11.

6 Musambachime, M., 'The Development and Growth of the Fishing Industry in Mweru-Luapula Area 1920–64: Its Social and Economic Effects', Seminar Paper, The University of Zambia, School of Education, Department of History, Seminar Series No. 9, 12 February 1975, p. 4.

7 Musambachime, 'The Agricultural History . . .', *op.cit.*

8 African Affairs, *1948 Annual Report*, p. 10; *1949 Annual Report*, p. 18; *1951 Annual Report*, p. 9; *1952 Annual Report*, p. 11; *1954 Annual Report*, p. 44; (Lusaka, Government Printer).

9 African Affairs, *1958 Annual Report*, (Lusaka, Government Printer), p. 28.

10 African Affairs, *1936 Annual Report*, (Lusaka Government Printer), p. 48; *1949*, p. 21; *1950*, p. 23.

11 African Affairs, *1947 Annual Report*, (Lusaka, Government Printer), p. 13.

12 In 1948 there were 220 village shop licences issued in Fort Rosebery District and 450 in Kawambwa District. In 1957 the figures were respectively 546 and 707 (African Affairs, *Reports* for years specified).

13 African Affairs, *1957 Annual Report*, (Lusaka, Government Printer), p. 28.

14 Musambachime, 'The Development and Growth . . .', *op.cit.*, p. 14; Native Affairs, *Annual Report*, (Livingstone, Government Printer, 1931, 1932 and 1934).

15 Musambachime, *ibid.*; African Affairs, *1960 Annual Report*, p. 32.

16 African Affairs, *1958 Annual Report*, (Lusaka, Government Printer), p. 28; *1961*, p.12; *1964*, pp. 2–4.

17 African Affairs, *1952 Annual Report*, (Lusaka, Government Printer), p. 11.

18 African Affairs, *1960 Annual Report*, (Lusaka, Government Printer), p. 25.

19 *Report on Intensive Rural Development in the Northern and Luapula Provinces of Northern Rhodesia, 1959–1961, op.cit.*; Magnus Halcrow, *op.cit.*; Government of the Republic of Zambia, *The Luapula Province Agricultural Stocktaking*, April 1965, compiled and produced by the Land Use Survey Section, 1959.

20 *Stocktaking, op.cit.*, pp. 73–4; *Report on Intensive Rural Development, op.cit.*, p. 25; *Nshila* (30 Sept. 1958), p. 21; African Affairs, *1958* and *1959 Annual Reports*.

21 *An Account of Disturbances in Northern Rhodesia, July to October, 1961, op.cit.*

22 Mulford (1967) *op.cit.*, p. 70.

23 Interview with M.P. elected in 1973, Interview no. 75 (all interviews from author's files); 25 Mar. 1975.

24 Mulford (1967) *op.cit.*, pp. 68, 78, 131, 137 and 151.

25 Mulford, *The Northern Rhodesia General Election 1962, op.cit.*, Appendix I; Northern Rhodesia Government Election Office, Analysis of Polling, Northern Rhodesia Election 1964, Table II, Jan. 1964; Election Results, 1968, Director of Elections, Lusaka (mimeo), and Referendum Results, 17 June 1969.

26 African Affairs, *1953 Annual Report*, (Lusaka, Government Printer).

27 *Ibid.*; Interview no. 75, 25 Mar. 1975.

28 African Affairs, *1953 Annual Report*, (Lusaka, Government Printer).

29 Interview no. 76, 26 Mar. 1975; 10 Apr. 1975.

30 According to some, activities of the administration's mobile unit invariably involved harassing and assaulting the villagers, stealing chickens, etc., in an attempt to demonstrate the power and force of government (Interview No. 75, *op.cit.* No. 77, 1 Apr. 1975 and 3 Apr. 1975).

31 Interview no. 77, *op.cit.*

32 Interview no. 77, *op.cit*; see Bates (1976), *op.cit.*, pp. 85–7 for a further discussion of this issue, particularly as it affected residents of the Upper Luapula Valley.

33 Bates' account suggests that party organisers may have come somewhat earlier than this and that the first to appear in Luapula was Banda. The information which we use here comes from A. Shapi's account of the organising activities which he and others were involved in. According to Shapi, no one had been sent officially by the party until he and D. Banda entered in the mid-'fifties (Bates, *op.cit.*, p. 80).

34 Interviews nos. 75 *op.cit.* and 77 *op.cit.* It was suggested by one of the early organisers that a number of businessmen joined the party in its first years as a means of expressing their opposition to a government which appeared to be impeding the progress of their enterprises.

35 Interview no. 75 *op.cit.*

36 Mulford (1967), *op.cit.*, p. 71; Interview no. 75 *op.cit.*

37 African Affairs, *1959 Annual Report*, (Lusaka, Government Printer), p. 29.

38 *Ibid.*, Interview no. 75 *op.cit.*; see Bates, *op.cit.*, p. 93 for an account of the manner in which Z.A.N.C. activities were maintained during this period, particularly in the area around Kasumpa village.

39 *An Account of Disturbances . . . 1961, op.cit.*

40 African Affairs, *1960 Annual Report*, (Lusaka, Government Printer), pp. 25–6.

41 *An Account of Disturbances . . . 1961, op.cit.* For their part the U.N.I.P. leaders told the people that they should go willingly to prison since the punishment for destruction of an identity certificate was only two weeks' imprisonment; they told the provincial administration to leave the doors of the prison open so that the people might enter voluntarily. According to one account, the prison soon filled up in Fort Rosebery but

the people continued to come. They went to the provincial and district offices, occupied them and said that they wanted to be arrested. Ultimately, the provincial administration declared that only provincial, constituency and branch officials of U.N.I.P. were subject to arrest (Interview no. 77; *op.cit*).

42   African Affairs, *1960 Annual Report*, (Lusaka, Government Printer), p. 25; Interview no. 75; *op.cit*.
43   African Affairs, *1956 Annual Report*, (Lusaka, Government Printer), p. 27.
44   *Northern News*, 22 Aug. 1961.
45   A similar argument linking political activism to economic depression is made by Bates, *op.cit*., pp. 87–91.
46   The only Luapulan who had been involved in the executive of the nationalist movement was T. Mukupo, who was active in A.N.C. in 1957 and 1958 but declined to break to Z.A.N.C. with Kaunda and Kapwepwe. He was elected an M.P. for Kawambwa Constituency in 1978. Though part of the central organisation of U.N.I.P., Shapi was involved at its lower levels.
47   Interview no. 75; *op.cit*.
48   Mulford (1967), *op.cit*., pp. 233–4.
49   *Ibid*., p. 236; Interviews nos. 18, 26 November 1973, and 75, *op.cit*.
50   Interview no. 75, *op.cit*.
51   Interview no. 10, 6 November 1973.
52   Several of the M.P.s elected in Luapula in 1973 argued that Luapulans had frequently been by-passed during the early years of independence when appointments were considered, precisely because the province's population had never been particularly troublesome (Interviews no. 17, 26 Nov. 1973 and no. 18, 26 Nov. 1973).
53   Interview no. 75, *op.cit*.
54   Minutes of U.N.I.P. Regional Conference, Mansa, *op.cit*. A slogan intended to express this feeling was 'Humanism is a book, each person should work where he belongs'.
55   Bates notes that the origin of the phrase *Tubulu* has been attributed to Kapwepwe, as well as to such Northern Province politicians as J. Chimba and J. Mwanakatwe. Having found no factual basis for any of these having formulated the phrase, Bates suggests that it was rather devised by the Luapula politicians themselves in order to foster the severing of bonds between the party organisation in Luapula and that in Northern Province (Bates, [1976], *op.cit*., pp. 229–30).
56   Memo to the President of the Republic of Zambia, from 7 M.P.s from Luapula Province, 21 Apr. 1969.
57   Memo to the President of the Republic of Zambia from the Copperbelt Luapula Delegation, 1970. Two of the signatories of this memo were elected to Parliament by Luapulan constituencies in 1973.
58   *Ibid*. Subsequent to the issuing of this petition, the secretary of the delegation was, according to his own account, suspended from the party for a year.

59 Comments along these lines were made by several Luapulan M.P.s and constituency officials at the U.N.I.P. Regional Conference in Mansa, April 1974; Minutes of U.N.I.P. Regional Conference, Mansa, *op.cit.*

60 No clear reasons were given for his suspension, but it took place immediately after he had toured Luapula, on his account for the first time since 1964. Allegedly his statements constituted a breach of his Cabinet position, because he had championed provincial interests (Interview no. 18; Press Release, 19 Apr. 1971; *Times of Zambia*, 19 Apr. 1971).

61 A. Shapi, however, was an under minister in Luapula, and then in Eastern Province, during the 1964–68 period, and two other Luapulan M.P.s were parliamentary secretaries and/or ministers of state. The title of Shapi's post changed over the years, first to the resident minister in the province and then to minister of state. It was not equivalent to the post of Provincial Cabinet Minister, which was created as a cabinet position in 1968.

62 Second National Development Plan *(SNDP)*, pp. 67, 81.

63 In contrast to the earlier Development Scheme, however, the First National Development Plan did give somewhat greater attention to agriculture.

64 *SNDP, op.cit.*, p.167.

65 *Ibid.*, p. 174, based on a survey by the Central Statistical Office.

66 It should be stressed that the linkages among points, as well as the substance of the argument, are not always valid, but the argument is an important one because its salience to some of the people of the province is high and because it continues to be articulated by some of the elected leaders of Luapula.

67 Kanta, *op.cit.*

68 Interviews with Mbereshi Constituency officials, 30 Nov. and 1 Dec. 1973, especially no. 44.

69 Based on inspection of applications for registration of U.N.I.P. branches and constituencies deposited with the Registrar of Societies. A non-random sample was taken of branches and constituencies registered in Mansa and Kawambwa districts in 1972, 1973 and 1974, and occupations of office-bearers were noted. At branch level, of 10 main branches, 5 women's brigades and 12 youth brigades, only 4 of those 27 bodies had any office-bearers with occupation listed as other than villager or housewife; only 4 per cent of all officers had occupations other than villager or housewife. At the constituency level, for 34 bodies (including 10 main bodies, 13 constituency youth brigades and 11 women's brigades), 16 included office-bearers with occupations other than villager or housewife. 7 of these were main bodies and another 8 were youth brigades. In total, of approximately 272 office-bearers in these constituency organisations, only 44, or 16 per cent were either self-employed or in wage employment. If the main bodies and the youth brigades are considered separately, the proportion of office-bearers either self-employed or in wage employment was 23 per cent. 17 of the 272 constituency officials listed themselves as workers, 8 as businessmen, 7 as councillors, 6 as bricklayers, contractors or carpenters and 4 as farmers. While a slightly

greater proportion of constituency than branch officials was employed, the great majority of both groups remained self-classified as villager or housewife.

70   Interview no. 66, 27 Feb. 1974.
71   Interview no. 59, 26 Nov.1973; Minutes of U.N.I.P. Regional Conference, Mansa, *op.cit.*
72   *Ibid.*
73   Interview no. 24, 29 Nov. 1973; Interview no. 14, 11 Nov. 1973.
74   Interview no. 14, 11 Nov. 1973.
75   Interview no. 15, 11 Nov. 1973.
76   The data reported here is compiled from a survey carried out by the writer during March and April 1974 with the assistance of Jonam Mwansa. Approximately 90 businessmen were interviewed throughout the province, most of these shop- and bar-owners.
77   This section focuses upon 6 of the 12 parliamentary constituencies in Luapula and on 2 districts, Mansa and Kawambwa. During the period of the campaign, from 26 October 1973 until 4 December 1973, the writer interviewed all of the candidates nominated in parliamentary contests in Mansa, Chembe and Mwansabombwe constituencies, as well as the three candidates who passed through the primary stage in Bahati and Kawambwa constituencies. District Governors and all regional party officials were interviewed in the 2 districts which include these 5 constituencies – Mansa and Kawambwa. In addition, as indicated previously, a number of constituency officials were interviewed in these two districts (with the assistance of Alick Munkonko). Detailed conversations were also held with several individuals who, while not directly involved in the campaigns, were particularly knowledgeable about local affairs and thus were able to provide very helpful background information of a relatively unbiased nature. The discussion in this section draws largely from both these interviews and conversations, and from personal observation of nominations, campaign meetings and the polling itself. Information concerning Mwense parliamentary constituency is based on the field work and report of Martin Kaluba Kanta who was present throughout the campaign, who interviewed candidates, officials, chiefs, lower level party officials and prominent residents and who additionally made detailed observations of several campaign meetings during the period. I am very grateful to him for allowing me to draw on this material.
78   Constituencies included here are Mansa, Bahati, Chembe, Mwense, Chipili, Mwansabombwe and Kawambwa.
79   The incumbent M.P.s are taken to fit into this category.
80   Interviews with Mbereshi constituency officials.
81   Interview no. 62, 1 Dec. 1973.
82   *Daily Parliamentary Debates*, 30 Jan. 1974, col. 692. It appears to have been the belief of some U.N.I.P. constituency officials as well that certain candidates were 'sent from Lusaka' (Minutes of U.N.I.P. Regional Conference, Mansa, *op.cit.*)
83   Interview no. 66, 1 Dec. 1973.

84 *Daily Parliamentary Debates*, 30 Jan. 1974, col. 692.

85 Zambian Information Service, Background Paper 130/75.

86 Interview no. 53, 7 Nov. 1973.

87 Campaign Meeting, 25 Nov. 1973, Mansa, *op.cit.*

88 Interestingly, the assumption that Kaushi had not spoken up for the people of his constituency and of Luapula as a whole was misplaced. Though not of a voluminous nature, his record in Parliament was one of periodic questioning of ministers concerning development projects scheduled for Samfya and Luapula as a whole.

89 Minutes of U.N.I.P. Regional Conference, Mansa, *op.cit.*

90 Interviews nos. 36, 3 Dec. 1973, 53, 7 Nov. 1973 and 59, 26 Nov. 1973.

91 Interview no. 66, 1 Dec. 1973.

92 *Ibid.*

93 Both Kayope and Chisembele had earlier in their careers been removed from positions they had held — Kayope in the Civil Service and Chisembele in the Cabinet — and effectively demoted. Another of the victorious Luapulan candidates had been suspended from the party for a year in 1970.

94 Molteno, *op.cit.*, for example, argues that in some instances the promotion of sectionalism essentially serves as a device for the promotion of individual politicians' careers.

95 *Daily Parliamentary Debates*, 30 Jan. 1974, col. 690.

96 *Times of Zambia*, 12 and 22 Mar. 1974.

97 G.S. Maipose, *op.cit.*, p. 57.

98 Some of the background information on M.P.s. elected in 1978 was provided by G.S. Maipose, to whom I am most grateful.

Western Province: tradition, economic deprivation and political alienation

Introduction

As the former Barotseland, Western Province in the early 'seventies had a particular salience for an understanding of the rural response to the one-party state. It is the country's most remote region and shares with Luapula a common experience of underdevelopment.[1] Unlike Luapula, however, it had a history of conflict with U.N.I.P. and in 1973 it was an opposition area, having supported the A.N.C. since 1968. It therefore presented the one-party state with a major test of its capacity to absorb and accommodate opposition. Moreover, in Barotseland, the traditional polity had enjoyed a good deal more autonomy and political power in the colonial period than had any other region, and in the independent state had continued to act as a focus of conflict in relations between the province and the centre. The influence of tradition has therefore also to be taken into account in any consideration of Western Province perceptions of their relationship with the Zambian state, and analysis of the province provides us with the opportunity to consider the relationship between tradition and economic change. We are primarily concerned with this and with the process whereby an awareness of cultural identity rooted in powerful traditional loyalties may interact with perceptions of economic deprivation and a sense of discrimination at the hands of other, culturally distinctive elements in society. In this essay we consider that process in the context of the recent political history of Western Province, culminating in the elections in 1973.[2]

The province is Zambia's second largest in area with its third smallest population.[3] It stretches west to the Angolan border and south to the Caprivi Strip, a vast, sandy flood plain intersected by the Zambezi and its tributaries on which its economy has always been dependent. Its most distinctive feature in the past was its isolation from the rest of the country.[4] The colonial authorities from an early stage regarded it as a labour reserve, and at any one time from the early 'thirties, 30 per cent of its able-bodied male population were working outside Barotseland, primarily, but not solely, in the South

African mines.[5] Early missionary endeavour ensured that the Lozi should be foremost in educational development in the colonial territory, thus providing a large proportion of the clerks and other white-collar employees along the line of rail. Young, educated Lozi also played a central role in the growth of urban nationalism. The province itself, however, remained isolated and underdeveloped. At independence, the population consisted primarily of subsistence cultivators and the general situation was one of dire poverty.[6]

Ethnically, Western Province is a highly complex area, with possibly fifty different groups with identifiable characteristics and dialects; but also with a high degree of fusion and assimilation between the many minority groups and the majority Lozi people whose traditional political system was the dominant influence in the area until the nationalist years.[7] It was the Lozi rulers with whom the British had come to terms at the end of the nineteenth century, and whom the Barotse Agreement had ensured a high degree of autonomy and power throughout the colonial period.[8] British rule in fact brought more changes to Lozi society than the Lozi themselves recognised. Nevertheless, their special Treaty relationship enabled them to retain their distinctive, highly-centralised traditional government, with its elaborate hierarchy of traditional chiefs and Indunas whose focal point was the Paramount Chief, or Litunga. It also enabled them to sustain the influence of tradition, or *sizo*, that held the Lozi together, and in which kingship as an institution played a particular role, symbolising the nation and an elaborate and deeply-rooted way of life. It was those traditional institutions, more than anything else, that set the Lozi apart as a distinctive group.[9]

The growth of African nationalism constituted a fundamental challenge to the traditional government, and from the late 'fifties the province was riven by separatist tendencies borne out of the attempts of the traditional leadership to retain its independence and privilege.[10] The most significant aspect of the nationalist years in Western Province was therefore the bitter struggle for power between the Lozi traditionalists, who dominated the Lozi government, and the Lozi nationalists whose militant politics, learned on the line of rail, played such a key role in the growth of U.N.I.P. The struggle for power left deep divisions within the Lozi ruling class, it failed to resolve the question of reform of the Barotse government itself,[11] and it continued after independence deeply to affect relations with the centre. Nevertheless, the Litunga, after a prolonged period of political manœuvring, in 1964 put his signature to the Barotse Agreement and ensured that Barotseland remained an integral part of the independent state.

The Barotse National Government was able to delay, but could not

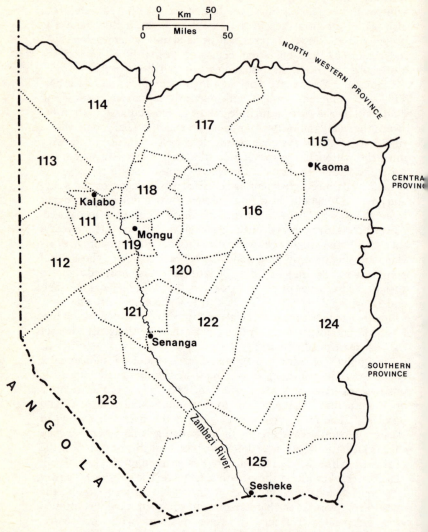

CAPRIVI (NAMIBIA)

Western Province: electoral constituencies, 1973 and 1978 (numbered as on the map of all constituencies, p. xiv). 111. Kalabo, 112. Sihole, 113. Sikongo, 114. Liuwa, 115. Kaoma, 116. Luampa, 117. Lukulu, 118. Luena, 119. Mongu, 120. Nalikwanda, 121. Nalola, 122. Senanga, 123. Sinjembela, 124. Mulobezi.

ultimately prevent, the penetration of the province by the political parties, and both the A.N.C. and U.N.I.P. became active from 1960. After four years' intensive political campaigning, U.N.I.P., had, by 1964, captured political control, having won two parliamentary elections, in 1962 and 1964, and in 1963 the elections for the Katengo, the reformed Barotse National Council. At independence, the party claimed Barotseland as a major stronghold, and there were four powerful Lozi national politicians in the independence Cabinet.[12]

Four years later, U.N.I.P. had lost its provincial base to the A.N.C., and at the introduction of the one-party state in 1973 the Western Province was a key opposition area. In the years of the multi-party state, moreover, electoral politics were characterised by steadily declining polls,[13] and in the general election in 1973, the provincial poll of 21.8 per cent was the lowest in the state. In 1978, that decline was reversed, with a poll of 44.1 per cent; nevertheless, once again Western Province registered the lowest poll, suggesting that in the one-party state U.N.I.P. failed to retrieve the legitimacy that it had won during the nationalist years.[14]

Western Province election results: 1962–78[13]

1962	75.5% and 81.4% polls (Barotseland West and Barotseland East)
1963	85% (Barotseland National Council)
1964	85% and 85.3% polls (Mankoya and Mongu-Lealui. Four uncontested seats)
1966	8.0–46.0% (local government elections, 71 uncontested and 39 contested wards)
1967	23% poll (parliamentary by-election, Lukulu)
1968	50.6–62.1% poll (10 contested, one uncontested seats)
1969	38.44% (referendum. Yes vote 14.22%)
1970	25% overall poll (local government elections)
1971	19.33–22.3% (parliamentary by-elections, three seats)
1973	21.8% (Parliamentary general election, poll ranging 12.5% to 28.4%, 4 of 15 seats uncontested)
1974	13.2%, 11.2% (by-elections)
1978	44.1%

It is with the political attitudes underlying that change that we are concerned here. We do not attempt a complete explanation, but rather to identify, across the province, the most salient aspects of the experience of those years which contribute to our understanding of the rural response to the one-party state.

The rise of opposition in the multi-party state

Relations between Western Province and the central government were dominated in the immediate post-independence years by two issues: the future of Lozi traditional institutions, and economic development.

On the first, the unwillingness of the Barotse leadership to accept proposals for reform led the central government in 1965 to proceed with the application to the province of the new local government system proposed for the whole country, and in the process to dismantle the formal structures of the Barotse National Government.[15] The changes were carried through in three successive stages between 1965 and 1969. First, the Local Government Act of 1965 abolished the Barotse Native Government, that had been the superior Native Authority, and the district councils, or *kutas*, through which it had maintained its administrative control. They were replaced by five elected District Councils established on exactly the same basis as the Rural Councils in the rest of the country and responsible to the Minister of Local Government in Lusaka. The subordinate administrative structure, based on the *Silalo* Indunas, was also abolished. The Chiefs Act of 1965 made the Litunga and subordinate chiefs in Barotseland subject to presidential recognition in the same way as any other chiefly order in the country. The Local Courts Act of 1966 repealed the Barotse Native Courts Ordinance and applied to Barotseland the same system of local courts as elsewhere, whose Court Presidents and Court Justices were now appointed by the Judicial Service Commission, not by the Litunga and Council.[16] Second, in 1969, after the referendum of that year, the government amended the Zambian constitution to terminate the Barotseland Agreement of 1964 and so to withdraw all rights, liabilities amd obligations previously existing under that agreement.[17] The third and final stage followed when the Western Province (Land and Miscellaneous Provisions) Act 1970, vested all lands in Western Province in the President and so legally destroyed the Litunga's control over land. Traditional land, fishing and other rights that had accompanied office were abolished. The change in the name of the Province, henceforth to be Western Province, signified the new order. The Litunga was now 'Just another chief'.[18]

None of these changes was implemented without fierce opposition from the Lozi traditionalists around the Litunga, who in 1966, for instance, campaigned to dissuade a sizeable element of the voters from registering for the local government elections, which were consequently conducted among a small electorate.[19] Their confrontation with the central government between 1965 and 1970 was, moreover, embittered by the fact that the ministers responsible for the implementation of these changes were those Lozi nationalist leaders who had opposed them for ten years. A good deal of the antagonism was thus personalised, in particular against two key Lozi Cabinet Ministers, Arthur and Sikota Wina. The Wina brothers had close family connections with the traditional royal court. Nonetheless, they had long been in conflict with the core traditionalist group, and at the level of the Lozi ruling class, this new confrontation may be seen as the culmination of the struggle that had dominated the nationalist years.[20] At the local level, however, the changes represented the triumph of the party over local traditional leaders, since U.N.I.P. now controlled the new Rural Councils, whose members and chairmen were predominantly local party activists.[21]

The second issue which quickly emerged as a source of local conflict was that of economic development. During the nationalist struggle, U.N.I.P. had laid the responsibility for the province's economic stagnation at the doors of the traditional establishment. At that time, they had promised a great deal if elected, and in 1965 they justified the local government reforms as a necessary change that would enable them to initiate development in the province.[22] The new government's proposals for the province in fact constituted a significant increase in investment above that of the colonial period by either the colonial or the Barotse government. The Transitional Development Plan (1964–66) provided £1,500,000 for Barotseland.[23] The first National Development Plan (1966–70) provided capital investment of £11,964,000 compared with Northern £30,426,000, Eastern £20,010,000, Southern £46,999,000, Luapula £11,108,000, and North-Western £10,760,000.[24] The Second National Development Plan (1972–76) allocation to Western Province for capital development was £12,077,000, which was not an unfavourable allocation in comparison with the other rural provinces: Luapula £10,455,000; North-Western £7,842,000; Southern £10,534,000; Eastern £10,668,000; Northern £10,750,000.[25] In 1967 a summer grazing scheme was commenced to overcome the shortage of grazing on dry land during the flood period; a maize scheme was begun in Kaoma; the National Beef Scheme project was set up, and in 1968 a state ranch was established at Senanga to breed stock for distribution to improve the quality of local herds.[26] There was also a creditable expansion in educational services, and especially the establishment of a secondary school in each district, most of them completed by the end of 1967.[27]

Nevertheless, economic investment proceeded more slowly than planned, and although in 1969 the official view was that there had been some progress on all fronts, the province had been unable to spend the full K27.2 million capital allocated in the first plan period.[28]

Western Province therefore shared with other rural areas the continuation of rural underdevelopment and the failure to achieve rapid change.

The failure of government to achieve rapid transformation quickly drew forth expressions of grievances against the centre that echoed those from elsewhere in rural Zambia. As early as 1965, there were signs of Lozi resentment at the failure of independence to bring immediate, tangible benefits.[29] In the case of Western Province, however, rural opposition was sparked off essentially by the central problem of employment, and by the government's decision in 1966 to prohibit any further labour migration to South Africa. It was that decision more than any other single government action which lay at the root of the opposition to U.N.I.P. that grew in the second half of the 'sixties.[30]

Recruitment of Lozi labour by the Witwatersrand Native Labour Association Ltd. (W.E.N.E.L.A.) had, for many years, been a major source of income for Barotseland, and many families were sustained by remittances from the South. In 1962, the total annual payout by W.E.N.E.L.A. in Barotseland had been £450,000. In 1964 4–5,000 men were working in South Africa and it had been considered officially that

WENELA revenue plays an important part in the general economy of the area, and unless and until this revenue can be replaced it is important that it continues.[31]

Thus the government's closure of the recruitment agency meant the loss of a major source of cash income for a significant proportion of the population in a region where there were few alternative opportunities. The abolition of W.E.N.E.L.A., moreover, increased an unemployment problem that had already existed at independence, and which even then included a growing number of primary school leavers who were 'unemployed and loafing around their villages, many bearing a grudge against the society in which they live'.[32] Such expansion in local employment as had taken place since independence had been almost entirely in the public sector, especially in local government. The Rural Councils did not, however, have the funds for major works programmes, and central government activity slowed down with the completion of its post-independence building programme. In 1968, the small increases in employment in agriculture and mining were offset by the decline in construction, which fell by half. There was a similar decline in commerce and transport, and at the end of 1968 there was less wage employment in the province than there had been in 1963.[33] 'People are now dependent on agriculture and cattle', the Assistant District Secretary in Sesheke reported in 1968; 'there is nowhere to get employment, especially for the young men, who complained bitterly at the Government failure to provide jobs.'[34] Neither cattle nor agriculture, however, was necessarily an easy alternative source of cash income. The official expectations that erstwhile Lozi migrants would turn to the cattle trade, ignored not only marketing constraints but also uneven distribution of ownership, and the fact that many of those who sought employment did not own cattle themselves.[35] Moreover, only in Kaoma district, which is the richest agricultural area in the region, was there any significant development of agriculture over these years. It was the overall failure of rural development itself which constituted the most serious constraint on the expansion of wage employment, as it was in other rural areas.[36]

The abolition of W.E.N.E.L.A. in 1966 contributed a great deal to the increased movement of Lozi to the line of rail in search of employment, so that whereas there had been an estimated 13,265 Lozi-speakers working in Northern Rhodesia in 1962, the 1969 census estimated approximately 70,000.[37] That movement served not only to intensify the sense of grievance among those Lozi who failed to obtain employment on the line of rail, but also to increase Lozi consciousness of their separate, cultural identity. On the one hand, they now came into greater competition for employment with other cultural groups, and especially with the Bemba on the Copperbelt, and the violent clash on the Copperbelt at Chililabombwe in 1968 was interpreted, as we have seen earlier, as a sign of Bemba dominance.[38] On the other hand, the factional conflict within U.N.I.P. in the period after independence was largely played out in terms of Lozi/Bemba rivalries, and resulted in the severe reduction of Lozi power at the centre of the party. Thus the dismissal of two Lozi ministers in 1966, the Lozi defeat at the hands of the Bemba/Tonga alliance at the Mulungushi elections in 1967, and a bitter demonstration against Lozi nationalist, Munu Sipalo, then Minister of Agriculture, in Kasama (Northern Province) in 1968, contributed also to a growing sense of discrimination, which reinforced the experience of Lozi work-seekers on the line of rail.

These several events help to explain the emergence of Lozi opposition to U.N.I.P. in 1968. Each year since independence, Western Province had been subjected to change which had disadvantaged one section of society or another. The abolition of the traditional authority had not only dismantled privilege but it had implicitly challenged tradition itself. It had not, however, resulted in the material benefits that Lozi nationalists had argued would follow. The fact that the changes had been introduced by Lozi ministers focused resentment upon them, and so persuaded an increasing number of Lozi, at different levels of society, of the need for an alternative Lozi leadership at the centre. The new affluence of many local U.N.I.P. activists also helped to focus resentment against the party at the local level.[39] Because economic grievances focused attention on the province, it also increased the sense of regional, and therefore of Lozi identity, so that economics and ethnicity reinforced each other.

Lozi opposition to the centre was first articulated by the United Party, formed in 1966. The party was started by Mufaya Mumbuna, formerly an A.N.C. M.P. for Mazabuka, who in 1965 after the passage of the Local Government Act, resigned from that party because he felt it could no longer protect Lozi tradition. Mumbuna had close associations with the traditionalists, since his father had been a senior Induna, and he had grown up in the Litunga's establishment; that association was subsequently important for his popular support. He argued, however, that his concern was not the privilege and power of a particular set of incumbents, but the deep attachment of the Lozi to tradition itself, which he insisted should be adapted, not abolished, in the interests of development.[40] Nalumino Mundia, however, who assumed the leadership of the party in 1967, focused on the economic difficulties that faced the province. He was himself from Kalabo district, which in the past had sent the largest number of migrants to the Rand mines, and which had suffered most seriously from the termination of W.E.N.E.L.A. and it was in Kalabo in 1967 that he first challenged U.N.I.P. on its failure to fulfil its election promises. In so doing, he articulated local disappointment at the slow pace of economic advance.[41] Anticipating the strategy that Simon Kapwepwe would adopt in 1971, he thus appealed to the economically dissatisfied.

Under Mundia's leadership, the U.P. extended its activities beyond Western Province, so that by 1968 the party had twenty branches scattered across the country, a few in each province except North-Western. Nevertheless, when it was banned in 1968, it was generally regarded as a Lozi party and there was no doubt of its influence in Western Province, or that its following, once it was banned, was transferred to the A.N.C. That support enabled the A.N.C. to defeat U.N.I.P. in the 1968 elections, when they won eight of the eleven parliamentary seats in the province. They campaigned, however, to a large degree independently of the A.N.C. national headquarters, so that their victory was essentially that of an alternative Lozi leadership, in the place of those Lozi in U.N.I.P. who were believed to have let their own people down.

How far the support for the A.N.C. in 1968 reflected support also for the traditionalists against the abolition of the Barotse Native Government is more difficult to assess. On the one hand, there was much to suggest the weakening of their influence. The Local Government Act had abolished the system of *Silalo* Indunas that had provided the

basic administrative framework through which the traditional government had maintained its authority, as well as communication and
control. The traditionalists failed, moreover, during this period to
provide any effective provincial leadership *vis-à-vis* the central government, appearing to be concerned rather with their own position
and privilege than with the needs of the province as a whole. There
was no evidence, for example, of their intervention as a group in the
W.E.N.E.L.A. issue.[42] The new Rural Councils had greater resources to
distribute at the local level than the *kutas* they replaced, and the
Barotse traditionalists had lost much of their power of patronage.
Mundia's Libonda home base was also the village of one of the royal
chiefs. Although he was still in restriction at the time of the election,
and so unable to campaign, his influence prevailed over others'.
Traditional backing did not help those candidates who had it in 1968,
or in the 1971 by-elections.[43]

On the other hand, the Litunga and Council continued to appoint
Indunas who remained as custodians of tradition, and who in this
respect retained a vital role in society. In numerous situations, central
government officers found the influence of the local Indunas
necessary to obtain local support for government development programmes. Their assistance proved essential, for example, to the
Veterinary Department's innoculation campaign at the time of the
bovine-pleuro pneumonia epidemic, and notwithstanding the
legislative changes in 1970, they continued to enjoy their traditional
authority over land. The capacity of the traditional chiefs as a force to
mobilise support at the local level could not therefore be discounted.

U.N.I.P.'s defeat in 1968 transformed the province into an opposition area. Provincial support for the A.N.C. was demonstrated further
by the 1969 referendum to make Parliament solely responsible for
amending the constitution (which they opposed) when 36,094 voted
against it and 23,225 voted in favour.[44] While the A.N.C. could not
prevent the passage of the land legislation of 1970, they successfully
exploited local opposition so as to increase their support in the local
government elections that year.[45] Although U.N.I.P. retrieved two
seats in the parliamentary by-elections in 1971, the minimal poll
suggested that provincial opposition, if not alienation, had further
increased.[46] Provincial relations with the centre were made more
difficult over this period by the accession to the Litungaship at the
end of 1968 of Godwin Mbikusita Lewanika, whose association with
the former Federal Government had earlier brought him into deep
conflict with U.N.I.P.[47] Old U.N.I.P. suspicions of Lozi separatist
tendencies were revived by rumours of South African involvement in
the region, at a time when the acceleration of the liberation struggle
in Angola gave the province an increased strategic importance.

The rise of the opposition in Western Province also had repercussions on Lozi representation at the centre, where only Sikota
Wina of the original Lozi ministers remained in the Cabinet. Moreover, in the face of the dual opposition of A.N.C. and traditionalists,
the government did not hesitate to intervene, for example in
appointments to traditional office. U.N.I.P. thus made it clear that
open opposition to the centre would not be tolerated.[48] At the same
time, however, they adopted a new two-pronged strategy in an
attempt to win back support. First, they tried to accelerate the implementation of development projects in the province, including the
tarred road to Lusaka. A special task force was set up to advise on
development.[49] Second, the party began to seek closer links with the
traditionalists, and to associate them more closely with the central
government.

The attempt to affect some reconciliation with the traditionalists
was suggested by a number of judicious appointments to provincial
office of Lozi who were likely to be more acceptable than their predecessors to the Lozi traditional circle, the key appointment being that
of Mr. Siyomunji, a nominated M.P., as Provincial Cabinet Minister.[50]
A number of traditional chiefs were also nominated as local
councillors, and during 1972–73 discussions took place on the possibility of the inclusion of traditional chiefs in the development committee structure.[51] Siyomunji set out with a good deal more diplomacy
than some of his predecessors to revive the legitimacy of the central
government in the eyes of the Lozi by associating the Lealui leadership more closely with his office,[52] his efforts culminating in June
1973 with the attendance of the Litunga at a meeting of the Provincial
Development Committee.[53] Finally, in the year leading up to the
introduction of the one-party state, efforts were made to associate
chiefs with the party. In the party reorganisation that preceded the
general election in 1973, a U.N.I.P. branch was established at each
chief's headquarters, and the traditionalists and the nationalists
appeared at last to have come together. How far such a strategy was
likely to restore popular support for U.N.I.P., rather than to involve
the traditionalists more explicitly in the inter-party conflict, was,
however, by no means clear. Hence, it was important that U.N.I.P.
made little effort to effect a reconciliation with A.N.C. in the Western
Province, prior to the one-party state. Western Province A.N.C. M.P.s
were not included in the Choma Agreement of June 1973, but were
left to negotiate separately their accommodation within the new
system. Those who accepted the changes made their peace with
U.N.I.P. at a public meeting in Mongu in August 1973, attended by
the Cabinet Minister, the Litunga and the Ngambela.[54] Neither they
nor their followers were permitted, however, to establish U.N.I.P.

branches in place of their own, and few emerged as U.N.I.P. party officials.

Opposition in the one-party state: the 1973 general election

In view of its recent history of political opposition, the most significant aspect for Western Province of the first general elections in the one-party state was the poll itself, which was the lowest in a decade of steadily-declining polls. It ranged from 12.5 per cent (in Sihole Constituency) to 28.4 per cent (in Sesheke), thus including some of the lowest turn-outs in the whole country. The overall poll for the province was 22.0 per cent compared with the national average of 39.4 per cent. The presidential poll, with a 77.4 per cent 'Yes' vote and 22.6 per cent 'No', produced the second highest vote against the President in the whole country. Moreover, the intense candidate participation that occurred elsewhere was lacking. Forty-one candidates were nominated for fifteen constituencies, a marked contrast with the other former A.N.C. stronghold, Southern Province, where there were ninety nominations for sixteen seats. Four of the fifteen constituencies had uncontested elections (Sesheke, Sinjembela, Nalolo and Senanga, the latter after the disqualification of a second candidate by the Central Committee), and only five constituencies produced a sufficient number of candidates to require a primary.[55] Campaign meetings were poorly attended, and the generally quiet atmosphere over the period, even in Mongu, the provincial headquarters, belied the idea that an election was in progress at all.

Not unrelated to the apparent lack of interest, not only in the election itself but in the opportunity to seek parliamentary office, was the degree of involvement in the selection process from the centre. The Central Committee vetoed three of the candidates successful in the primary elections, which in one case led to the remaining candidate being elected unopposed.[56] Of considerably more importance, however, was the influence of Lozi leaders holding key positions at the centre in either party or government, who intervened to support a number of candidates. They did so, it seemed, essentially in their personal, private capacity, and the process of consultation was for the most part informal; it was implicitly directed to ensure candidates acceptable to U.N.I.P.[57] Their success varied a good deal between districts, and in Kaoma they were unable to overcome local party opposition to their own choice. Nevertheless, their influence ensured that, although there were no official party candidates, the final list of nominations in most constituencies included a candidate, whom we shall term the 'preferred candidate'. Thus, while there was no 'party slate', the party to a considerable extent maintained the same control over nominations that it had exercised in the multi-party state.

Specifically, eleven candidates were preferred, including all out-going M.P.s. No serious attempt appeared to be made to accommodate the former A.N.C. leaders, three of whom, including Mundia, were still in detention in August 1973. No A.N.C. candidate was a preferred candidate. Nor were any concessions apparently made to the traditional leaders at Lealui, and the nominations themselves suggested that the old conflict between the Litunga and the Lozi nationalists continued to play its part in determining local alliances.[58] Local party interests were to some extent accommodated, not least in the uncontested seats. Local interests, however, represented the Rural Councillors, the party constituency and branch chairmen, the trustees and the local traders. The limitation of popular support of those interests was suggested by events in Sinjembela, where their candidate was elected unopposed. In that case, a would-be contestant successfully brought an election petition in which he claimed that local party officials had prevented him from lodging his nomination.[59] He went on, in 1974, to win the by-election that followed.[60]

Of those candidates who finally contested the primaries, seven were sitting M.P.s, four of them ministers. Seven were teachers, six were civil servants, ten were local party officials and ten were business-men. Two had previously stood unsuccessfully for A.N.C., one in 1971. Three were former A.N.C. M.P.s who had crossed the floor in 1970. Only Mumbuna had been an A.N.C. opposition M.P. at the time of the declaration of the one-party state. Eleven, as noted, could be identified as 'preferred candidates'. Six might have been said to have been 'acceptable' to Lealui, but neither A.N.C. nor tradition was strongly represented among the candidates who presented them-selves, first for the primary and then for the general election. Instead, the people of Western Province were offered a group of candidates, most of whom had a long association with the party believed to be responsible for the backwardness of the province and the alleged discrimination against the Lozi. To many, it must have appeared to be no choice at all, which may well have made many decide not to vote.

The fifteen M.P.s returned in the general election included all eleven 'preferred candidates', including the two ministers and two ministers of state; the two former A.N.C. M.P.s who had crossed the floor in 1970 (and one of whom was one of the assistant ministers); and a former nominated M.P. (in the independence Parliament), who had been defeated when he stood for election in 1968. The other four might be called the 'local choice'. One was Mumbuna, the second an unsuccessful A.N.C. candidate in 1968 in Kaoma (where he now won), and two had no obvious party connections. The majority of the new

Western Province M.P.s were still therefore drawn from the old U.N.I.P. circle that had originated in the early 'sixties. While this might have constituted a 'victory' for the party, in the face of the low poll it scarcely represented a change of political heart in the province. The eleven 'preferred candidates' (who included the four returned unopposed) received a total of 11,221 votes, which in a total electorate of 197,000 could scarcely be interpreted as an enthusiastic swing back to U.N.I.P., or a positive acceptance of the new one-party situation. The vote in favour of President Kaunda was 31,282, which might fairly be interpreted as support for the government; but 9,135, 22.6 per cent voted against him. One is forced, therefore, to conclude that the voting results indicated a continued rejection of U.N.I.P. as a party, with all the implications that held for a withholding of legitimacy from the government. The strategies of 1971–73 had not, it appeared, overcome the alienation from U.N.I.P. that had been expressed in 1968, 1969 and 1970.

If we are to understand the difficulties that now faced U.N.I.P. in Western Province, it becomes important to consider the underlying attitudes that helped to determine the grass-roots response. We have suggested above two key issues that exercised the public mind in the province, both of which had played their part in leading to U.N.I.P.'s earlier defeat: on the one hand, the failure of economic development and on the other hand, the awareness of local identity, which that had increased. It therefore becomes necessary to follow those two issues through into the one-party situation, and to consider the extent to which one or the other, or both, were responsible for the continuing alienation of the grass roots.

We may first consider the influence of the traditionalist leaders, with whom, as we suggested above, U.N.I.P. had attempted to make some public identification in the period prior to the introduction of the one-party state. The strategy of 1971–73 had undoubtedly been based on the assumption that the party must benefit from the associa-tion. Moreover, while U.N.I.P. had been unwilling to countenance Lealui nominees, a number of candidates had links with the traditional ruling class. M. Mututwa (the unopposed candidate in Sinjembela) had in the early 'sixties been an Induna in the Barotse Native Government and a member of the Saa-Sikalo. L.N. Luyanga (whom Mumbuna defeated in Luena Flats) had also been an Induna, and still maintained a keen interest in the organisation of traditional ceremonies such as the annual Kuomboka, the ritual journey of the Litunga from the plain capital to the higher capital at Limulunga each March. Mr. Mumbuna's family associations with Lealui and his deep attachment to tradition have been mentioned. Dr. Bull (who was returned unopposed in Nalolo) enjoyed close associations, through her

father, with the royal chieftainess at Nalolo, the Mulena Mukwae
Makwibi, and had won the admiration of many for her book on Lozi
history. M. Silumesii had connections by marriage with the royal
family as also did J.B. Siyomunji. Other candidates' campaign
speeches also revealed the belief that to succeed they must demonstrate their attachment to tradition,[61] but the clearest symbolic demonstration of the attempt to restore U.N.I.P.'s legitimacy through the
support of the traditional leaders was the occasion of the President's
meeting in Mongu, when the Litunga and his Indunas were all present. Notwithstanding the brusque recognition accorded them by the
President, the Litunga had seconded the vote of thanks for the President's speech, in the course of which he assured him that his Indunas
were determined to ensure a high 'Yes' vote in the presidential election.[62]

The election results therefore raise doubts of the continued dominance of the traditional leaders at grass-roots level, and their ability to
mobilise political support. Whereas in 1966 they had had sufficient
influence to dissuade people from voting in the local government
elections, by 1973 their influence was, it appeared, insufficient to
persuade the villagers to vote in the opposite manner, notwithstanding that they remained the custodians of *sizo*.[63]

It becomes necessary, therefore, to identify the role of tradition
more carefully. We need then to distinguish between, on the one
hand, *sizo*, tradition in its deepest sense, standing for a way of life and
a specific set of values which offered protection for a particular
identity, and on the other, the traditionalists themselves. Attachment
to *sizo* in most cases ensures attachment and loyalty to those who
hold traditional office. But in Western Province, events had brought
some of those office holders into popular disfavour. The very association of the traditional leaders with the party popularly seen as responsible for the disadvantaged position of the Lozi itself, challenged
their earlier pre-eminence. During 1973, there were at least two disputes involving traditional chiefs and Indunas, one in Sesheke and one
in Lubonda, which were specifically matters of local politics, and
which suggested a popular antagonism to some of the traditional
office-holders involved. Hence, respect for *sizo* did not necessarily
ensure support for those who held traditional office.[64] The weakening
popularity of the traditional leaders had in fact been suggested by their
response to the Chona Commission, when, seeking the restoration of
traditional institutions, they had indicated their need for an external
support to ensure their continued authority.[65] They were now a dependent group compared, for example, with Mufaya Mumbuna whose
respect for *sizo* was accompanied also by his established record as a
man who had challenged government for its lack of economic inputs

into the province. Appeal to *sizo* and articulation of a sense of economic deprivation were in his case intimately connected.

Thus we must turn to the second major issue in the province, the issue of economic development, which emerged as a recurring theme at public meetings. Small as the attendance was, the response was invariably the same: complaints were voiced at the continued lack of development in the province in general and in the particular constituency. Such a sense of economic neglect, if not deprivation, was articulated wherever election meetings were held. 'What was the use', the question usually went, 'of electing a Member of Parliament, when nothing ever changed.'[66]

In 1973, government spokesmen could point to certain important recent developments in the province. The tarring of the Mongu –Lusaka road had been completed and Western Province was now linked to Lusaka by a magnificent highway. The road from Livingstone as far as Sesheke had been tarred, so that communication with the Southern Province had also improved, certainly for the southern parts of Western Province. The abattoir in Mongu, which promised improvements for the cattle industry, had been completed (although it had not in fact come into operation, owing to the delays in the arrival of power from Livingstone). The cattle epidemic had been successfully eradicated and cattle sales resumed and expanded.[67] Educational services had certainly expanded. Between 1966 and 1970 there had been a 36 per cent increase in the number of primary places available, and 80.7 per cent of the 7–14 age group were enrolled in primary school. There was a full secondary school in each district except Lukulu, and an enrolment in 1973 of 5,075.[68]

Notwithstanding those achievements, however, for the majority of villages little had changed. Every district faced an increased school-leaver problem, since only 18–20 per cent of Grade VII pupils continued into Form I. A large proportion of primary schools were still 'pole and dagga', and facilities were grossly inadequate. Internal communications remained poor, Kalabo for example still being virtually cut off from the rest of the province for several months in each year.[69] Marketing facilities were inadequate, even for those farmers around Mongu who had begun to grow vegetables for the township market. If its title of 'Cinderella Province' had been usurped by Luapula, Western Province nevertheless demonstrated in acute manner all the failures of rural development.

The problems of rural development that faced Western Province were felt by Zambia's rural areas as a whole. As in 1966, however, so in the early 'seventies the sense of economic deprivation in Western Province was heightened by another major policy change on the part of central government that affected only the Lozi: the legal change in the status of Lozi land, opposition to which had won the A.N.C. considerable support in 1970 and 1971.[70] The government had argued that the land law changes were necessary in the interests of justice, equity and development, and that traditional land law in Western Province had tended to be an obstacle both to the enjoyment of full rights by all the Lozi people, and also to the efficient use of resources.[71] So far as the relationship between land tenure and agricultural or other development was concerned, there had always been a certain amount of disagreement.[72] There were significant differences in land ownership among the Lozi; and it might fairly be argued that it was the traditional ruling class who were most affected and most concerned about the 1970 legislation. Many villagers might have therefore, welcomed the change. Nevertheless, the changes represented in many respects a frontal attack on their whole way of life. In the Western Province of Zambia, as much as anywhere in Africa, land remained a sensitive political issue, and to appreciate the reaction fully it is necessary to consider briefly land use in that province as it had evolved over many years.

In the first place, good land is both limited and unevenly distributed over Western Province. It had always, therefore, been of great value, and traditional ownership and inheritance customs recognised this fact.[73] In the second place, land provided the crucial basis for the cohesion of the social system. Ownership of mounds (in the flood plain) and the control it gave over productive activities in the Plain, which were the main integrating principles in the Lozi kinship structure, had not entirely disappeared in the early 'seventies. In the third place, traditionally the Paramount Chief, the Litunga, was the 'owner of the land' of Barotseland, but his subjects, whether Lozi or not, all had rights to as much land for cultivation and for building on as they needed. Once they had been granted land, their rights were protected, even against the Litunga himself. Since the 'fifties at least, people had enjoyed well-protected rights to both cultivated, resting and even abandoned land. However, by the early 'sixties, the combination of population pressures upon good land, and the deterioration of the drainage system, had resulted in increasing cultivation of forest land and the increasing subdivision of gardens; consequently most Lozi villagers had very small acreages. They were therefore deeply concerned for a basic security of tenure, which customary law assured them, for essentially economic reasons.

In the early 'seventies therefore, at a time when the end of W.E.N.E.L.A. and the continued failure of rural development had created new economic difficulties for many Lozi, underlying the concern at the changes in land law was not only the chiefly fear of the loss of privilege but the subsistence farmer's concern for security.[74]

Faced with this situation, U.N.I.P. needed to supply the kind of ideological force that could overcome doubts and mobilise the population to greater effort, as well as to create better communications between government and people. We need, therefore, to consider also the position and role of the party in Western Province at that time. The elections showed that in 1973 U.N.I.P. had neither the party machinery nor the manpower to mount an effective campaign that might have won people over and mobilised support for the new system.[75] The party organisation at district and branch level varied from area to area, but generally in Western Province branches were small, in many cases consisting only of the officials. The attempt to set it in order prior to the elections and to ensure that all branches were registered for the primary elections, led in August/September to a burst of activity and to a situation in which the local party had two kinds of branches: those that had been long established (the minority) and those created at that time. The older branches consisted characteristically of a small group of long-standing U.N.I.P. members who constituted essentially a 'local club'. There was little evidence of any continuous party activity. In Mongu District, and this was generally the case, there was little regular communication between the regional office and the villages, the Regional Secretary not having visited some of his rural constituents for the previous two years.[76] In addition, many party officials were out of touch with the villagers and their arrogance offended the local people.[77] It was the District Governor who had provided communication between the district and the village, not the party.

The party's weakness in part reflected the limited electoral activity that had taken place over the previous eight years. In the 1964 election, U.N.I.P. had won five of the seven seats uncontested, without any electoral campaign. The party organisation remained rudimentary, and there was little to testify to a vigorous local party machine. U.N.I.P.'s control of the Rural Councils, which from 1965 consisted predominantly of known U.N.I.P. loyalists, provided an alternative to a party structure, and the councillor was an important channel of control as well as communication with the local level.[78] But the party organisation had not benefitted. The 1968 general elections and the 1971 by-elections had been harder fought, but the considerable assistance from the national leadership on the latter occasion suggested a weak local machine.[79] In 1970, moreover, U.N.I.P. had lost control of the council in several districts, notwithstanding that all Council Chairmen (nominated by the minister) were U.N.I.P. supporters.

There was little to show, therefore, of a viable local level party organisation. In 1964, U.N.I.P. had claimed that Senanga was a 'one-party district' and that organisation was 'very smooth'. Party officials had also admitted, however, that card sales were poor and that the women's and youth leagues were very disappointing. They regarded the district as a one-party district because the U.N.I.P. candidate, M. Sipalo, had been returned unopposed. Senanga District, nine years later, at the time of the 1973 Mulungushi conference, was reported to have thirteen U.N.I.P. branches and no party constituencies.[80] In the brief period between the August Mulungushi conference and the end of September 1973, seventy-four branches, all with three wings, were registered.[81] There was nothing, however, to indicate any extensive recruitment of members during that exercise. In effect, the exercise consisted of the selection of eight branch officials.[82] Elsewhere in the province, the registration of new branches similarly concealed a weak party structure.[83]

The local party was, however, as elsewhere, a powerful mechanism of control over access to resources. Although U.N.I.P. councillors tended, in the more remote areas, to be cultivators, they also included local traders, and the provincial leadership was closely identified with the local business class. The patterns of patronage did not, therefore, appear very different from elsewhere. They promoted factions at the local level, and the impression was that they also explained, in part at least, the factional alignments within the old ruling class.[84]

The local party's image in 1973 remained, therefore, that of a minority group, and to a considerable extent a closed group anxious to protect its own position. Many of the officials who formed the branches were indeed long-standing party members, who remained jealous of their positions. They still believed in the old 'rules of the game', by which candidates for elective office, whether at local or national level, must be 'the best and most responsible Party men in the locality',[85] and not a few of them resented the idea that former A.N.C. members were to be welcomed to the fold. During the campaign period, for example, the District Governor at Mongu had to resolve at least one local branch dispute arising between 'old U.N.I.P.' and would-be 'new men' from A.N.C. And at a large meeting of leaders and officials in Kalabo, addressed by a member of the Central Committee, one elderly man was ruled out of order because he challenged the wisdom of welcoming former A.N.C. members into the party.[86] Such attitudes at the local level increased the difficulties of winning over former opposition followers in the one-party situation, for reasons unconnected with tradition.

Factional rivalries at the local level also weakened the local organisation. In Kaoma, for example, such rivalries cost the U.N.I.P. 'old guard' the seat. Kaoma, unlike other districts in Western Province, had a long and continuous record of loyalty to U.N.I.P., but in the 1968 elections neither of the party's candidates had been a local man. Local U.N.I.P. leaders now felt that it was time their loyalty should be rewarded, with the result that they rejected the candidate proposed from the centre. Two local candidates put themselves forward, splitting the 'loyal U.N.I.P.' vote, and leaving the third candidate, a former A.N.C. man, to win.[87]

The increased emphasis upon local interests, particularly in the more remote districts, drew greater attention to ethnic cleavages. Up to this point, we have spoken of Western Province primarily in terms of its Lozi inhabitants, the Lozi being the dominant group who had always formed the superior political force. Western Province, however, as we pointed out at the beginning, has a diverse and complex population, and there had always been a tension between the dominant Lozi and the other smaller ethnic groups. In Kaoma District, Mbunda- and Nkoya-speaking people especially had long resented what they regarded as Lozi domination. In Kalabo District, where the so-called 'minority tribes' outnumbered the Lozi, Makoma opposition to the traditional authority had led them at an early stage in the nationalist struggle to support U.N.I.P.[88] In 1973, the greater emphasis upon locality resulted in the articulation of economic grievance in terms of those smaller ethnic groups. Changes in constituency boundaries in Kalabo, moreover, changed the ethnic composition of two of them significantly, and so increased the importance of ethnic support.[89] In Kalabo in 1968, two of the three successful A.N.C. candidates had been Lozi, suggesting that perceived economic deprivation overrode any ethnic particularism.[90] In 1973, however, in Sikongo Constituency, which included Kalabo township, the Lozi minister of state (who was believed to be a preferred candidate) was opposed by a Makomo party youth official. In the event, the minister of state won, in a low 17.4 per cent poll. The contest reflected, however, the perceptions of neglect felt by Makomo traders, at the hands of a party which they had previously supported, and their desire for a local and therefore a Koma man. The local party termed the situation 'tribalism', to which it attributed both the low poll and the overall absence of popular involvement.[91] But the feeling was more essentially parochialism. Kalabo illustrated the way in which a sense of economic deprivation could reinforce local and therefore ethnic identity, producing a parochialism which is often mistaken for simple 'tribalism'.

The local divisions within the party reflected, however, the parochialism of the local élite rather than of the rural population itself. The Kalabo electorate was a rural, subsistence society whose most serious problems related to the lack of communications within the district, which were highlighted by the concentration of development in

Kalabo township, the district centre, at the expense of the periphery. Development since independence had brought the district a secondary school and a hospital, the latter officially opened in September 1972. Both, however, were in Kalabo township, and in the district beyond, little change occurred. The district as a whole remained a net importer of food. Thus, while the contest between the candidates themselves might be explained in terms of economic interests translated into local and therefore ethnic terms, the low poll must be considered also in the light of such rural underdevelopment, and the apathy, if not alienation, of a scattered, isolated subsistence population.[92]

One other factor must also be taken into account, which affected all the border districts of the province. Stretching to the Angolan border, Kalabo district had suffered, since the escalation of the liberation war in Angola, from successive border incursions by both Portuguese and liberation forces. There had also been a large influx of Angolan refugees, some of whom had ethnic ties with the local population. Villagers had in many cases fled from their border villages.[93] Others had reacted angrily to the imposition of a cattle cordon along the border, designed to control the movement of cattle and therefore of disease.[94] Those difficulties, and the presence of Zambian armed forces in the province, could not fail to create local hostility towards the centre, and reinforce perceptions of neglect.[95] A similar situation prevailed in Sesheke and Senangan in the southern part of the province.

The 1978 elections

The introduction of the one-party state did not, therefore, persuade the Lozi in 1973 to restore to the centre or to the party the support they had so clearly withdrawn in 1968. Moreover, the further decline in the poll in three by-elections in 1974 showed the electorate still apathetic, even in Kalabo where Mundia, released from detention, now successfully contested a seat.[96] The failure of political confidence that had led the Lozi to reject U.N.I.P. in 1968 remained. None of the new Western Province M.P.s, moreover, with the exception of Mundia, had the national stature or experience to build effective links between the province and the centre. While they sought to articulate their constituents' needs at the centre, their capacity to do so was limited.

Two important changes in relations between the province and the centre occurred in the following five years. On the one hand, Lozi influence at the centre declined further, notwithstanding the appointment of a Lozi member of the Central Committee, Daniel Lisulo, as Prime Minister in 1978. The new Cabinet in 1973 included four ministers from Western Province, and that level of representation was maintained through successive Cabinet reshuffles and ministerial changes. In 1977, Mundia returned to government when Kaunda appointed him Minister for North-Western Province. Nevertheless, with the exception of Lisulo, none of the Lozi held a key ministerial office, and the concept of provincial balance that kept them in the Cabinet did not necessarily give them real power. Moreover, Sikota Wina's dismissal from the Central Committee in 1976, whatever the reason, symbolised a final and fundamental loss of Lozi position at the centre. Only Mundia and Arthur Wina, now representing Livingstone, remained of that group of powerful Lozi nationalists who had taken office in 1964.

On the other hand, the government presence increased in Western Province, and there was a more visible demonstration of the powers of the State. This was in part the result of the continued military presence in the province. It was epitomised by the successive detentions and trials of Western Province villagers charged with treason for alleged assistance to the South Africans. What was now clear, however, was the dominance of central government.[97]

It is difficult to identify any clear-cut response among the Lozi to these changes, or how far they affected either popular perceptions of economic deprivation or the position and influence of tradition. Hitherto in the one-party state, attachment to *sizo* had remained strong; but as we have seen, there had been signs that the incumbent traditional office-holders no longer provided the leadership required. In 1973, the U.N.I.P. leadership was to some extent faced with the consequences of its own deliberate policy of dismantling traditional institutions. The policy of abolition, rather than adaptation, had perhaps been more successful than expected in weakening the traditional leaders' influence. It had been less successful in restoring or creating loyalty to the party at a time when the Lozi continued to suffer a further loss of power and status at the centre, and economic stagnation at home. Mundia's victory in 1974 in Kalabo, given the ethnic composition of the constituency, suggested that economic deprivation and geographical isolation were now the major determinants of rural apathy.[98]

If we look briefly at the outcome of the second general election in 1978, we may come closer, however, to identifying the basis of alienation over these years. The election results in 1978 suggested that U.N.I.P. had to some extent retrieved its position since 1973. First, there was a significant increase in the number of candidates standing to seventy-nine. Only one candidate was elected unopposed. Primaries were required in all save two constituencies. Although the average Electoral College vote was only 370, in most cases this represented an increase over 1973, suggesting some increase at least in party activity at the local level. Second, the poll increased in all constituencies, in some instances dramatically, as in Kalabo where it rose from 16–53.2 per cent; the average poll was 44.1 per cent. The 'No' vote in the presidential election declined from 22.6–19.9 per cent. A substantial proportion of the electorate appeared, therefore, to have given greater support to the party in the one-party state, at a time when the national economic crises had meant, for Western Province as for other rural areas, a further decline into economic stagnation.[99]

The evidence does not allow us to draw any firm conclusions or to offer a full explanation. A number of points may, however, be made. First, the increased voter participation in the general elections was undoubtedly related to the increase in polling stations, from 190 to 298.[100] Local party officials had insisted in 1973 that the low poll was largely a consequence of the lack of transport and the long walk that people faced to polling stations, in which they had been correct. Second, notwithstanding the apathetic response to the Kalabo by-election of 1974, Mundia's return to Parliament, and in 1977 to Cabinet office, must have persuaded some Lozi at least to look with more confidence towards the centre.[101]

Such confidence, however, was by no means evident in all parts of the province. The change in rural response was perhaps less significant than it seemed. Just over 50 per cent of the electorate remained aloof, either unable or unwilling to vote. The 19.9 per cent 'No' vote was the third largest vote against Kaunda, and in seven of the fifteen constituencies, just under half the 'No' vote in fact increased. The background of the M.P.s elected must also be borne in mind. Seven of the ten M.P.s who stood for re-election were successful, suggesting a degree of public satisfaction with their performance or their own firm grasp of the local party machine.[102] In four of the fifteen constituencies, however, the voters in the general election overturned the Electoral College choice, voting into office the candidates who had come only second or third in the primary poll.[103] Of the three incumbent M.P.s who were defeated, one was a minister who had been returned unopposed in 1973. Finally, at least four of the successful candidates were men with strong past associations with the U.P./A.N.C. opposition, three of them having been formerly A.N.C. M.P.s. Two others, perhaps three, might have been considered to have tradition on their side, although traditionalist links obviously did not benefit the minister who lost his seat. Support for the successful candidates thus derived from different loyalties, but it did not necessarily mean support for U.N.I.P.

While it is difficult to identify any clear pattern of voting, the distribution of the poll, and especially of the increased 'No' **vote** suggested, however, the continued importance of isolation and rural deprivation as an influence upon local response. This was not universally the case. Kalabo, for example, had the second highest poll in the province, and its 'No' vote declined significantly. Nevertheless, the constituencies with polls well below the provincial average, and an increased 'No' vote coincided to a significant extent with the rural periphery which had suffered most from the economic stagnation of these years.[104]

In the five years between the two elections, Western Province had suffered the same economic stagnation that had hit all rural areas as Zambia's economic crisis grew. Not all parts of the province, however, had been affected in the same way. Central-government spending on a number of highly visible, predominantly infrastructural projects, benefited mainly the provincial centre and to some extent the other townships. Mongu, the provincial headquarters, gained a new Indeco mill, a tall National Insurance Company building and television. It now had electricity linked up to Livingstone, and the abattoir came into operation. The cattle industry, however, continued to suffer from inadequate marketing and the crippling shortage of transport that affected the whole province. A new, tarred highway was constructed from Mongu to Senanga, but the great majority of the population still lived very distant from an all-weather road. The road construction undoubtedly brought more employment into the province, if only temporarily, but the opportunities were geographically restricted, and in 1974 total provincial employment had been only 11,360, 3.0 per cent of the national total.[105] Western Province appeared also to be falling behind in educational facilities, and the great majority of people were far from any health centre.[106] The province became more rather than less dependent, especially in food, this dependence symbolised most clearly by the great pyramid of bags of maize stored at Mongu. Border areas were subject not only to insecurity and attack but also to famine.[107]

Underlying these changes could be discerned the further impoverishment of the rural periphery, reflected in the movement of people not only to the line of rail but to the urban areas within the province itself. Between 1969 and 1980, Western Province had the lowest provincial population increase in Zambia, a 1.6 per cent rate of growth against the national average of 3.1 per cent. Its urban population, however, grew at a rate of 18 per cent, reflecting a significant shift towards urbanization at the expense of rural development.[108] The resulting increased gap between rural periphery and rural centre within the province must be borne in mind, therefore, as a continued source of rural alienation in these years. Other changes were important, not least the further decline of Lozi influence at the centre, the death of the Litunga in 1977 and the accession of his successor, and the increased military and government presence. At the end of the 'seventies, however, political alienation seemed more closely linked with the failure of rural development.

Notes

1 Laurel van Horn, 'The Agricultural History of Barotseland, 1840–1964' in Robin Palmer and Neil Parsons (eds.), *The Roots of Rural Poverty in Central and Southern Africa* (London, Heinemann, 1977).

2 This essay is based on a much longer paper of the same title written in 1974 for which research was carried out in Western Province in the course of 1972 and 1973, including the period of the elections from October to December 1973.

3 The 1969 Census gave the population as 410,000 (Government of Zambia Report of the 1969 Census) and the Preliminary Report of the 1980 Census as 487,988. Central Statistical Office (Lusaka, January 1981).

4 Mulford (1967), *op.cit.*, Chapter VI.

5 Great Britain, *Report of the Commission to Enquire into the Financial and Economic Position of Northern Rhodesia*, Col. No. 145, 1938 (Pym Report).

6 Republic of Zambia, H.A.M. Maclean, *An Agricultural Stocktaking of Barotseland* (Lusaka, Government Printer, 1965).

7 M. Gluckman, 'The Lozi of Barotseland in Northwestern Rhodesia', E. Colson and M. Gluckman (eds.), *Seven Tribes of Central Africa* (Manchester, Manchester University Press, 1951). For a major reappraisal of the early Lozi colonial experience, see Gwyn Prins, *The Hidden Hippopotamus*, (Cambridge, Cambridge University Press, 1980).

8 Gluckman.

9 See, for example, LAB/C40, Zambian Archives, for a *Report* on his visit to the Copperbelt by the Barotseland Labour Induna, 1943, decrying the bad influence upon Lozi of the town, and the dangers of urban life to the maintenance of Lozi custom.

10 Mulford (1967), *op.cit.*; Gerald M. Caplan, *The Elites of Barotseland 1878–1969 Political History of Zambia's Western Province* (London, C. Hurst and Co., 1971).

11 Caplan, *op.cit.*, from whom I borrow the term 'ruling class'. See also Mulford (1967), *op.cit.*

12 Arthur and Sikota Wina, Nalumino Mundia and Munu Sipalo.

13 For full details see Director of Elections, *Election Results, 1962–64*, 1968 and by-elections. Also *Results* of Referendum, 1969. All mimeo.

14 Director of Elections, *Election Results*, 1973 and 1978, *op.cit.*

15 Tordoff (ed.) (1974), *op.cit., passim.*

16 Act No. 69 of 1965, The Local Government Act 1965, which, *inter alia*, repealed the Barotse Native Authority Ordinance; Act No. 67 of 1965, The Chiefs Act; Act No. 20 of 1966, Local Courts Act.

17   The Constitution (Amendment) (No. 5) Act, 1969. See also, K.D. Kaunda, *I Wish to Inform The Nation, op.cit.*

18   Act No. 65 of 1969. The phrase 'Just Another Chief' was used in 1965 after the Local Government Act was passed and is quoted in Caplan, *op.cit.*, p. 212.

19   Personal communication. The actual conduct of the 1966 local government elections meant that such details as turn-out were not centrally registered.

20   In 1965 Sikota Wina was Minister for Local Government and Arthur Wina the Minister of Finance. The Minister of Justice responsible for the changes in the court system was Dr. Kabaleke Konoso. Konoso, like the Wina brothers was a member of the Lozi traditional ruling class, who had been prominent in the nationalist struggle, and had been elected unopposed on a U.N.I.P. ticket for Sesheke Main Roll constituency in 1964. Arthur Wina was M.P. for Mongu Lealui. Sikota Wina was, however, M.P. for the Copperbelt constituency of Luanshya/Kalalushu. In 1969 Sikota Wina, now Minister of Information, Broadcasting and Tourism, had the responsibility for explaining the referendum which led in due course to the changes in land title.

21   Of whom 77 (out of 110) were elected unopposed in 1966.

22   See, for example, *Daily Parliamentary Debates*, 7 Sept. 1965, for Sikota Wina, as Minister of Local Government and his defence of the Barotseland changes:

It is only in this manner that the population of our people in Barotse Province shall move into fresher waters. I hold the belief that whether a man be Lozi, Tonga, Bemba or Ngoni, his primary concern is for food to fill his stomach; clinics to heal his wounds; schools to educate his children; and development to generate employment so that his wife can dress as well as the wives of Honourable Members of this House . . . [It is] only a small and dying section of the traditional element in Lealui alone who still look through the blurred spectacles of the nineteenth century. The Barotses, Mr. Speaker, are no longer interested in being regarded as museum specimens, or to be regarded as a pure preservation of old happy Africa as seen through the eyes of Stanley . . .

23   Republic of Zambia, *An Outline of the Transitional Development Plan, 1964–66* (Lusaka, Government Printer, 1965).

24   *Republic of Zambia, First National Development Plan 1966–1970* (Lusaka, Government Printer, 1967), p. 81.

25   *S.N.D.P.*, pp. 181–7.

26   *Progress Evaluation Report* on the First Four Year Development Plan, Western Province, Agricultural Sector, December 1969 (mimeo).

27   *S.N.D.P.*, p.169.

28   *Ibid.*, p. 167. See also above, Chapter 6, and Bates (1976), *op.cit.*

29   Caplan, *op.cit.*, p. 214.

30   *Times of Zambia,* 29 Mar. 1966. See G.N. Sumbwa, *The Impact of Wenela Closure on the Makoma People of Western Province,* University of Zambia History Research Paper, 1974, p. 3.

31 F.N. Heath (Acting Resident Commissioner), *Memorandum on Economic Development for Barotseland*, Mongu, 10 October 1960 (mimeo). Also Maclean, *Stocktaking, op.cit.* J.A. Hellen, *Rural Economic Development in Zambia, 1890–1964* (Munich, Weltforum-Verlag, 1968), p. 249 estimated 44 per cent of taxable males absent through labour migration in 1961, 22 per cent in South Africa.

32 Maclean, *Stocktaking, op.cit.*, p. 12.

33 *Annual Reports*, Labour Department, Western Province 1965–8. On employment generally see M.D. Veich, *Employment and the Labour Force: Regional Analysis* (Lusaka, 1970)(mimeo).

34 *Tour Report*, 1967, Mongu Provincial Headquarters (mimeo).

35 On the question of ownership of cattle, their distribution and attitudes towards sale, see Maclean, *Stocktaking, op.cit.*

36 See, for example, *S.N.D.P.*, p. 11.

37 Maclean, *Stocktaking, op.cit.* 1969 Population Census, *op.cit;* cf. Bates (1976), *op.cit.* for movement out of Luapula after 1964.

38 See above, Chapter 5.

39 Caplan, *op.cit.*, p. 214.

40 Based on personal interviews, but see also his parliamentary speeches, e.g. *Daily Parliamentary Debates*, 7 Dec. 1965. On the United Party, I am grateful to Mr. Kasolo, University of Zambia politics student, for use of his paper, *'The Rise and Demise of the United Party'* (mimeo), the findings of which accord substantially with my own. See also Caplan, *op.cit.*, p. 216–17; and Tordoff and Scott, *op.cit., passim.*

41 Kasolo, *op.cit.* A good many people in Western Province, and especially Kalabo, still remembered Mundia's speeches in 1973. See also *Daily Parliamentary Debates*, 10 Aug. 1965.

42 Although Mundia, while he was himself Minister of Labour in 1965, had held discussions with the traditional chiefs and the Litunga, on the implications of government's desire to abolish W.E.N.E.L.A.

43 For 1968, see Molteno and Scott, *op.cit.*; for 1971, see Gertzel *et al* (1972), *op.cit.*

44 Director of Elections, Referendum, Tuesday 17 June 1969. *Summary of Results*, Lusaka, Office of Director of Elections, (mimeo)

45 Former A.N.C. leaders were all agreed that their opposition to the land changes won them significant support in the 1970 local government elections. Although they won a majority in several councils, all council chairmen, appointed by the Minister for Local Government, remained U.N.I.P.

47 Caplan, *op.cit.*, p. 216; Mulford, *op.cit.*, Ch. VI.

48 For example, in September 1972, when the then Ngambela (Chief Minister) resigned after reportedly advising the Litunga not to meet the President at the airport when the latter visited the Province.

49 See Cherry Gertzel, 'Two Case Studies in Rural Development', W. Tordoff (ed.), *Administration in Zambia* (Manchester University Press, 1980). The Task Force did not in fact produce any new initiatives.

50 Siyomunji had formerly been a civil servant and dipolomat before his appointment to Parliament in 1968. Since he had never contested office

on a U.N.I.P. ticket, it was unlikely he had incurred the same kind of approbrium that the Lozi U.N.I.P. ministers had earlier aroused. No Lozi had previously been Provincial Cabinet Minister or (before 1969) Resident Minister, so that the appointment was an important departure from previous practice.

51 For example, Chief Lukama, appointed with three others to Mongu Rural Council in November 1973. Also Nalisa and Sibolika, appointed to Sesheke, 1972, were both traditional Indunas.

52 One previous minister, for example, had been reported in the press in 1970 as threatening to suspend all developments in the province to show that it was not the opposition that brought progress. *Times of Zambia*, 22 Sept. 1970.

53 Western Province PDC Meeting, 14–15 June 1973.

54 *Times of Zambia*, Aug. 1973.

55 Director of Elections, Results of Primary and General Elections, 1973 (mimeo). Senanga District as a result had no parliamentary election at all, except in that northern part of the district included in Nalikwanda Constituency, which it shared with Mongu.

56 In Senanga; the other two constituencies were Sikongo and Mulobezi.

57 The Lozi Central Committee members also attended the Provincial Political Committee at which nominations were discussed.

58 Not least due to the fact that the Wina brothers remained the dominant U.N.I.P. influence over the provincial party organisation.

59 *Zambia Daily Mail*, 1 June 1974.

60 Director of Elections, *Parliamentary By-elections*, 24 October, 1974.

61 One candidate had told the writer he intended to stress his support for tradition, as well as to emphasise that a vote for a former A.N.C. member would not lead to imprisonment.

62 The writer was present at this meeting, which was reported *Times of Zambia*, 16 Nov. 1973. The Litunga and Indunas were accorded a very cursory recognition.

63 It is possible, of course, that the traditionalists, while publicly supporting the new one-party regime, had secretly campaigned against it, in which case the low poll would be evidence of their continued political influence. But there was nothing to suggest this strategy, certainly during the campaign. Circumstantial evidence suggests indeed that the traditionalists were themselves now counting on U.N.I.P. support.

64 Both disputes concerned frictions within the local traditional leadership group.

65 Summarised in *Times of Zambia*, 21, 22 and 27 Apr. 1972.

66 At each meeting the writer attended, such complaints were made. Reports of similar complaints were received from observers at other meetings.

67 Ministry of Planning and Finance, *Economic Report, 1973*, pp. 171–2.

68 Ministry of Education, Western Province. Lukulu had been created as an administrative district only in 1970.

69 *Times of Zambia*, 8 Oct. 1973. For the development position generally in this period, see *Minutes* of Provincial and District Development Committees.

70   See above, page 224.
71   K.D. Kaunda, *I Wish to Inform the Nation, op.cit.*
72   Heath, *op.cit.*
73   This summary on the land position is based on M. Gluckman, *Economy of the Central African Plain* (Manchester University Press for Rhodes-Livingstone Institute, 1941); D.U. Peters, *Land Usage in Barotseland* (Lusaka, 1960) (1956) and Maclean (1965), *op.cit.* Also, on discussions with a number of traditional leaders.
74   *Daily Parliamentary Debates,* 29 Sept. 1970, col. 280. Up to 1973, there had been no change in the procedure for settlement of land matters, which still went to the traditional chiefs, Indunas, headman or to the Litunga. However, steps had been taken to set land aside for the townships throughout the province, and to make them state land areas.
75   This conclusion is based on observations over five weeks during the election campaign, as well as during earlier visits to the province, and on discussions with officials.
76   F. Aaongola, *Elections in Mongu Constituency,* University of Zambia (mimeo).
77   In Sefula, for example, where villagers complained loudly about the behaviour of party officials.
78   See *Government Gazette,* 2 Nov. 1965, for full lists. Report to the National Council, 1964.
79   Ministers F. Mulikita, J. Mutti and J. Siyomunji, and ministers of state, Misheck Banda and F. Liboma, toured the province. See Gertzel *et al* (1971), *op.cit.*
80   Registrar of Societies, 1972. Branch figures were given by the minister at the meeting of 19 August.
81   Primary Roll Register, Senanga District, November 1973.
82   Under the Societies Act, a society required ten members for registration.
83   A comparison of the Primary Roll Register and the 1973 Reports indicated the following position and change from 1972–73. Kaoma, 65 (55 with 3 wings) branches, May 1973; 339 in September 1973 (including all three wings); Mongu, 96 (32 with 3 wings) in May 1973, 7, at least 234 in September 1973; Lukulu, 13, 74. Sesheke, 0, 65; Kalabo 104, 311.
84   It is not irrelevant, for example, that Chief Lukama, one of the traditional chiefs nominated as a Rural Councillor in 1973 (see fn. 51 above) was also a businessman and had stood (unsuccessfully) as a U.N.I.P. candidate in the 1971 by-elections.
85   In the past, of course, the Central Committee had made the final selection of candidates from loyal party members, but especially for local government elections, the District Political Committee had exercised considerable control over selection.
86   Meeting at Kalabo, 19 November 1973.
87   The results in Kaoma Constituency were J.K.M. Kalaluka, 1,444; K.M Kalyangu, 1,169; B.C. Liwoyo, 826. Liwoyo was a small businessman, local councillor, a constituency party official, a longstanding U.N.I.P. member who had lived in the district for the greater part of his life, and was resident at the time of elections. Kalyangu had been a founder

member of U.N.I.P. in the district and a political activist against the traditionalists in the early 'sixties, after which he moved into a succession of political appointments outside the district. Both were Mbunda-speaking. Mr Kalaluka, at the time a Shell representative in Chipata, had unsuccessfully contested the seat in 1968 for A.N.C. He was Nkoya-speaking.

88 Sumbwa, *op.cit.* The minority groups were in fact the majority of the population of Kalabo District. See *Census of Population and Housing 1969* Final Report, Vol.II(h), Table 41.

89 Liuwa constituency, which replaced the former Libonda, and included part of Lukulu district, was now divided almost equally between Lozi and Luvale. Sikongo, the new constituency, had a mixed population of Makoma, Nyenga, Mwenyi and Mbunda.

90 See 1968 election results. The three A.N.C. M.P.s were Mundia, Silumesi and Sianga.

91 Meeting of 19 November 1973, at which the author was present. There was a small 'demonstration' outside the District Governor's office after the announcement of the Central Committee's disqualification of the third candidate, which resulted in a charge against one of the Koma traders for allegedly insulting the District Governor and Regional Secretary, both Mbunda.

92 In the case of Kalabo, the paucity of polling stations, the distances involved and the lack of transport, undoubtedly contributed to the size of the poll.

93 *Times of Zambia*, 2 Feb. 1972.

94 *Ibid*, 2 May 1972.

95 Between 1970 and 1973, a number of Sesheke villagers were found guilty of assisting South African forces. See especially the evidence given in the treason trial against the former Mayor of Livingstone, the former Sesheke M.P., and others, in 1975. For example, in *Zambia Daily Mail*, 23 Apr. 1975.

96 The Senanga and Sinjembela by-elections were made necessary by a retirement and a successful election petition, that in Kalabo by the death in an accident of the sitting M.P.

97 *Africa Research Bulletin*, Political, Social and Cultural Series October 1–31, 1978.

98 This is difficult to prove conclusively, given that it is impossible to identify the actual ethnic composition of the voting. However, the disposition of the constituency, the activity during the campaign, and impressionistic evidence suggests this was so. Mundia's reputation as a long-standing opponent of central government was his most important asset on that occasion.

99 Director of Elections, *Election Results*, 1978, *op.cit.*

100 Compare the Register of Voters 1972 and 1978.

101 Mundia was appointed Cabinet Minister for North-Western Province in February 1976. See *Zambia Daily Mail*, 21 Feb. 1976.

102 They were Nakonde (Sihole), Kalaluka (Kaoma), Mumbuna (Luena), Ikacana (Nalikwanda), Bull (Nalolo), Mukwe (Senanga), and Limbo (Sinjembela).

103   In Kalabo, Liuwa, Luampa and Sesheke.
104   The seven constituencies in which the 'No' vote increased were Kaoma,
      Luampa, Lukulu, Nalolo, Sinjembela, Mulobezi and Sesheke.
105   *Third National Development Plan, 1979–1983*, p. 79.
106   *Ibid.*, p. 73, p. 80.
107   See, for example, *Daily Parliamentary Debates*, 4 Feb. 1975, Col. 704,
      and 5 Feb. 1975, Col. 806.
108   1980 Census of Population and Housing, *Preliminary Report*, January
      1981, Table 1, Table 2 and Table 4. Also p. 15, A–3. Population of Small
      Urban Townships.

Conclusion
Conflict in the one-party state

The introduction of the one-party state removed the danger of fragmentation that had threatened U.N.I.P. in 1971, but it did not eliminate political opposition, as the rise of dissent through the 'seventies showed. Hence the management of conflict remained the primary task of the one-party state, leading to the further extension of control, and a further concentration of power at the centre. Zambia thus appeared to repeat the trend towards the more authoritarian state that had been the wider African experience, suggesting the difficulty of absorbing the different elements of Zambian society into the single party structure without a severe constraint upon participation. Since the capacity to absorb and accommodate opposition was the most severe test presented to the one-party state, we look finally therefore at the underlying conflict, as it had emerged by 1981, eight years after the Second Republic had come into being.

The lines of political debate throughout the 'seventies revealed the continued importance of local-central relations in Zambian politics. The political weight of provincial groups was to some extent reduced by the new electoral system, which increased the emphasis upon more parochial loyalties and cleavages at the constituency level thus reducing the capacity of M.P.s to act as a provincial block. Nevertheless, the political and administrative organisation of the one-party state still encouraged parliamentary leaders to mobilise support on the basis of provincial identity and parochialism reinforced perceptions of regional deprivation. The decline of the party emphasised the role of M.P. as the link between locality and centre. This contributed to an increased emphasis upon local needs in the parliamentary debate, and a willingness on the part of M.P.s to challenge national programmes on the basis of provincial and local needs. Early in the first parliament for example, M.P.s opposed with some success the government's Intensive Development Zone programme because they wanted 'a more equal distribution of development resources over the country as a whole'.[1] The debate about 'provincial balancing' within the party and the Cabinet reflected a similar concern to ensure recognition of local interests. It was also frequently articulated in the language of 'tribalism'. A Western Province M.P. for example attributed the economic underdevelopment of his province to 'this cancer we call tribalism'.[2] The critics of 'provincial balancing' rejected it on the grounds that it meant appointment to political office on the grounds of 'tribe not merit'.[3] Provincial cleavages thus remained a source of political competition and groupings within the party continued to be identified in provincial terms. The careful balance of provincial representation that Kaunda maintained at the centre reflected his response to the resulting pressures.[4]

Underlying the focus upon district and province was the more fundamental issue of relations between urban and rural regions. While it was true that a majority of M.P.s in both 1973 and 1978 were urban residents, so far as parliamentary representation was concerned the rural provinces had won some important advantages out of the one-party state, since the changes in electoral boundaries in 1973 had been in their favour.[5] Equal provincial representation within the party had also been to their advantage, and their influence was explicit in the decision in 1978 to amend the method of presidential election to require equal provincial support for any presidential candidate. In contrast, the urban electorate had lost position at the centre. This was true in particular of the Copperbelt, for which two general elections in the 'seventies, following the U.P.P. crisis of 1971–72, produced major changes in political representation at the centre, both in legislature and executive. By 1979 the Copperbelt nationalist generation had been removed from both Central Committee and Cabinet.[6] Copperbelt M.P.s were as vigorous in defence of their urban constituents' interests as were those from the rural provinces but their numbers were small.[7] Moreover in terms of population it could be argued that the Copperbelt was under-represented at the centre. The actual rate of urban migration which had swelled the cities and towns along the line of rail in the 'sixties and the 'seventies slowed down. Nevertheless the proportion of the urban to the total population had increased continuously since independence: 20.5 per cent in 1963, 29.4 per cent in 1969, and 43.0 per cent in 1980.[8] By 1980 the Copperbelt and Lusaka provinces together accounted for more than a third of the country's population. The Copperbelt province alone had a population of 1,248,888, 22 per cent of Zambian society.[9] It remained moreover central to the economy and thus to economic recovery. There was therefore a serious imbalance between the region's economic importance and its political power at a time when its urban population had suffered a real decline in living standards as a result of the economic crisis. It was not surprising therefore that the strongest opposition to equal provincial representation was expressed by Copperbelt M.P.s.[10]

The Copperbelt therefore in many respects presented the most serious problems of incorporation into the one-party state. This was reflected in the continuing difficulties that U.N.I.P. encountered after 1973 as the party attempted to restore its provincial organisation and membership.[11] The limitations of Central Committee control were evident when local party officials led the opposition to government's price increases in 1974.[12] U.N.I.P.'s sense of insecurity was implicit in party leaders' allegations of continued U.P.P. activity as the source of opposition, which in turn sustained attention upon the lines of cleavage that had weakened and divided the party in the past. The fear that the Copperbelt would emerge as a base for renewed factional conflict at the centre was indeed explicit in backbench allegations in 1975 of 'private meetings' held there by 'top leaders'.[14] Lastly the old rivalries between the party and the unions remained a source of tension. Industrial unrest in the face of continuing economic crisis presented government with the most serious challenge to its control. In 1975 the M.P. for Wusakile warned both party and government of growing disillusionment among miners at the failure of the formal machinery of industrial relations to ensure their economic well-being and the consequent potential for strike action:

Sir, the miner today is slowly getting back to the days of Katilungu unionism . . . during the good old days of the leadership of Mr. Katilungu they had recourse to strike action when they wanted an increase . . .[15]

As we have seen the confrontation between labour and the party in 1981 demonstrated the continued power of the miners in the one-party state and the potential of urban labour as a source of opposition.

The Copperbelt was not only however a working class constituency. It was also the location of much of the increased Zambian enterprise that followed the economic reforms of 1969–1972.[16] Copperbelt businessmen were prominent in that 'politically conscious and active indigenous owning class' that had emerged by the mid-'seventies. Their potential for political opposition had been demonstrated in 1971 when some had joined the U.P.P. The Copperbelt party had, as we have seen, been largely transformed as businessmen, assumed a more prominent role in the provincial political leadership.[17] Copperbelt M.P.s in both parliaments included a small but significant number of businessmen with local party connections. They articulated the needs not only of their working class constituents but also of the business class and were prominent among backbench critics of economic policy.[18] They shared many of the ideas and policy preferences of the professional and managerial elements of the Copperbelt's expanding middle class. The Copperbelt was thus also a potential arena for the articulation of bourgeois dissent.[19]

Urban dissatisfaction with government and party policy at a time of continued economic crisis was demonstrated by the outcome of the second general election in 1978. In spite of party apprehension that it would be otherwise the Copperbelt vote increased from 40 per cent to 72.9 per cent suggesting that U.N.I.P. had regained some of its former capacity to mobilise the urban electorate. The increased electoral participation suggested also that the one-party system itself had now been accorded a greater legitimacy than in 1973. The 'Yes' vote in the presidential election of 80.3 per cent could also be fairly interpreted as widespread support for Kaunda at a time of acute national crisis. However, there was also a significant increase in the opposition vote. The 'No' vote increased, in the higher poll, from 11.4 per cent to 19.7 per cent. There was also a distinct coincidence between a high poll and a high 'No' vote, suggesting that increased electoral participation reflected increased opposition to the centre. A substantial minority thus sought to use the electoral system to express their desire for change. Fourteen of the nineteen constituencies registered an increased 'No' vote, distributed widely across mining, non-mining and rural constituencies alike. The seven highest 'No' polls were, however, in mining constituencies, ranging from 22.9 per cent to 43.7 per cent. Finally, electorate choice diverged from party preference more than had been the case in 1973, with eight of those candidates who had won their primaries being defeated in the general election. Party control over the electorate was therefore to that extent reduced.

The first five years of the one-party state thus saw an increase in urban electoral opposition. Against the background of economic decline it is not unreasonable to relate such opposition to a widespread urban frustration at economic hardship, held in check by a sense of loyalty to the national interest at a time when Zambia faced an acute external threat. What is more difficult to determine is the extent to which this also related to increased perceptions of class interests as opposed to a general economic discontent. The structure of the one-party state was a constraint, as we have seen, upon class associations in the rural area, and inhibited specific interests or class groups from seeking power through the electoral process.[21] It also inhibited the participation of working class candidates in the parliamentary elections so that it is difficult to identify a working class vote. Nevertheless, the expansion of trade union membership over these years suggested a greater willingness among urban workers to organise on the basis of a class interest and it is not difficult to understand why this might be so. The dominant characteristic of Copperbelt society remained the social inequality, not only between African and expatriate but within African society itself. U.N.I.P.'s increased petty bourgeois and bourgeois image widened the gap between the leadership and the mass of urban society and challenged Kaunda's emphasis upon the party as one of 'workers and peasants'. It was the labour movement that concentrated attention on the 'bread and butter issues of food, shelter and clothing' which could not fail to increase perceptions of social and economic inequality.[22] The united front presented by the Z.C.T.U. and M.U.Z. in the crisis of 1980–81 further emphasised a greater sense of working class solidarity along the line of rail as the underlying basis for industrial action. Against the increased 'No' vote on the Copperbelt in 1978 the strike in January 1981 moreover takes on a further significance. It demonstrated not only the miners unwillingness to accept party control but their willingness to use direct industrial action when political action had failed.

The changes on the Copperbelt in 1978 thus suggested that the one-party state had produced a potential for more specifically class-based action on the part of urban labour.[23] At the same time the preponderance of Bemba speaking people at all levels of Copperbelt society meant the continued overlap of ethnic and economic interests. This sustained the same factional interests that had dominated the intra-party debate in the earlier years, and which the one-party state had reduced but could not eliminate. Hence Copperbelt politics ultimately focused on the role of the Bemba in national politics, and the charge of a Bemba opposition.[24]

The predominance of Bemba speakers in the Copperbelt work force, among the growing Zambian entrepreneurial class, encouraged the interpretation of both labour and bourgeois dissent in ethnic terms. The focus on the Bemba was however ensured by the conflict that surrounded Kapwepwe's return to U.N.I.P. which also drew attention to provincial and therefore ethnic competition. Although Kapwepwe made no public appeal for ethnic support his stature as Bemba as well as national leader ensured that his attempt to challenge Kaunda's leadership should have an ethnic dimension. Thus one Copperbelt D.G., immediately after Kapwepwe's decision to contest the presidency had been announced, described it as a tragedy for the Bemba because 'Kapwepwe is a tribal leader and other tribes will think he is trying to form a tribal government'.[25] The treatment meted out to him in 1979, when he was charged with managing a banned party, heightened the sense of discrimination among Bemba-speakers and his death in 1980 produced a powerful demonstration of Bemba identity which focused attention on the potential for Bemba political action.[26]

Charges of a Bemba opposition were encouraged in a number of different ways between 1973 and 1980, and not least by the concentration of disqualifications in the 1978 elections in the Bemba-speaking provinces.[27] Nevertheless there was little evidence of a cohesive Bemba-speaking opposition in either party or Parliament, and no sign of a new accord between the three Bemba-speaking provinces.The use of ethnicity to label opposition as illegitimate also obscured the extent to which ethnic loyalties were interwoven with other interests. In the circumstances of uneven development, where ethnic identity was so interwoven with class and occupation, it was often difficult to know where any of these categories began or ended. The boundaries between class and ethnicity frequently overlapped, so that tribalism was often the form of conflict rather than its essence. Hence it is useful to bear in mind that the U.P.P. in 1971, under Kapwepwe's leadership, had been a protest by some disadvantaged groups, or by those who perceived themselves as disadvantaged.[28] It was in this context that his presidential challenge in 1978 was now of fundamental significance in the continuing party conflict. His platform in 1978 which emphasised the demands of the private sector suggested that his appeal was to the emergent business class.[29] However his standing as a Bemba leader ensured him support from far more diverse interests that shared a common dissatisfaction with party policy. He offered an alternative leadership to such dissatisfied groups.

The lines of political conflict therefore focused on the presidency itself. The structure of the one-party state ensured that this should be so. Moreover the dominant position of the president in both party and government ensured that the loss of governmental credibility in the face of the continuing economic decline must ultimately focus upon Kaunda himself. The problem that faced Zambia at the beginning of the 'eighties therefore was ultimately that of presidential power. The one-party state while it provided for electoral participation and for the expression of protest, had further increased the power and autonomy of the executive. It was executive power therefore that remained the central issue in 1981. The executive, as the locus of power, thus became the focus of dissent as well as the symbol of national unity.

As Zambia moved into the 1980s she therefore faced the possibility of continuing political conflict. The environment within which the one-party state had to operate had deteriorated since the inauguration of the Second Republic and the country faced its worst economic crisis since independence. On the one hand, the continuing crisis in the copper mining industry combined with the aftermath of the drought, as well as internal inefficiences, meant an increased scarcity of resources and limited room for manœuvre. On the other hand, the increased social and economic inequalities had called into doubt the capacity of the state to introduce the major changes of economic policy required. At the same time Zambia remained subject to severe external pressures. The end of the Zimbabwe war had reduced but had not eliminated the external threat at a time when Zambia's economic dependence upon the South had increased. In the face of both external and internal crisis the policy debate was bound to continue.

In the face of these pressures it was difficult to anticipate how Kaunda would react to a further challenge to the executive. While the second presidential election had demonstrated his own continued popular support, the weakness of his position reflected his relationship to the party. Throughout the 'seventies he had insisted on the centrality of the party in the one-party system, and linked it persistently with the presidency. The party, however, was in conflict with Parliament and trade unions and with significant elements of society as a whole. Control over recruitment to office had enabled him to reduce intra-party conflict but it had pushed opposition out of the party and largely destroyed the credibility of the Central Committee, which he insisted must remain supreme. To open up the party to change was, however, to acknowledge the legitimacy of the policy debate that had emerged in the 1970s, and therefore of the opposition. This Kaunda had shown himself unwilling to do. While some of the policy changes instituted in the 1970s suggested concessions to emerging class interest, he had refused to capitulate on the central 'socialist' objectives to which the party still adhered. What seemed more likely therefore was that he would continue to use the power of the state to maintain control and so move further again along the path to greater concentration of power.

Notes

1   Cherry Gertzel, 'Two Case Studies in Rural Development' in W. Tordoff (ed.), *Administration in Zambia* (Manchester, Manchester University Press, 1980).
2   *Daily Parliamentary Debates*, 5 Feb. 1975, col. 813.
3   *Ibid.*, 7 Feb. 1980, cols. 1292–1294.
4   *Ibid.*
5   *Chona Report* paras. 80–81. Maipose, *op.cit.*, p. 58.
6   See Tordoff (ed.), 1980, *op.cit.* p. 14 for the regional balance in the Cabinet 1973–77.
7   See for example *Daily Parliamentary Debates*, 5 Feb. 1975.
8   1980 Census of Population and Housing, *Preliminary Report*, p. 3.
9   *Ibid.*
10   *Daily Parliamentary Debates*, 6 February 1980, cols. 1264–1270.
11   See above chapter 5. *Daily Parliamentary Debates* 20 Aug. 1980, col. 1025.
12   *Ibid.*, 6 Dec. 1974; *Times of Zambia* 2 Dec. 1974.

13 *Times of Zambia* 21 Aug. 1974, 14 Oct. 1974.

14 *Daily Parliamentary Debates* 6 Feb. 1975, col. 895.

15 *Daily Parliamentary Debates* 5 Feb. 1975, col. 801

16 See above Chapter 3. Also Baylies and Szeftel, *op.cit.*

17 See above p. 141.

18 See for example *Daily Parliamentary Debates*, 20 February 1975, cols. 1575–1578.

19 It was significant that Elias Chipimo made his critical speech, which urged a return to the multi-party state, to a Law Society dinner held on the Copperbelt.

20 Director of Elections, *1978 Parliamentary and Presidential Election Results.*

21 See above p. 67.

22 *Sunday Times* 10 May 1981.

23 This does not however mean that the working class was yet strong enough to win.

24 See for example *Observer* 18 Oct. 1981. Also Tordoff 1980, *op.cit.*, quoting Szeftel, 1978, *op.cit.*

25 *Times of Zambia* 4 Aug. 1978.

26 *Observer* 18 Oct. 1981.

27 See above p.38

28 See above p. 51.

29 *The Economist* 14 Aug. 1978.

Appendix I

Occupation/position of candidates and winners
estimated percentages with unknowns removed,[a] 1973

Occupation/ position	All candidates (%)	All losers[b] (%)	Losers primary (%)	Losers general election (%)	Winners (%)
Incumbent M.P.	13.5	7.1	4.4	10.4	34.4
Wage and salaried employee	37.1	37.0	40.5	35.8	35.0
Business only	31.8	34.8	33.6	34.4	22.5
Professional	2.1	1.9	3.4	0.7	2.7
Chief	1.6	1.5	0.9	2.1	1.8
Progressive farmer	3.2	4.4	6.0	3.6	—
Subsistence farmer	1.1	1.5	1.7	0.7	—
Retired or unemployed	4.5	5.9	6.0	4.3	0.9
Unknown, but unpaid local government official	5.1	5.9	3.4	7.9	2.7
Total	100.0	100.0	99.9	99.9	100.0
All non-incumbents with business interests	36.8	38.5	37.9	38.0	30.6
All candidates with business interests	42.1	40.7	39.6	41.0	45.8
Number of unknowns in each category	136	127	61	55	9

Notes:
a. Unknown cases have been distributed among all other categories except incumbent M.P. in proportion to the distribution among known cases.
b. All losers include disqualified candidates.

Appendix II

Further breakdown of wage and salaried employees among candidates and winners, 1973

a. All candidates

Type employment	Number	All employees (%)	All candidates (%)	Number with business interests
Civil servant	59	42.4	11.0	7
Teacher/headmaster	25	18.0	4.7	2
Regional secretary or district governor	9	6.5	1.7	4
Diplomat	2	1.4	0.4	1
National level trade union leader	5	3.6	0.9	—
Executive/managerial	11	7.9	2.1	1
Other	28	20.1	5.3	1
Total	139	99.9	26.1	16

b. All winners

Type employment	Number	All employees (%)	'New' M.P.s (%)	Number with business interests
Civil servant	18	46.2	22.0	5
Teacher/headmaster	9	23.1	11.0	—
Regional secretary or district governor	4	10.3	4.9	2
Diplomat	1	2.5	1.2	1
National level trade union leader	1	2.5	1.2	—
Executive/managerial	3	7.7	3.7	1
Other	3	7.7	3.7	—
Total	39	100.0	47.7	9

BIBLIOGRAPHY
of sources cited in the text

Printed Primary Sources

Northern Rhodesian/Zambian Government (in chronological order)
Government of Northern Rhodesia, Native Affairs, 'Annual Reports', 1931, 1932, 1934 (Livingstone, Government Printer, 1931, 1932, 1934)
Government of Northern Rhodesia, African Affairs. 'Annual Reports', 1948–1964 (Livingstone, Government Printer, 1948–64)
Government of Northern Rhodesia, 'Report on Intensive Rural Development in the Northern and Luapula Provinces of Northern Rhodesia, 1959–1961' (Lusaka, Government Printer, 1961)
Government of Northern Rhodesia, 'Report of the Commission of Inquiry into Unrest on the Copperbelt in the Months of July and August 1963' (Lusaka, Government Printer, 1963)
Government of Northern Rhodesia, 'Report of the Committee of Inquiry into the Stoppage of Work Among Teachers in the Western Province during the Months of July and August 1963' (Lusaka, Government Printer, 1963)
Government of Northern Rhodesia, 'The Luapula Province Agricultural Stock-taking', compiled and produced by Government of Northern Rhodesia Land Use Survey Section, 1959 (Lusaka, 1965)
Republic of Zambia, The Government Gazette (Lusaka, Government Printer, 1964–1975)
Republic of Zambia, Ministry of Labour, 'Annual Report', 1964–75
Republic of Zambia, 'Annual Reports, Labour Department, Western Province, 1964–1968'
Republic of Zambia, Ministry of Rural Development, 'Statistical Bulletins, 1964–1973' (Lusaka, 1964–1973)
Republic of Zambia, 'An Agricultural Stocktaking of Barotseland', compiled by H.A.M. Maclean (Lusaka, Government Printer, 1965)
Republic of Zambia, Office of the President, Central Planning Office, 'An Outline of the Transitional Development Plan' (Lusaka, Government Printer, 1965)
Republic of Zambia, Cabinet Office, 'Manpower Report: A Report and Statistical Handbook on Manpower, Education, Training and Zambianisation, 1965–66' (issued by the Cabinet Office) (Lusaka, Government Printer, 1966)
Republic of Zambia, Ministry of Mines and Co-operatives, Research Unit of Community Development, 'The People of "Zambia City" ', 1966 (mimeo)
Republic of Zambia, 'Agricultural and Pastoral Production, 1967', Vol. I (Lusaka, Government Printer, 1968)

Republic of Zambia, Livingstone Labour Conference: A Survey of Industrial Relations in Zambia (Lusaka, 1967)

Republic of Zambia, Central Statistical Office, Report on Employment and Earnings 1963–1968 (Lusaka, 1969)

Republic of Zambia, Report to the Government of Zambia on Incomes, Wages and Prices in Zambia, Policy and Machinery (Turner Report) (Lusaka, Cabinet Office, 1969 and ILO, Geneva 1969)

Republic of Zambia, Second National Development Plan January 1972 – December 1976 (Lusaka, Ministry of Development Planning and Guidance, December 1971)

Republic of Zambia, Report of the National Commission on the Establishment of a One-Party Participatory Democracy in Zambia (The Chona Report) (Lusaka, Government Printer, 1972)

Republic of Zambia, Government Paper No. 1 of 1972, Report of the National Commission on the Establishment of a One-Party Participatory Democracy in Zambia, Summary of Recommendations accepted by Government (White Paper) (Lusaka, Government Printer, 1972)

Republic of Zambia, Central Statistical Office, Census of Population and Housing 1969. Final Report, Vol. 1, 'Total Zambia', (Lusaka, Central Statistical Office, November 1973)

Republic of Zambia, Director of Elections, Primary Elections 1973, Provisional Results of Nominations and Poll (n.d. 1973)

Republic of Zambia, Director of Elections, General Elections 1973, Results

Republic of Zambia, Central Statistical Office, Report on Employment and Earnings, 1969–1974 (Lusaka, 1974)

Republic of Zambia, Central Statistical Office, Preliminary Report. Sample Census of Population 1974 (Lusaka, 1975)

Republic of Zambia, Central Statistical Office, Industry Monographs, Nos. 1–6 (Lusaka, Central Statistical Office, August 1975 through March 1976)

Republic of Zambia, Report of the Special Parliamentary Select Committee appointed 14 October 1977 (Lusaka, Government Printer, 1977)

The Republic of Zambia, Report of the Commission of Inquiry into the Affairs of the Zambian Railways (The Mumpanshya Report) March 1978 (Lusaka, Government Printer, 1978)

Republic of Zambia, Report of the Committee on Parastatal Bodies, presented to the Fifth Session of the Third National Assembly, Committee appointed 31 January 1978 (Lusaka, Government Printer, 1978)

.Republic of Zambia, Director of Elections, Presidential and Parliamentary General Elections Results, 1978 (Lusaka, Elections Office, May 1979)

Republic of Zambia, Director of Elections, Parliamentary General Elections, Summary of Primary Elections Results (Lusaka, Elections Office, May 1979)

Republic of Zambia, Central Statistical Office, 'Monthly Digest of Statistics', XI, 1 (1980); XVI, nos. 4–9 (1980)

Republic of Zambia, 1980 Census of Population and Housing, Preliminary Report (Lusaka, Government Printer, January 1981)

Great Britain

Great Britain, 'Report of the Commission to Enquire into the Financial and Economic Position of Northern Rhodesia', Col. 145, 1938

Great Britain, Advisory Committee on the Review of the Constitution of the Federation of Rhodesia and Nyasaland, 'Report', Appendix VI. 'Survey of Developments since 1953', Command Paper No. 1149 of 1959 (London, HMSO, 1959)

Great Britain, The Barotseland Agreement 1964, Command Paper No. 2366 of 1964 (London, HMSO, 1964)

United National Independence Party (U.N.I.P.)

United National Independence Party, Manual of Rules and Regulations Governing the 1973 General Elections, issued by the Central Committee of U.N.I.P., n.d. [1973]

United National Independence Party, 'Minutes of the U.N.I.P. Regional Conference, Mansa', 13–15 April 1974

United National Independence Party, National Council Resolution 4, 'Deliberations, Proceedings and Resolutions of the Fourth National Council', Lusaka, 20–5 April 1974

United National Independence Party, The Cause of the People is the Cause of the Party, Guidelines for the Central Committee (Lusaka, 1974)

United National Independence Party, Manual on Party Organisation, Financial Control and Development Administration (Lusaka, U.N.I.P., 1975)

United National Independence Party, 'Progress Report December 1975', presented to the meeting of the National Council by Secretary-General, Hon. A.G. Zulu, M.C.C., 8 December 1975

United National Independence Party, Progress Report 1973–78 by the Central Committee.

United National Independence Party, *Constitution*, November 1970

United National Independence Party, *Constitution*, August 1973

United National Independence Party, *Constitution*, February 1979

Zambia Information Services

The Year Ahead (n.d. but January 1976)

Parliamentary Records

Daily Parliamentary Debates 1964–1981

Private and Parastatal Enterprise Reports

Bank of Zambia, Report, 1973; Report 1980

Indeco, Annual Report

Zambia Mining Year Book 1973

Legislation

Republic of Zambia Act No. 69 of 1965, The Local Government Act 1965

Republic of Zambia Act No. 36 of 1971, The Industrial Relations Act 1971

Republic of Zambia Act No. 18 of 1977, The Industrial Development Act 1977

Constitution of Zambia: Appendix 3 to The Laws of Zambia (1965 edition)

Republic of Zambia Act No. 47 of 1966, The Constitution (Amendment) (No. 2) Act 1966

Republic of Zambia Act No. 33 of 1969, The Constitution (Amendment) (No. 5) Act 1969

Constitution of Zambia: Schedule to The Constitution of Zambia Act, No. 27 of 1973

Republic of Zambia Act No. 22 of 1975, Constitution of Zambia (Amendment) Act 1975, 29 December 1975

Republic of Zambia Act No. 10 of 1980, Constitution of Zambia (Amendment) Act 1980, 29 September 1980

Printed Secondary Sources

Allen, W, Gluckman, M., Peters, D.U., Trapnel, C.G. *et al.* Land Holding and Land Usage Among the Plateau Tonga of Mazabuka District: A Reconnaissance Survey, 1945. Rhodes-Livingstone Papers, No. 14, Manchester University Press, 1948.

Anglin, D.G. and T.C. Shaw. Zambia's Foreign Policy: Studies in Diplomacy and Dependence (Boulder, Colorado, Westview Special Studies in Africa, 1979).

Baldwin, R.E. Economic Development and Export Growth. University of California Press, 1961.

Bates, Robert. Unions, Parties and Political Development: A Study of Mineworkers in Zambia. Yale University Press, 1971.

Bates, Robert H. Rural Responses to Industrialisation. Yale University Press, 1976.

Baylies, C. 'Zambia's Economic Reforms and their Aftermath: The State and the Growth of Indigenous Capital'. The Journal of Commonwealth and Comparative Politics, XX, 3 (1982).

Baylies, C., and Szeftel, M. 'The Rise of a Zambian Capitalist Class in the 1970s.' The Journal of Southern African Studies, 8, 2, (1982).

Berg, E.J., and Butler, J. 'Trade Unions.' Political Parties and National Integration in Tropical Africa. Edited by James Coleman and Carl Rosberg. University of California Press, 1964.

Berger, Elena L. Labour, Race and Colonial Rule. Clarendon Press, 1974.

Bienen, Henry. 'One Party Systems in Africa.' Authoritarian Politics in Modern Society. Edited by Samuel Huntington and Clement Moore. Basic Books, 1970.

Bienen, Henry. 'Political Parties and Political Machines in Africa,' in The State of the Nation: Constraints on Development in Independent Africa. Edited by Michael Lofchie. University of California Press, 1971.

Boissevain, Jeremy. 'Of Men and Marbles: Notes Towards a Reconsideration Of Factionalism.' A House Divided? Anthropological Studies in Factionalism. Memorial University of Newfoundland, Social and Economic Papers, No. 9, 1977.

Bratton, Michael. The Local Politics of Rural Development: Peasant and Party-State in Zambia. University of New England Press, 1980.

Brelsford, W.V. Copperbelt Markets: A Social and Economic Study. Lusaka, Government Printer, 1947.

Burawoy, Michael. The Colour of Class on the Mines: From African Advancement to Zambianisation. Manchester University Press, 1972.

Butler, D. and D. Kavanagh. The British General Election of October 1974, Nuffield College Series of Election Studies, 10, (London, Macmillan, 1975).

Caplan, Gerald M., The Elites of Barotseland 1878–1969: Political History of Zambia's Western Province. (London, C. Hurst and Co., 1970).

Chambers, Robert, and Singer, Hans. Poverty, Malnutrition and Food in Zambia. Country Study for World Development Report IV, 1980, University of Sussex.

Chazan, Naomi, 'African Voters at the Polls: a Re-examination of the Role of Elections in African Politics', Journal of Commonwealth and Comparative Politics, XVII (1979).

Chipimo, Elias. Speech given at Law Society Dinner on the Copperbelt, April 1980. National Mirror, 99 (1980)

Chikulo, B. 'Elections in a One-Party Democracy.' Development in Zambia, edited by B. Turok. Zed Press, 1979.

Chikulo, Bornwell. 'The 1978 Zambia Elections.' The Evolving Structure of Zambian Society. Proceedings of a Seminar held in the Centre for African Studies, University of Edinburgh, 30 and 31 May 1980.

Cliffe, Lionel, editor, One Party Democracy (Nairobi, East African Publishing House, 1967)

Coleman, Francis L. The Northern Rhodesian Copperbelt, 1899–1962. Manchester, University Press, 1971.

Coleman, James, and Rosberg, Carl (eds.). Political Parties and National Integration in Tropical Africa. University of California Press, 1964.

Curry, Robert L. Jnr. 'Zambia's Economic Crisis: A Challenge to Budgetary Politics.' Journal of African Studies (UCLA), 6, 4, (1979–80).

Daniel, Philip. Africanisation, Nationalisation and Inequality: Mining Labour and the Copperbelt in Zambian Development, (Cambridge, Cambridge University Press, 1979).

Dumont, Rene, and Mottin, Marie France. Towards Another Development in Rural Zambia. Lusaka, 1979, mimeo.

Eisenstadt, S.N., and Roneger, Louis. 'Patron-Client Relations as a Model of Structuring Social Exchange.' Comparative Studies in Society and History, 22, 1, (1980).

Elliot, Charles, editor. Constraints on the Economic Development of Zambia. Nairobi, Oxford University Press, 1971.

Epstein, A.L. Politics in an Urban African Community. (Manchester University Press, 1958).

Epstein, A.L. Ethos and Identity. Tavistock Publications, 1978.

Fincham, R., and Zulu, G. 'Labour and Participation in Zambia.' Development in Zambia, edited by B. Turok, Zed Press, 1979.

Finer, S.E., 'The Statesmenship of Arms', Times Literary Supplement, 17, February 1978.

First, Ruth, The Barrel of a Gun, (London, Penguin, 1971).

Frank, Andre Gunder. Capitalism and Underdevelopment in Latin America. Monthly Review Press, 1967.

Gertzel, C. The Politics of Independent Kenya. Heinemann, 1971.

Gertzel, C., et al. 'Zambia's Final Experience of Inter-Party Elections: the By-elections of December 1971.' Kroniek van Afrika, 2, 2 (1972).

Gertzel, C. The Political Process in Zambia: Documents and Readings, Vol. II, The Presidential System (University of Zambia, 1973).

Gertzel, C. 'Labour and the State.' Journal of Commonwealth Political Studies, XIII, 3 (1975).

Gertzel, Cherry, 'Industrial Relations in Zambia to 1975', Industrial Relations in Africa. Edited by Ukandi G. Damachi, H. Deiter Seibel and Lester Trachman. Macmillan, 1977.

Gertzel, Cherry, 'Two Case Studies in Rural Development', in W. Tordoff, (ed.), Administration in Zambia (Manchester, Manchester University Press, 1980).

Gluckman, M. Economy of the Central African Plain. The Rhodes-Livingstone Papers No. 7. Manchester University Press for Rhodes-Livingstone Institute, 1941.

Gluckman, M. 'The Lozi of Barotseland in Northwestern Rhodesia'. Seven Tribes of Central Africa. Edited by E. Colson and M. Gluckman. Manchester University Press, 1951.

Lord Hailey. Native Administration in the British African Territories, Part II. HMSO, 1954.

Halcrow, Magnus, Development Commissioner. Recent Advances in the Northern and Luapula Provinces of Northern Rhodesia. Lusaka, Government Printer, 1959.

Hall, R. The High Price of Principles: Kaunda and the White South. Hodder and Stoughton, 1969.

Hall, Richard. The High Price of Principles. Penguin, 1973.

Hallett, Robin. 'The South African Intervention in Angola, 1975–76'. African Affairs, 77, 308 (1978).

Harries-Jones, P. 'The Tribes in the Town'. The Tribes of Zambia. Edited by W.V. Brelsford. Lusaka, Government Printer, 1965.

Harries-Jones, Peter. Freedom and Labour. Blackwell, 1975.

Heisler, Helmuth. 'The Creation of a Stabilised Urban Society: A Turning Point in the Development of Northern Rhodesia/Zambia.' African Affairs, 70 (1971).

Hellen, J.A. Rural Economic Development in Zambia, 1890–1964. Weltforum-Verlag, 1968.

Henderson, Ian. 'The Copperbelt Disturbances of 1935 and 1940.' Journal of Southern African Studies, 2, 1, (1975).

Hyden, Goran. Political Development in Rural Tanzania. East Africa Publishing House, 1969.

Huntington, Samuel and Clement Moore, editors, Authoritarian Politics in Modern Society (New York, Basic Books, 1970).

Hyden, Goran, and Leys, Colin. 'Elections and Politics in Single-Party Systems: the case of Kenya and Tanzania.' British Journal of Political Science, 2, 4 (1972).

International Labour Organisation (ILO). Incomes, Unemployment and Inequality. Geneva, ILO, 1972.

International Labour Organisation (ILO). Narrowing the Gaps, Jobs and Skills Programme for Africa. Addis Ababa, ILO, 1977.

Jacobs, W. Richard. The Relationship Between African Trade Unions and Political Organisations in Northern Rhodesia/Zambia, 1949–61. Geneva, ILO, 1971.

Johnson, C.E. African Farming Improvement in the Plateau Tonga Maize Areas of Northern Rhodesia. Department of Agriculture, Northern Rhodesia, Agricultural Bulletin No. 11. Lusaka, Government Printer, 1956.

Kandeke, Timothy K. Fundamentals of Zambian Humanism. Lusaka, Neczam, 1977.

Kaunda, Kenneth David, Dr. Humanism in Zambia and a Guide to its Implementation. Lusaka, Zambia Information Services, 1967.

Kaunda, Kenneth David, Dr. His Excellency the President. Towards Complete Independence. Speech by His Excellency the President to the U.N.I.P. National Council held at Matero Hall, 11 August 1969.

Kaunda, Kenneth David, Dr. His Excellency the President. I Wish to Inform the Nation. Lusaka, Zambia Information Services, 1969.

Kaunda, Kenneth David, Dr. His Excellency the President. 'Take up the Challenge . . .'. Speeches made by His Excellency the President to the U.N.I.P. National Council, Lusaka, 7–10 November 1970. Lusaka, Zambia Information Services, 1970.

Kaunda, Kenneth David, Dr. His Excellency the President. Opening Address to Sixth General Conference of U.N.I.P. Mulungushi, 8 May 1971. Lusaka, Zambia Information Services, 1971.

Kaunda, Kenneth David, Dr. His Excellency the President. Opening Address to U.N.I.P. National Council, Mulungushi Hall, 4–6 March, 1972. Background, 8/72. Lusaka, Zambia Information Services.

Kaunda, Kenneth David, Dr. 'A Nation of Equals' — The Kabwe Declaration: Addresses to the National Council of U.N.I.P. at the Hindu Hall, Kabwe, 1–3 December, 1972. Lusaka, Zambia Information Services, 1973.

Kaunda, Kenneth David, Dr. His Excellency the President. 'The "Watershed" Speech'. Address by His Excellency the President to the U.N.I.P. National Council, 30 June–3 July 1975. Lusaka, Zambia Information Services, 1975.

Kaunda, Kenneth David, Dr. His Excellency the President. Address by His Excellency the President to a meeting of the Supreme Council of Z.C.T.U. at State House, Sunday 10 August 1975. Background, 40/75. Zambia Information Services.

Kaunda, Kenneth David, Dr. His Excellency's Broadcast to the Nation, 28 January 1976. Zambia Information Services.

Kaunda, Kenneth David, Dr. His Excellency the President. Address to the Emergency Session of Parliament, 14 October 1977. Daily Parliamentary Debates, 14 October 1977.

Kaunda, Kenneth David, Dr. His Excellency the President. Press Conference by the President, Dr. K.D. Kaunda at the Reopening of the Southern Route, Background, 10/1978. 17 October 1978. Zambia Information Services.

Kuczynski, R.R. Demographic Survey of the British Colonial Empire, Volume II. Oxford University Press, 1949.

Lamb, Geoff. Peasant Politics. Julian Friedman, 1974.

Legum, Colin, editor, Zambia: Independence and Beyond – The Speeches of Kenneth Kaunda. London, Thomas Nelson and Sons, 1966.

Lenin, V.I.U. The Development of Capitalism in Russia. Moscow, Progress, 1956.

Lewis, Roy. 'Kenneth Kaunda', Round Table, (July 1967)

Lewis, W. Arthur. Politics in West Africa. Oxford University Press, 1965.

Leys, Colin. 'Politics in Kenya: The Development of Peasant Society.' British Journal of Political Science; 1 (1971).

McCulloch, Merran. A Social Survey of the African Population in Livingstone. Rhodes-Livingstone Papers, No. 26. Manchester University Press, 1956.

MacLean, H.A.M. An Agricultural Stocktaking of Barotseland. Lusaka, Government Printer, 1965.

Macpherson, Fergus. Kenneth Kaunda of Zambia: The Times and the Man. Lusaka, Oxford University Press, 1974.

Maimbo, Fabian J.M., and Fry, James. 'An Investigation into the Change in the Terms of Trade Between the Rural and Urban Sectors of Zambia.' African Social Research. University of Zambia Institute for African Studies. 12 (1971).

Martin, Anthony. Minding Their Own Business. Hutchinson, 1972.

Mitchell, Clyde. The Kalela Dance. The Rhodes-Livingstone Institute Paper No. 27. Manchester University Press, 1956.

Mitchell, J.C. African Urbanisation in Ndola and Luanshya. Rhodes-Livingstone Communication, No. 6. Rhodes-Livingstone Institute, 1954.

Mlenga, Kelvin C., editor. Who's Who in Zambia. Zambia Publishing, 1968.

Molteno, Robert. 'Cleavage and Conflict in Zambian Politics.' Politics in Zambia. Edited by W. Tordoff. Manchester University Press, 1974.

Molteno, Robert, and Scott, Ian. 'The 1968 General Election and the Political System.' Politics in Zambia. Edited by William Tordoff. Manchester University Press, 1974.

Morgan, David Gwyn, 'Zambia's One-Party State Constitution', Public Law (Spring, 1976).

Mulford, David C. The Northern Rhodesia General Election 1962. Nairobi, Oxford University Press, 1964.

Mulford, David, C. Zambia: The Politics of Independence, 1957–1964. Oxford University Press, 1967.

Musambachime, M. 'Labour Migration from Mweru-Luapula 1900–24: A Study of African Response to Wage Labour'. Zambian Land and Labour Studies, Vol. II. Edited by R. Palmer. National Archives Occasional Paper No. 2. Lusaka, National Archives, September 1974.

Nelkin, Dorothy, 'The Economic and Social Setting of Military Takeovers in Africa', Journal of Asian and African Studies, II, 1967.

Ohadike, Patrick O. Development of and Factors in the Employment of African Migrants in the Copper Mines of Zambia, 1940–1966. University of

Zambia, Institute for Social Research. Zambian Papers, No. 4, 1969.

Perrings, Charles. Black Mineworkers in Central Africa. Heinemann, 1979.

Perrings, Charles. 'A Moment in the Proletarianisation of the New Middle Class: Race, Value and Division of Labour in the Copperbelt, 1946–1966.' Journal of Southern African Studies, 6, 2 (1980).

Peters, D.U. Land Usage in Barotseland. Lusaka, Rhodes-Livingstone Institute, 1960.

Pettman, Jan. Zambia: Security and Conflict. Julian Freedman, 1974.

Prins, Gwyn, The Hidden Hippopotamus. Cambridge, Cambridge University Press, 1980.

Quick, Stephen. 'Bureaucracy and Rural Socialism in Zambia.' Journal of Modern African Studies, 15, 3 (1977).

Rainford, Roderick. 'The Teaching of Humanism to Adult Students in the University Extra-Mural Programme.' Bulletin, No. 3 (1968) Institute of Social Research, University of Zambia.

Rasmussen, T, 'Political Competition and One-Party Dominance in Zambia,' Journal of Modern African Studies, 7, 3 (1969).

Riker, William H. The Theory of Political Coalitions. Yale University Press, 1962.

Roberts, Andrew. A History of the Bemba. Longmans, 1973.

Robson, Peter, and Lury, D.A. The Economics of Africa. Allen and Unwin, 1969.

Rose, Richard, editor, Electoral Behaviour: a Comparative Handbook. New York, Free Press, 1974.

Rotberg, Robert. The Rise of Nationalism in Central Africa: The Making of Malawi and Zambia, 1873–1964. Harvard University Press, 1966.

Sandbrook, Richard. 'Patrons, Clients and Factions: New Dimensions of Conflict Analysis in Africa.' Canadian Journal of Political Science, 5 (1972).

Saul, John. 'Background to the Tanzanian Election 1970'. Socialism in Tanzania. Edited by Lionel Cliffe and John Saul. East African Publishing House, 1972.

Schmidt, Steffen W., Scott, James C., Lande, Carl and Guasti, Laura, editors. Friends, Followers and Factions. University of California Press, 1977.

Scott, Ian. 'Party Functions and Capabilities: The Local Level U.N.I.P. Organisation during the First Zambian Republic (1964–1973).' African Social Research, 22 (1976), 107–29.

Scott, Ian. 'Middle Class Politics in Zambia.' African Affairs, 77, 308 (1978).

Scott, Ian, and Molteno, Robert. 'The 1968 Election.' Politics in Zambia. Edited by William Tordoff, Manchester University Press, 1974.

Silverman, M. and R.F. Salisbury, editors, A House Divided? Anthropological Studies of Factionalism, Memorial University of Newfoundland, Social and Economic Papers, No. 9, 1977.

Sklar, Richard. 'Political Science and National Integration — A Radical Approach.' Journal of Modern African Studies, V, 1 (1967).

Sklar, Richard L. 'Zambia's Response to the Rhodesian Unilateral Declaration of Independence.' Politics in Zambia. Edited by W. Tordoff. Manchester University Press, 1974.

Sklar, R. Corporate Power in an African State. University of California Press, 1975.

Sklar, R. 'The Nature of Class Domination in Africa.' Journal of Modern Africa Studies, 17, 4 (1979).

Southall, T. 'Zambia: Class Formation and Government Policy in the 1970s.' Journal of Southern African Studies, 7, 1 (1980).

Szeftel, Morris. 'The Political Process in Post-Colonial Zambia: the Structural Basis of Factional Conflict.' The Evolving Structure of Zambian Society. Proceedings of a Seminar held in the Centre of African Studies, University of Edinburgh, 1980.

Tordoff, William, editor. Politics in Zambia. Manchester University Press, 1974.

Tordoff, William. 'Residual Legislatures in Tanzania and Zambia.' Journal of Commonwealth and Comparative Politics, XV, 3, (1977).

Tordoff, William, and Molteno, Robert. 'Parliament.' Politics in Zambia. Edited by William Tordoff. Manchester University Press, 1974.

Tordoff, William, and Molteno, Robert. 'Government and Administration.' Politics in Zambia. Edited by William Tordoff. Manchester University Press, 1974.

Trotsky, L.D. History of the Russian Revolution. Sphere, 1967.

United Nations. Report on the UN/ECA/FAO Economic Survey Mission on the Economic Development of Zambia. The Seers Report. Ndola, Falcon Press, 1964.

van Horn, Laurel. 'The Agricultural History of Barotseland, 1840–1964'. University of Zambia History Seminar, 1973–74, Paper No. 14 (mimeo). Published in The Roots of Rural Poverty in Central and Southern Africa. Edited by Robin Palmer and Neil Parsons. Heinemann, 1977.

Veich, M.D. The Population of Zambia: Internal Migration 1963–69. Lusaka, n.d., mimeo.

Veich, M.D. Employment and the Labour Force: Regional Analysis. Lusaka, 21 July 1970, mimeo.

Willianis, M. 'State Participation and the Zambian Economy', in World Development, 10 (October 1973).

Wilson, Godfrey. An Essay on the Economics of Detribalisation, Parts I and II. Rhodes-Livingstone Papers Nos. 5 and 6. Livingstone, Rhodes-Livingstone Institute, 1941 and 1942.

Young, Crawford. 'Patterns of Social Conflict: State, Class and Ethnicity', Daedalus (Spring, 1982) (Issued as Vol. III, No. 2 of the Proceedings of the American Academy of Arts and Sciences).

Zambia Episcopal Conference, Christian Council of Zambia and Zambian Evangelical Fellowship. Marxism, Humanism and Christianity. Lusaka, 1979.

Zolberg, Aristide. Creating Political Order: The Party States of West Africa. Rand McNally, 1966.

Zulu, Justin, B. Zambian Humanism: some major spiritual and economic challenges. Lusaka, Neczam, 1970.

Newspapers, Research Bulletins and Press Releases
 i) United Kingdom
      Africa Confidential (London)
      Africa Contemporary Record (London)
      Africa Research Bulletin, Political, Social and Cultural series, and Economic, Financial and Technical series, 1964– (Exeter)
      Economist (London)
      Financial Times (London)
      Guardian (London)
      Observer (London)
      The Times (London)

 ii) Northern Rhodesia/Zambia
      Northern News, 1965
      Nshila 1958–1959
      Sunday Times of Zambia, 1970–1982
      Times of Zambia, 1965–1982
      Zambia Mail, 1965–1970
      Zambia Daily Mail, 1970–1982

iii) Zambia Information Services
      Background Papers
      Press Releases

Miscellaneous
City of Kitwe, City Council Development Plan.
City of Kitwe, Kitwe Social Survey.
Constitution of the United Progressive Party, Lusaka, 1971 (mimeo).
Heath, F.N. (Acting Resident Commissioner). Memorandum on Economic Development for Barotseland. Mongu, 10 October 1960 (mimeo).
Progress Evaluation, Report on the First Four Year Development Plan, Western Province. Agricultural Sector. December 1969.
National Institute of Public Administration (NIPA). Speech by Mr. A. Milner, Secretary-General to the Government of Zambia, to the National Institute of Public Administration. June 1973.
National Institute of Public Administration. Speech by Chairman of the Electoral Commission to the Second Briefing Session of Registration Officers at National Institute of Public Administration. 25 March 1975 (NIPA, mimeo).

Unpublished Seminar Papers
Aaongola, F. 'Elections in Mongu Constituency.' mimeo, University of Zambia, n.d.
Gertzel, Cherry. 'District Administration in Zambia.' Seminar Paper, University of Zambia, 1971.
Kandeke, Timothy K. 'The Development of Zambian Humanism as a socio-economic and political ideology in Zambia.' Manuscript, Lusaka, n.d.

Kanta, Martin. General Study of Mwense District, University of Zambia, Course Research Paper, February, 1974.

Kasolo. 'The Rise and Demise of the United Party.' Undergraduate Political Science Paper. University of Zambia, n.d.

Maipose, G.S. 'Institutionalisation of One-Party Participatory Democracy in Zambia: A Case Study of the Electoral Process During the 1978 Presidential and Parliamentary General Elections.' University of Zambia, 1980.

Musambachime, M. 'The Agricultural History of Mweru-Luapula Area to 1940.' Mimeo, University of Zambia, Library, n.d.

Musambachime, M. 'The Development and Growth of the Fishing Industry in Mweru-Luapula Area, 1920–1964: Its Social and Economic Effects'. Seminar Paper, University of Zambia, School of Education, Department of History, Seminar Series No. 9, 12 February 1975.

Sumbwa, G.N. The Impact of Wenela Closure on the Makoma People of Western Province, University of Zambia, History Research Paper, 1974.

Tipple, A.G. 'Squatters and Housing.' Seminar Paper, University of Zambia, September 1974.

Turok, B. State Capitalism: The Role of Parastatals, University of Zambia, n.d. but 1979 (mimeo).

Unpublished Theses

Baylies, C. 'The State and Class Formation in Zambia.' Ph.D. thesis, University of Wisconsin, 1978.

Szeftel, M. 'Conflict, Spoils and Class Formation in Zambia.' Ph.D. thesis, University of Manchester, 1978.

Index